GLOBAL
SOUTH
ASIA

Padma Kaimal
K. Sivaramakrishnan
Anand A. Yang
SERIES EDITORS

Privileged Minorities

Syrian Christianity, Gender, and Minority Rights in Postcolonial India

SONJA THOMAS

UNIVERSITY OF WASHINGTON PRESS

Seattle

Privileged Minorities was made possible in part by a grant from the Association for Asian Studies First Book Subvention Program.

UNIVERSITY OF WASHINGTON PRESS
www.washington.edu/uwpress

LIBRARY OF CONGRESS CATALOGING-IN-PUBLICATION DATA
Names: Thomas, Sonja, author.
Title: Privileged minorities : Syrian Christianity, gender, and minority rights in postcolonial India / Sonja Thomas.
Description: Seattle : University of Washington Press, 2018. | Series: Global South Asia | Includes bibliographical references and index. |
Identifiers: LCCN 2018002613 (print) | LCCN 2018004513 (ebook) | ISBN 9780295743837 (ebook) | ISBN 9780295743820 (hardcover : alk. paper) | ISBN 9780295743844 (paperback : alk. paper)
Subjects: LCSH: Syriac Christians—India—Kerala—Social conditions. | Minorities—India—Kerala—Social conditions. | Women—India—Kerala—Social conditions. | Kerala (India)—Social conditions.
Classification: LCC DS432.S965 (ebook) | LCC DS432.S965 T47 2018 (print) | DDC 305.6/8154095483—dc23
LC record available at https://lccn.loc.gov/2018002613

Cover photograph: Annamma Vellaplamuryil. Photograph by Thomas Matthew Theempalangad.

Contents

Acknowledgments

I finished the bulk of this manuscript during the 2015–2016 academic year, when I was also fortunate enough to be caring for my aging father, Dr. Thomas Matthew Theempalangad. My dad was once a seminarian; later he studied to be a doctor. He had a deep appreciation for the Aramaic language and Eastern rite Christian traditions. When I was a child, after evening prayers and the rosary, we'd read from the Bible. My dad would then quiz us on passages or ask us theological questions. My five siblings and my mother would often tire of the back-and-forth debates, but I never did. I know now that he was the reason I chose to study issues of religion and secularism in South Asia. My dad passed away in February 2016. This book could not have been written without his insights, his help with translations, or his incredible photo archive. Dad, I miss you terribly.

During the same academic year, I was fortunate to be a visiting scholar at Lehigh University in the Department of Women, Gender and Sexuality Studies and the Department of Religion Studies. To Monica Miller and Chris Driscoll, I am in awe of your collaborative spirit and have benefited immensely from our conversations on how to translate interdisciplinarity to the discipline-structured academy. To Chiara Minestrelli, Michael Raposa, Ben Wright, Rob Rozehnal, Khurram Hussain, Jodi Eichler-Levine, Annabella Pitkin, Nandini Deo, and Marian Gaumer, every conversation I had with each and every one of you was so insightful. I am grateful to have met and collaborated with you. A special thank you to all those involved with the Religion Studies Brown Bag Series; the Women, Gender and Sexuality Studies lunch lectures; and the Feminisms Beyond the Secular conference.

To my mentors at Rutgers University—Jasbir Puar, Elizabeth Grosz, and Ethel Brooks—I am amazed at how your guidance during my graduate school years continues to shape me. I am proud to be your student. To Kathleen Powers, I miss you and our conversations, and I wish I could tell you how much your insights shaped this project and continue to shape my other research as I go forward. To Radhika Balakrishnan, thank you for the work that you do; I am forever grateful for the opportunities you've opened up for me, and for the mentorship you offer to women of color in academia.

Mona Bhan, you are the scholar I aspire to be! I cannot tell you how much your friendship and your collaboration mean to me, and I'm looking forward to many a future South Asia conference.

I first began envisioning this project in the fall of 2011 at the American Institute of Indian Studies workshop. I'd like to thank the AIIS and all involved in the workshop. Thanks to Paul Josephson, John Holt, Jason Petrulus, Sharleen Mondal, Chris Driscoll, David Stroll, Megan Cook, Paula Harrington, and SherAli Tereen for feedback on chapters. Thanks also to my feminist collaborators in the Women's Studies PhD group, including (but not limited to) Jenny Musto, Ashley Glassburn Falzetti, Vange Heiliger, Andrea Breau, and Laura Foster. I remember a time, years ago, when we voiced our hope that, with our first collaborative conference, we were making lifelong scholarly connections. I'm so incredibly happy to know that this has indeed been the case. I'm grateful to all of you for your continued efforts to help build antiracist feminist spaces for Women's Studies PhD graduates. To Keely Sutton, thank you for your help in understanding caste and class dynamics within the Mappila Muslim community. And to Swapna Thottathil, I so appreciate your insights into the Syrian Christians in Malabar and the class disparities within the community. Thank you all.

At Colby College, I have thrived under the mentorship of Lisa Arellano, Walter Hatch, Nikky Singh, Anindyo Roy, Mark Tappan, and Lyn Mikel Brown. Thank you for making this job worth every minute. Thank you to my research assistant, Mansi Hitesh, for your keen eye. Thanks as well to my friends and colleagues Dean Allbritton, Bibiana Fuentes, Elsa Fan, Urmi Engineer, and Sahan Dissanayake. And I am grateful for my endless conversations with Elizabeth LaCouture and Jason Petrullis about this project and so much more. You make Maine winters bearable.

In India, I benefited from the guidance of J. Devika and the Centre for Development Studies. Thanks to P. T. Chacko's family for access to his private library; to my immediate and extended family, especially the Ampalathumkal family; to Joy Theempalangad for help in locating members of the community who were integral to my research; and to the Kananthanam family. I thank all of you for letting me into your lives and for your help in making this book a reality. I am especially grateful to the Ampalathumkal family, the Powathil family, the Moolayil family, the Theempalangad family, and the Pulickal family for letting me use their family photos. To Serin George, I want to say that your photographs are beautiful, and I am so in awe of your work. To the faculty of the AIIS program in Malayalam—Arun, Bindu Teacher, and Prema Teacher—thank you for putting up with my whining over reading and writing Sanskrit-based Malayalam words and for encouraging me to work on those verb endings to get my conversational skills up to damn-near-native-speaker quality. Thanks to two brilliant linguists, S. Prema and Sri Kumar, for help in translating the circular letters, work that I could not have done myself—you do know that I tend to complain and get very frustrated with the Sanskrit-based words that no one uses in colloquial Malayalam.

To Larin McLaughlin, Mike Baccam, Laurel Hecker, and Julie Van Pelt at the University of Washington Press, thank you for your patience and guidance through this process. And to all involved in the Global South Asia series, I'm so very honored to be a part of this.

Thank you to my siblings, Diana Thomas, Helen Davis, Aisha Thomas, Tommy Thomas, and Mallika Towne, and to my mother, Mary Thomas. Yes, I'm the only "nonsciencey" one, but I do appreciate all your feedback. And, finally, to my daughter, Thresia Mary Reddy: You are the best thing that ever happened to me. I love you so much.

Privileged Minorities

Introduction

ON A PLEASANT SUNNY DAY IN THE SOUTH INDIAN STATE OF KER-
ala, I interviewed Claramma, an elderly Syrian Christian woman. A widow,
she lived alone. She wore a distinctive white garment traditional for upper-
caste Christian women. Claramma especially wanted to tell me about the
hardships she had faced as a woman after her marriage in 1936. On the one
hand, Claramma's life was confined to the home, and she endured constant
surveillance from family members if she deviated from the "good woman"
norm. On the other hand, Claramma had participated in a number of protests for Christian minority rights, and these outings allowed her to leave
the home while still acting within traditional gendered norms:

> Claramma: In my time, it was hard for women. My father told me, "You
> are a girl—you shouldn't have to learn anymore," and they took me
> out of school. Oh, how I cried! I wouldn't drink anything. But who
> was there to tell? They married me off at sixteen, and then I came to
> this family. I was the oldest girl here. That meant I had to do all the
> housework. My mother-in-law had a baby right when I had my oldest,
> and I had to look after both babies. My mother-in-law did not make
> her daughters work, but she abused me and made me do so much
> housework! In the household where I was born, I had two brothers
> and a sister, and then [when I was already a member of this family]
> my father died. I begged my father-in-law to let me go and help them,
> but [my new family] would never let me leave the house. I couldn't
> even leave the house for a bath! My mother-in-law would tell the
> neighbors what a bad match I was, and I was scared that the neighbors
> might see me leaving the house. What could I do? . . .
>
> Sonja Thomas: Did you see any of the protests in 1959?
>
> Claramma: Oh, the protests in 1959! [Christians] forced [the Communist
> government] out. The education minister, too, we forced out. My
> younger sister went to Kottayam to protest, and my boy went too.

I saw everything the protesters did. They broke a cacoose pipe [sewer pipe] and sprayed it all over. What fun! The priests would tell us about it at mass, and we would all gather and march in protest. We even went all the way to Thekkady to protest!

ST: You could go to a protest, but not to your own family's house? Not to the stream bath?

Claramma: Oh, but this was different. This was for our minority rights.[1]

What interests me in Claramma's discussion of her opportunities for mobility is the assumed place of women within certain identitarian realms of belonging. In Claramma's experience, both as a woman and as a member of the Christian minority, what is possible for her in terms of political action? What is possible for her as an upper-caste/middle-class woman? And what is possible for her as a member of a Christian minority?

In this book, I question how identity-based categories such as "Christian," "minority," and "woman" have been mobilized in postcolonial India, and I problematize the presumed link between numerical subordination and political vulnerability. I examine a privileged religious minority community that has routinely invoked secular constitutional protections in India and has thus played an integral role in defining minority rights in the nation-state—Kerala's Syrian Christians.

Christians are only 2.3 percent of the population of India, but they constitute 18.4 percent of the population of Kerala; as for Syrian Christians, they number slightly over 6 million and make up just under 50 percent of Kerala's Christian population.[2] Although demographically a minority, the Syrian Christians are not exactly a subordinated community. They are a caste-, race-, and class-privileged minority that has historically held power and benefited economically and socially from its privileged positions. In my analysis of the Syrian Christians, I specifically look at the interplay between privilege and subordination in the secular Indian state's protection of women and numerically challenged religious minorities.

"Women" and "minorities" are categories that in and of themselves are not homogeneous but are stratified by caste, class, race, and religious differences. Often, belonging to a minority community or a feminist collective can provide marginalized groups with a platform to address social inequalities. But group belonging itself demands homogenization. An investment in one category could reap benefits for one stratum within a group while crosscutting forms of oppression can be concealed or may even be deepened because of that very investment. For example, as I discuss in chapter 2, the traditional white clothing worn by Claramma is not just about "Christian" clothing or "women's" clothing but embodies a long history of symbiotic relations between upper-caste Hindus and upper-caste Christians in its difference from Dalit and lower-caste women's clothing. Claramma's in-laws' insistence that she keep in close proximity to the house is indicative of a life not shaped by agricultural labor but a kind of domesticity mediated by caste and class privilege. As I discuss in chapter 4, the 1959 protest that Claramma was allowed to participate in represented a subset of privileged minority interests not shared by other minorities, such as Dalit Christian, Muslim, or tribal groups. Thus, in this book, I'm attentive to the ways in which inequalities within groups shape wildly different experiences in religious movements, political movements, and in feminist and rights-based activism.

Despite their small numbers, the Syrian Christians are an important community to examine, especially because they complicate conventional ways of understanding minorities, secular protections, vulnerability, and subalternity in India. Christians as a whole are such a minuscule minority in India that they are often overlooked in scholarship on minority rights. When they are present, there is an almost automatic sliding of "Christians" into a "subaltern" category. In her work on Christian fishing communities in South India, Ajantha Subramanian has argued that within subaltern studies specifically, the subaltern is problematically depicted as outside secular society and having a religious outlook as a foundational worldview. Subramanian argues that this view of subaltern life is a scholarly fetishizing of religiosity.[3] I would add that this sort of fetishizing of religiosity problematically tends to homogenize all Christian minorities as subaltern. This may especially be true because scholarship on Christianity in South Asian studies often focuses on conversion with a heavy focus on Dalit Christianity.[4] Conversion is intimately tied to the resistance of casteism, and there can be an uncritical romancing of that resistance as we fetishize the worldviews of Christians. As Abu-Lughod's classic critique tells us, in the romance of resistance there can be a focus on finding and explaining resistance itself rather than an examination of power.[5] As an indigenous Christian community that is both upper-caste and class-privileged, the Syrian Christian community complicates normative images of Christian subalternity and offers us a different narrative concerning conversion and resistance to casteism.

Syrian Christians trace their conversion to the year 52 CE, when St. Thomas the Apostle arrived on the Kerala coast and reportedly converted Brahmins to Christianity. Because the Syrian Christians practiced their mass in Aramaic or Syriac, the label "Syrian" was used to distinguish them from Christians converted by Western missionaries using the Latin rite.[6] Both Portuguese missionaries in the sixteenth century and British missionaries in the nineteenth century converted Hindus and Muslims largely from the lower castes. Today there remains a glaring caste difference between the upper-caste Syrian Christians and other denominations of Christians in Kerala.

The Syrian Christians are considered a forward caste by the Kerala state and do not qualify for reservations. There is also a class difference between Christians, as the Syrian Christian community is relatively affluent, leading all other religious communities in Kerala in landownership.[7] The Syrian Christians are also known for banking, rubber tree cultivation, and private education, all of which have been extremely profitable for the community since 1947.[8] There are, of course, class differences within the community. For example, cash crop farming in northern Kerala was made possible by lower-class Syrian Christian peasants who migrated in the early twentieth century from southern Kerala, participating in the dangerous reclamation of jungle land and taking part in a very risky business gamble.[9] But, as this example shows, Syrian Christians are generally seen as risk takers with business acumen, both within and outside the community. Their entrepreneurship is encapsulated in the somewhat disparaging, somewhat envious Malayalam phrase often used to describe the community: "Kamizhnu veenal, kalpanam" ("Even when he's fallen facedown, he stands up holding a coin").[10] I refer to the community as Syrian Christians and see the term as representing Christians claiming a St. Thomas origin story and an upper-caste/middle-class status.

The protection of minority religions in postcolonial India through secular constitutional articles and policies laid the groundwork for a particular minority rights politic in the nation-state. This politic shapes what I call "dominant minority culture," where caste, class, and racial divides between minority populations are often glossed over in conventional readings of minority/nonminority relations. In addition, the figure of the modern woman—both marginalized in a patriarchal society and yet idealized as wife and mother in service to the (Hindu) nation—has profoundly shaped the parameters for what it means to be a "good woman" in postcolonial India.[11] In Kerala specifically, a normative "dominant woman" paradigm has emerged that privileges upper-caste and middle-class experiences over and against other expressions of womanhood mediated by caste, class, race, and religion.[12]

Chapters in this book examine how a dominant-woman paradigm overlays and interacts with dominant minority culture, separating women into their respective communal groups and disconnecting the political struggles of vulnerable minorities from each other. As Claramma's narrative articulates, her capacity to act is shaped by how she, her family, and the larger community upholds a particular version of female sexual morality shaped by upper-caste/middle-class privileges and frames what becomes viewed as acceptable political participation for women in minority rights movements. Tracing the intricacies of that agency allows us to understand how intersectional oppression functions, to see how solidarity movements may be hindered because of dominant-women/dominant-minority paradigms, and to question how social change is envisioned, acted upon, and ultimately actualized.

GENDER, CASTE, AND RELIGION IN SOUTH ASIAN FEMINISMS

For decades, feminist activism in India was aimed at shaping progressive laws but did not necessarily lead to revolutionary social change. As a consequence, South Asian feminists have begun to question feminism's reliance on the state as a site of progress. For example, Flavia Agnes and Shoba Venkatesh Ghosh ask, "If law is not the sole arbiter that determines women's rights, what are the other locations that we need to engage with for the determination of women's rights?"[13] Srila Roy has discussed the widening of South Asian feminisms attuned to and shaped by changing discourses on development, globalization, militarization, and communalism and expressed through other locations, such as social media, nongovernmental organization (NGO) work (and critique of NGO work), and grassroots initiatives.[14] In this widening of South Asian feminisms, studies have become much more attentive to the intersections of gender and caste.[15] This book reflects the influence of such scholarship, especially as it has emerged from South Asian feminisms over the past twenty years.

In previous studies of colonial India, gender was equated with upper-caste Hindu women's experiences, while studies on casteism focused on the experiences of Dalit men.[16] This resulted in the absence of Dalit women from colonial histories while it simultaneously separated gender-based violence from caste violence. As Anupama Rao explains, "The specific relationship of stigmatized existence with sexed subjectivity accentuates the consistent illegibility of sexual violence as caste violence, even as it renders sexual violation a definitive aspect of gendered Dalit personhood."[17] For Rao, an analysis of the multiple and changing dimensions of caste is crucial to the ability to truly understand gender inequality in postcolonial India.[18] Thus it is important not just to add Dalit women's voices to a women's movement or a canon of literature but to interrogate the ways in which brahmanical patriarchy legitimates its power through controls over women's bodies and their sexuality, over reproduction, and over casted labor and what counts as legitimate knowledges.[19]

This nuanced feminist scholarship on the intersections of gender and caste has led to a call for South Asian feminisms to engage with the concept of intersectionality and Black feminist thought.[20] Intersectionality itself has largely been used in Western-world contexts and specifically to understand Black women's experiences of oppression in the United States. As Julia Roth has argued, there may be an impetus for feminist scholars researching and working on the Global South to use intersectionality in order to be recognized and acknowledged by scholars in the Global North.[21] In the case of South Asia, this means adding the category of caste to the list of normally discussed intersections of race, class, and gender. Intersectionality then acts as a mere corrective to studying the internal problems of a given geographical area. In turn, it can unintentionally isolate certain forms of oppression, such as caste in India and race in the United States, as categories that can be equally compared—a problem I address in chapter 3. Instead, Bandana Purkayastha has argued that "in places where caste or religious or ethnic hierarchies—with their own set of ideologies, interactions, and institutional structures—are more salient, we should consider the relative importance of these axes of domination within those countries (and the extent to which these structure transnational social lives) as we use intersectional frameworks."[22] Applying intersectionality without an analysis of these axes of domination reduces the theory of intersectionality to a mere diagnostic of determining where intersections are located in people's experiences of oppression. As I see it, the point of intersectionality is not to diagnose where the intersections of race, class, caste, gender, and religion are at work in India but to go back to Kimberlé Crenshaw's important critique of how certain experiences of oppression can be privileged over others in attempts at redress, leading to an inability to adequately fight for or even imagine social justice.[23]

South Asian feminisms are in desperate need of such a dynamic analysis of power and subordination because once one intersection is examined, the multidimensional matrix becomes limited through a single-axis frame. South Asian feminist scholarship on caste is a good example of this. Caste can be understood only through one vector: Hinduism. Studies on Christianity almost reinforce this because, as mentioned, many works on Christianity focus on conversion and Dalit Christianity. The term "Dalit Christian" makes it seem as though caste originates from Hinduism and is merely transplanted from Hinduism to Christianity. But caste doesn't stop at the moment of conversion, nor is the concept of caste limited to Hindu caste formations. Caste continues to operate within Christianity and is enforced socially, economically, and politically through shared upper-caste Christian and upper-caste Hindu interests. Reading Dalit Christians as people who experience caste as former Dalit Hindus only tethers caste to Hinduism and, in turn, shapes how South Asian feminisms view religion as a static category within intersectional scholarship on caste and gender.

Even the most nuanced South Asian feminist studies that attempt to talk about the intersections of caste and gender suffer from this rigidity. In this book, I rely heavily on work by Prem Chowdhry and by Uma Chakravarti—both of whom discuss the intersections of caste and gender, although both make it seem as if caste is articulated primarily in Hinduism and is therefore best studied within Hinduism.[24]

Chowdhry's analysis of intercaste marriages focuses more on (Hindu) intercaste marriages than on interfaith marriages. Chowdhry argues that (Hindu) caste becomes more important and more worthy of study than religion because of how caste is articulated by community members over and against religion: "Although the media tends to highlight the difference in religions, the local populace is characteristically reticent in these matters. They tend to highlight different/unequal or inter-caste and status equations rather than those of religion. Religion is important but not locally 'exploited' in such matters. . . . Why and how are differences of religion subsumed under caste, class and community concerns? These questions need an in-depth and separate study."[25] This reading of how community members speak about religion glosses over the fact that minority religions are often subsumed into caste because religions in India are informed and regulated by upper-caste Hinduism. In Kerala specifically, this happens constantly. For example, in chapter 5, I look at a protest over a school textbook that presented a story about an interfaith marriage between a Muslim man and a Hindu woman. When the marriage was discussed by the public and in the media, it was called an "intercaste marriage." But this subsuming of religion under caste is possible only because of the taken-for-granted notion that Muslims in Kerala have historically been associated with lower-caste agricultural labor and fishing, an association that allows for the collapsing of religion and caste-based occupations onto a lower-caste identity. Thus, while the community may highlight caste, religion is still invoked through connections between debased caste-based occupations associated with particular religious communities. In light of the way in which religion is still implicitly invoked through assumptions concerning labor and caste, I would argue that religion requires as dynamic an analysis as South Asian feminisms now give to caste and gender.

Similar to Chowdhry's analysis, Chakravarti's lays out the argument that caste is best understood through an examination of how it functions within Hinduism; for Chakravarti, caste "pervades the Muslim and Christian communities in India who have kept their caste identities even within the new fold," but she "focus[es] on caste within Hindu society as its articulation is best understood by looking at its origins and elaborations through time in Hindu society as its reference point."[26] In other words, the intersections of caste and gender are better understood through how Hindus experience caste and gender because Hinduism is the source of caste. I assume that studies on caste and gender can then be extrapolated onto Muslims and Christians because they experience caste only as former Hindus. As I will show throughout this book, the political mobilization of Christians and the idea of a "Christian culture" is *entirely* determined by caste, making it completely possible to argue that caste is best elaborated in Christianity. For, as Uma Narayan reminds us, "in general, the *origins* of a practice or concept seldom limit its *scope of relevance*."[27] More apt than the "Hinduism as the source" reason for focusing on caste within Hinduism is the fact that upper-caste Hinduism acts as the invisible referent for scholarship on the marginalized and vulnerable "other" in South Asian feminisms.

Elsewhere I have discussed the problem of the upper-caste Hindu referent, which tends to mark Dalit-caste Hindus and Muslim women as the primary oppressed "other" and, in turn, mark Christian and Adivasi women as limit cases in relation.[28] The upper-caste Hindu referent forecloses the possibility of understanding intersectional gender- and caste-based oppression outside the dominant script on vulnerability in South Asian feminisms. That is, because South Asian feminisms tend to, however unintentionally, rely on the upper-caste Hindu referent when imagining caste-based discrimination and minority religion, the frame for understanding how the intersections of gender and caste function in postcolonial India is overdetermined. The very idea that an intercaste marriage is separate from an interfaith marriage is a case in point. In actuality, one can marry across castes and religions simultaneously (an upper-caste Christian marrying a lower-caste Hindu), just as one can marry within a minority religion and not the same caste (an upper-caste Christian marrying a lower-caste Christian). In other words, an intercaste marriage can also be an interfaith marriage, just as a marriage within a religion other than Hinduism can be an intercaste marriage. But because South Asian feminisms tend to see Muslim women as the primary *religious* "other," and Dalit women as the primary *caste* "other," such a nuanced intersectional analysis of mixed marriage fails to register. This is why Ritty Lukose has argued that "there is a dynamic relationship between the production of 'caste' and the production of 'religion' (as Hindu) that requires exploration."[29] What is needed is not a separate study of why religion is subsumed under caste. Rather, what is needed is a different view, one that not only can allow feminist scholars to fully interrogate where intersections of caste and gender are manifested and/or politicized but can also allow feminist scholars to examine the relationship between the production of caste and the production of religion and how these work together to engender and consolidate brahmanical patriarchal power, not just within Hinduism but across any religious group that can access social and economic positions of power.

One of the challenges in conducting such an intersectional analysis is that it requires an undoing of secular definitions of minority, definitions that tend to link numerical subordination with political vulnerability. Numerical subordination can lead to majority rule in politics, resulting in the tyranny of the majority and the exclusion of a minority voice in a democratic system. When a minority community is particularly targeted by the dominant majority, the exercising of individual rights can be threatened, which may further an entire minority community's political disenfranchisement. Numerical subordination can also lead to the erasure of minority culture through demands for minority communities to assimilate to the dominant culture. Secular protections for minorities can ensure that the playing field is a bit more level for vulnerable, numerically challenged populations. Secularism in the Indian context therefore created a particular relationship between the majority and the minority, whereby minorities belong to the nation as citizens but are unequal to the majority as *protected* citizens.[30]

Indian secularism not only works to protect minority religions from the dominant majority, it also attempts to protect women of all religions by providing women with an alternative to religion.[31] This is especially the case for religious personal laws in India that govern marriage, inheritance, and divorce. All of India's religious personal laws are patriarchal, as Amrita Chhachhi has argued, and these patriarchal laws reinforce the patrilineal and patrilocal family.[32] Secular law, then, can provide women with an alternative to these patriarchal religious laws. But while secularism may provide women with an alternative to religion theoretically, it is not clear that this always happens in practice. Community norms and gendered expectations could undermine any kind of protection a woman would have under secular law, as was the case in the aftermath of the Shah Bano ruling and the replacement of the Travancore Christian Succession Act.[33] Evident tensions emerge that center on definitions of who, exactly, is actually protected by Indian secularism. Does the secular state protect women (within minority religions)? Or does the secular state protect (patriarchal) minority religions? And are the two necessarily opposed to one another?

INDIAN SECULARISM AND KERALA'S
(SO-CALLED) RELIGIOUS EXCEPTIONALISM

Anupama Rao has examined how Dalit enfranchisement engendered a particular kind of minority identity predicated on historical suffering and discrimination, which constitutionally made Dalits objects of state protection. Rao explains that Dalits "altered the shape of Indian democracy as they creatively redeployed founding assumptions regarding the subject of rights and the terrain of politics."[34] When it comes to the Syrian Christians and minority rights, different questions emerge. The Syrian Christians, although demographically a minority, are not exactly a subordinated community, nor do they have any sort of claim to historical suffering or discrimination, as is the case for Dalit minority rights. But as a protected minority, they are a community that has also altered the shape of Indian democracy. What I explore in this book is not exactly the other side of the Dalit minority coin but rather the other side of how "vulnerable" is perceived by the state and invoked by minority communities in secular India.

South Asianists have long discussed how Indian secularism functions in the modern nation-state, and my focus on religious minorities in postcolonial India draws on many of these debates.[35] Claims to nation-statehood are often predicated on secularism, which is especially the case for postcolonial nations.[36] In many ways, the non-West was (and continues to be) depicted as religious and backward, and a commitment to secularism was seen as a necessary move toward national unity for many postcolonial nations.[37] But in India, the championing of secularism was not only about combating an imperialist view that portrayed the non-West as inherently religious. It was also oriented toward (supposedly) protecting vulnerable minority communities after the horrific communal violence of Partition. A commitment to secularism became a moral imperative and signaled a break from India's communal past. Thus, with the ratification of the constitution, in 1950, India adopted a number of constitutional articles aimed at protecting minorities.[38] For example, Article 30(1) of the Indian constitution gives religious and linguistic minorities the right to establish and administer their own schools. This article, which will be discussed throughout this book, is supposed to protect minorities by providing them with an enclave for the production and reproduction of minority culture in the face of the dominant majority. However, the constitution never defined what constitutes a minority community, and so contestations over who gets to enjoy secular constitutional protections often play out in the courts.[39]

It's curious that while postcolonial scholarship in South Asian studies has been almost obsessed with critiquing state-sponsored secularism, the one arena where these debates occur most often in people's daily lives—education—has not been adequately examined.[40] Because the definition of what constitutes a minority school necessarily engages with the question of who qualifies as a minority, education becomes the realm where state-sponsored protections are officially contested. If Muslims occupy the special place of "national minority" because of Partition and the creation of Pakistan, I would argue that Christians are the *underexamined* national minority because of their prominence in private education in India.[41] But few want to enter into the "nitty gritty of administration and regulation" associated with Article 30(1).[42] Article 30(1) often comes into contention with Article 29(2), which holds that no educational institution that receives state aid can deny admission to a student on the basis of the student's religion. Article 29(2) restricts the scope of Article 30(1) by limiting the autonomy that aided schools have in admitting students. That is, if a minority school receives state aid, it cannot serve minority students alone or it would be in violation of Article 29(2).[43] However, if a minority school does not receive state aid, can Article 30(1) be used to reverse-discriminate by admitting only minority students?[44] And, if so, is Article 30(1) actually protecting minorities or giving minorities special favors? Can a sect or offshoot of a majority religion attempting to establish its own schools be considered a minority community?[45] And who determines when a sect is no longer part of the majority religion? These types of questions have all made education one of the most important, if not confusing, arenas for determining what minorities are, what vulnerability is, and how state-sponsored secular protections function. The highly educated state of Kerala—which has consistently boasted the highest literacy rates in India, and where education has long been part of state politics—becomes one of the most important regional sites for examining secularism and minority rights in India today.[46]

However, much of the literature on secularism in South Asian studies is oriented to North Indian communalism and ethnic conflict between Hindus and Muslims. There is an assumption that the South Indian state of Kerala is a picture of religious harmony—a harmony that is often referenced but little interrogated. Interaction between religious communities in Kerala does not resemble the communalism we've come to recognize in South Asian studies, and for this reason "community" politics in Kerala are more often discussed than "communalism."[47] Ashotosh Varshney has concluded from his comprehensive study of ethnic conflict in India that, because of communism and intercommunal engagement in the state, the meaning of the term "communalism" changed in Kerala to "community" or "ethnicity."[48] Ashis Nandy has argued that the Hindu Right has not had an impact on Kerala, because the Hindu majority of Kerala does not have a minority complex as it does in North India; Nandy posits that Kerala people understand themselves as Muslims, Christians, or Hindus only theoretically.[49]

I do not want to enter into a debate over whether religion in Kerala should be discussed through the word "communalism." Rather, it is my intention to try to understand the role of *privileged* minorities in determining a minority rights discourse in a national frame. Kerala's so-called religious exceptionalism prevents us from engaging with how minorities in the region have shaped secular debates in India. It is true that religious harmony (*mathamaithri*) is seen as one of the state's finest achievements. The pride in *mathamaithri* for Malayalees is reflected in everything from members of different religions sharing food with neighbors during Kerala's holiday, Onam, to the *mathamaithri* poster often displayed in Kerala's private buses (figure I.1). However, the valorization of religious harmony masks intersectional caste and class power dynamics that play out between religions. Indeed, the Syrian Christian hierarchy has been quite friendly with Narendra Modi and the Bharatiya Janata Party (BJP) central government, despite the attacks on Dalit Christians and churches in North India.[50] The civic connections between upper-caste Hindus and upper-caste Christians—at the expense of casted or classed communities—should not be mistaken for religious harmony.

FIGURE I.1. *Mathamaithri* poster, 2014. Photograph by the author.

OVERVIEW OF THE CHAPTERS

Although this book examines the effects of brahmanical patriarchy and intersecting social inequalities, it is also attentive to the ways in which people can both defy and comply with patriarchal systems. Its chapters challenge the dominant assumption that equates numerical subordination with political vulnerability. The book also brings together elements that, until now, have not been in conversation with each other—clothing, Aryan/ Dravidian racial divides, education, textbooks, mixed marriages, protests for minority rights—and it instigates that conversation precisely because these seemingly disparate elements inform the struggles of minorities and women in postcolonial India. Ultimately, the book's feminist analysis contextualizes the lack of feminist solidarity between privileged and disenfranchised minority women, and it argues for more effective forms of rights-based activism.

Chapter 1 discusses the history of the Syrian Christians and their relationship to Hindus, Muslims, and other Christian denominations in Kerala. Although Christians appear to be a united minority group in India, Christian denominations have been quite definitively separated from one another by caste and class divisions among themselves as well as by the shared caste and class interests of upper-caste Christians and Hindus. The chapter lays out this complex denominational history in order to fully interrogate movements for minority rights and dominant minority culture. This historical background is followed by a discussion of the Kerala model of development and of Syrian Christians' support for the Congress Party from the time of Indian Independence to the present day.

Chapter 2 presents a "clothes reading" of the material practice of dress, analyzing how and why Syrian Christian women's communal clothing was replaced in postcolonial India by the sari and then by the *churidar* that Indian women wear today regardless of caste or religion. Regarding dress as an embodied practice, the chapter examines the ways in which clothing concretely marks the limits of intersectional group inclusion and exclusion. The chapter traces how sartorial choice became a way for lower-caste and Dalit women to protest social oppression. Rather than fixating on dress as a form of caste resistance, the chapter then examines another, less discussed sartorial change: the change from communal dress to the pan-Indian and purportedly secular sari.

Chapter 3 deals with the concept of the Aryan race and with racialized oppression in South Asia. The field of South Asian studies engages with questions of racial division primarily through separate studies on linguistics, communalism, and colorism. But this narrow, topic-specific approach to the study of race cannot fully explore how racialized discrimination actually functions in South Asia. The chapter traces the ways in which Syrian Christians' claims to upper-caste Hindu Brahmin origins have allowed the entire community to additionally access an Aryan racial identity, and it explains how mythic origin stories legitimize continued discrimination against dark-skinned bodies on the basis of entrenched social hierarchies. The chapter provides a nuanced account of how the intersections between religion, color, and class not only shape assumptions concerning the sexual availability of low-caste/dark women but also and simultaneously place communal restrictions on upper-caste/fair women's mobility in the public sphere.

Chapter 4 offers a detailed historical analysis of Christian minority culture and protests aimed at securing minority rights. To facilitate an understanding of what constitutes a dominant minority culture, the chapter first examines Christian opposition to both the 1958 Kerala Education Bill (KEB) and the 1958 Kerala Dowry Prohibition Bill (DPB). What follows is a discussion of Christians' involvement in the 1959 *vimochana samaram*, the liberation struggle (with women as key participants) that ousted Kerala's first state ministry and tested India's commitment to secular protections for religious minorities. The protest proved pivotal to the development of a very particular discourse of minority rights in India. The chapter also reveals how "minority," a label that united all Christians as the protest unfolded, became an invented identity, one that was defined by dominant minority culture and created at the expense of subordinated lower-caste Christian and tribal minority communities.

Chapter 5 furthers this analysis of minority rights by examining two more protests: one in 2007, against the regulation of self-financing colleges, and a 2008 protest—led by the Syrian Christian community and characterized as a second *vimochana samaram* by clergymen—that concerned a textbook's story about an interfaith marriage, as described earlier. The chapter also provides a detailed examination of endogamous marriages and questions the way in which purportedly religious sentiments are profoundly shaped by specific readings of upper-caste morality, which in turn are informed by the regulation of female sexuality.

The book concludes with a discussion of postsecular feminisms and the study of women's participation in religious movements. I offer thoughts on how feminists can approach the study of agency, religion, and spirituality and pose a final question: What sort of social change can be brought about when a woman who belongs to a privileged minority community, and who is governed by communal norms that are patriarchal, takes part in public life through a religious movement that may reinforce boundaries between privileged and subordinated women?

RESEARCH METHODOLOGY AND BACKGROUND

In this book, I draw most often on literature from the interdisciplinary fields of women's studies and South Asian studies. I engage South Asian postcolonial theory and feminist theory throughout the book, but especially in discussions of how to understand the concept of differences and multiple intersecting oppressions. The book also speaks to and draws from many other disciplines, including anthropology, sociology, history, education, religious studies, critical race studies, and social work. I look at a wide variety of texts, such as Legislative Assembly debates, communal group and government pamphlets, political rally chants, textbooks, print media, movies, novels, religious rituals and religious texts, and material culture. This multifaceted interdisciplinary approach enables me to investigate dominant social worldviews and conventional ways of knowing that often confound or negate important connections between seemingly disparate sites of analysis.

Through the course of this research, I conducted over eighty interviews, mostly in the Malayalam language, the official language of the state of Kerala. Over 90 percent of the Kerala population speaks, reads, and writes Malayalam.[51] I translated these interviews into English. The majority of the participants were Syrian Christians, although I did interview Hindus, Muslims, and other Christians as well. My research sites were centered in the Travancore region, the former princely state of the southern half of Kerala.[52] Archival research was conducted at the Nanthacode State Archives, the Kerala Legislative Assembly library, the Kerala University library's newspaper archive, the Centre for Development Studies, the *Malayala Manorama* newspaper archive, and private libraries.

I am a South Asian American, which gives me both insider and outsider status in relation to my research on the Syrian Christians. I am an outsider to the community as an American citizen and a heritage Malayalam speaker with a distinct accent and peculiar syntax. I was often told by research participants that I needed to better learn "my" language. Perhaps most profoundly, my outsider Malayalam made me fearful that I would be perceived as an urban or Western woman, with all the stereotypes and assumptions that come with those labels. On hearing my accented Malayalam, one man followed me down the street in Thiruvananthapuram, asking if I was from Delhi or Bangalore or the United States. When I tried to ignore him, he got more aggressive, with lewd language, and propositioned me for sex. Once I was followed by two men down an alley on my way to the bishop's house to interview a priest. When one grabbed my wrist, I screamed, attracting the attention of another man, who chased the two attackers off. Shakily, I thanked the man, only to have him yell at me for being careless and walking alone. When I spoke to friends and relatives about how much the attack had rattled me, I was told again and again, "This is not America—you should not travel alone." Sarah Caldwell has similarly discussed how her very body was made to conform in Kerala as she conducted fieldwork:

> In my daily efforts to comport myself as an acceptable appropriation of a Malayalee lady, I was constantly conscious of every curve of my body bespeaking its sexual potential, under the devouring gaze of men and boys in public. Were my breasts too noticeable, were they properly covered? Was I moving my hips too much as I walked, or was I sufficiently restrained in my body language to imply dignified propriety? I hoped I wasn't smiling or laughing too broadly, encouraging immodest thoughts in the minds of males I met. My sari, God knows, was never pulled down

far enough to cover my ankles and feet sufficiently—my lady friends would always tug at it to get it just a little lower. This constant attention to my dress and muting the sexual speech of my female body had sensitized me to the importance of control in every aspect of womanhood in Kerala.[53]

Unfortunately, these realities of being a female researcher and an "outsider" in fieldwork are all too common and, as many feminist ethnographers have argued, they should be discussed more openly in South Asian studies specifically and in the academy more broadly.[54]

But I am also an insider, as a person of South Asian descent. I am often read by my research participants as an Indian national. I cannot say that I wasn't delighted when my Overseas Citizenship of India qualified me for same-day access to the library at the Centre for Development Studies. In addition, I was often perceived as belonging to the Syrian Christian community by research participants. This may have allowed for an openness during the interviews that arguably wouldn't have been present if I had been perceived as a complete outsider.

I was born and raised in the state of Montana, near the North Dakota border. My parents come from a Syro-Malabar Catholic tradition, associated with the largest denomination of Syrian Christianity. We prayed the rosary, offered novenas, and read the Bible, and we sang Malayalam devotional songs every night in my family. As a result, my childhood was thoroughly shaped by upper-caste Indian Catholicism.

In the 1980s and 1990s, first the Bismarck Diocese in North Dakota, and then the Billings–Great Falls Diocese in Montana, began sponsoring Indian Catholic priests who served in the dioceses' understaffed rural parishes.[55] Many of those priests came from Kerala, and somehow they managed to find our home, where my mother cooked such traditional Syrian Christian cuisine as *palappam* and *kachiya moru*. In the early 1980s, my father even invited one of the visiting priests to perform a full Syro-Malabar mass in Aramaic at our local church.

My rural South Asian American Catholic upbringing was, I suspect, very different from the experience of many other Indian Americans, who grew up in more urban areas that had a Hindu/North Indian subculture, and where there were ethnic religious enclaves and networks of Indian American family friends living nearby.[56] But my insular Syrian Christian upbringing also provided me with an unusual "insider" perspective on my interdisciplinary research.

1 Syrian Christians and "God's Own Country"

ACCORDING TO THE *KERALOLPATTI*, THE SOUTH INDIAN STATE OF Kerala was created by the god Parashuram, an avatar of Vishnu. After slaughtering the Kshatriyas twenty-one times over in response to the death of his father, Parashuram threw his ax into the Arabian Sea. From where he sat at Gokarna to where the ax landed at Kanyakumari, lush and fertile land emerged from the water. Parashuram gave the land to Arya Brahmins in penance for his rage and declared that those living in Kerala would be equal to those in heaven.[1] To protect the land, he gave the Brahmins weapons. Thirty-six thousand Brahmins settled in sixty-four villages with Parashuram's blessing to reign over the other castes in Kerala. Slavery and tenancy were introduced.[2] Parashuram also assigned Sudra women to Kerala Brahmin men to satisfy their sexual cravings.[3] As a mark of respect, Sudra women were to appear with their breasts uncovered because their "greatest pleasure should be giving pleasure to" Brahmin men.[4] God's own country.

This story of the creation of Kerala has had a remarkable permanence in the Kerala imaginary. The *Keralolpatti* is most certainly "a Brahmanical document par excellence," which was used to legitimize caste dominance in a land where Hindu Brahmins had to rely on certain relationships to the Nayar caste, Christians, Jewish and Arab traders, and local kings and rulers.[5] Many histories use the *Keralolpatti* to reconstruct the region's history and explain the rise of Brahmanical power, patriarchal practices, and the class divisions that characterized the area from roughly the ninth century to the early twentieth century.[6] The story affected how the British determined upper-caste Hindu landlords' rights and Muslim and lower-caste Hindu tenants' relationships in Malabar in the late nineteenth century.[7] Even today, the Parashuram story acts as a romantic backdrop for a backward time that was overcome through Kerala's emergence into secular modernity.

Archaeological and linguistic evidence does support the theory of Aryan migration to Kerala, which occurred somewhere between the seventh and ninth centuries as South Indian culture began to move from the more egalitarian Sangam age to a temple-oriented society characterized by a caste-based division of labor. Temple lands were exempted from tax and were never attacked, which became especially important during the Chola-Chera wars of the eleventh century. Landowners gradually signed over their lands to temples for protection, and temples themselves became the biggest landowners in medieval Kerala.[8] As temple lands were under the control of Brahmin priests, this land was essentially amassed by the Namboodiri Brahmins.

The Namboodiri Brahmins separated themselves from other Brahmins in South India by adhering to the teachings of Sankara, an ascetic who lived from 788 to 812 CE. Namboodiris followed the strict sixty-four rituals given in the *Sankara Smriti*, which included rules on dress, ornamentation, washing, and purity rituals. Although the Namboodiri Brahmins were few in number, with landed privileges and a monopoly over ritual knowledge, "Brahmin" became the point of reference from which other castes fixed their social status.[9] As Robin Jeffrey explains, "Possession of land complemented ritual status and brought power."[10]

The Namboodiris were patrilineal, and the eldest Namboodiri son was required to marry within the caste. This ensured that the *illam*, or Brahmin property, was kept within the caste. Over time, this led to further consolidation of lands, so that vast tracts could be in the hands of a single Namboodiri family. But the custom of Namboodiri women marrying only the eldest Namboodiri male led to very strict gender roles within the Namboodiri community. Namboodiri women were called *anterjanams*, or "those who live inside," because their movements were restricted to the confines of the Namboodiri complex. Many young Namboodiri women were married as second and third wives to older Namboodiri first sons. Some became early widows and were forced to follow strict purification rituals and lead austere lives.[11]

Although technically considered Sudra, the Nayar caste supported the temple-based social system and functioned as an upper-caste martial class.[12] As supporters and enforcers of this temple-based system, many Nayar families were granted tracts of land. In contrast to the patrilineal Namboodiris, the Nayar caste was largely matrilineal, with inheritance determined through the female line.[13] Nayar women entered into marriage alliances with Namboodiri Brahmin second and third sons, forming a sort of socio-economic kinship alliance between the upper-caste Hindus.[14]

In Kerala, the four-caste system of Brahmin, Kshatriya, Vaisya, and Sudra does not hold. As Prema Kurien explains, "Kshatriyas were rare and Vaisyas nonexistent. The Nayar caste took the place of Kshatriyas, but they were regarded as Sudras by the local Brahmins. The Ezhavas came below the Nayars followed by the slave castes."[15] This caste arrangement created a huge divide between what was considered high and low and led to strict social dictates. Not only was untouchability practiced, unseeability was as well. A Dalit was not allowed within sixty feet of a Namboodiri Brahmin. Over time, distance pollution was even practiced among Dalits themselves.[16] Regulations encompassed not only personal space but also clothing and ornamentation practices, which visually demarcated peoples from each other in public spaces (see chapter 2). Restrictions were also placed on worship as lower castes were not permitted to worship the high Hindu gods, such as Shiva and Vishnu, but were relegated to demon worship. Temple entry for lower castes was denied. Namboodiri Brahmins were exempted from land taxes, while lower castes had to pay taxes and fees even for the right to use an umbrella or a palanquin.[17] By the late nineteenth century, there were over five hundred divisions and subdivisions of caste placed within a complex social regulatory system, prompting Swami Vivekananda to describe Kerala as a "lunatic asylum."[18]

The history of Syrian Christianity in the region is tied to this insane caste hierarchy. As mentioned in the introduction to this book, the Syrian Christians trace their conversion to the year 52 CE, when St. Thomas the Apostle arrived on the Kerala coast and reportedly converted Brahmins to Christianity. The Syrian Christians established themselves as a landowning merchant class, with a status that most closely matched that of the upper-caste Hindu Nayars in the region.[19] Some theorize that the Syrian Christians stood in for Kerala's missing Vaisya caste.[20] Proselytization was not really a feature of Syrian Christianity, as the community supported the temple-oriented society and thus refrained from converting Hindus of any caste. The Syrian Christian community was rewarded by the landowning upper-caste Hindus with land and caste privileges. Their privileged status is documented especially in the eighth-century Syrian Christian Copper Plates, which granted the community particular rights, including freedom from certain taxes, rights to trade, and land rights.[21] They were most definitely considered an intermediary caste, based on their temple position as "purifiers." One touch from a Syrian Christian male was considered to have purifying effects on caste-polluted objects, making the Syrian Christians, quite literally, a community that stood between upper- and lower-caste Hindus. Like Kerala's Namboodiri Brahmins, the Syrian Christians were patrilineal within a larger matrilineal society, and they practiced dowry.[22] They also had a public penitential system similar to that of the Namboodiri Brahmins.[23] Syrian Christian churches were built in the fashion of Hindu temples.[24] The Syrian Christians were allowed to have their own private armies and, like upper-caste Hindus, were allowed to possess slaves. In fact, the Syrian Christians supported the slave-caste system to such a degree that the community worked against anticaste and antislavery movements in the early twentieth century.[25]

The alliances between the Namboodiri Brahmins, the Syrian Christians, and the Nayars created a combined power that Uma Chakravarti has called the "king-brahmana duo" or "priest–dominant caste duo" where "Brahmana *men* had a monopoly over ritual knowledge and Kshatriya *men* over the means of coercion."[26] Since there was no Kshatriya caste in Kerala, both the Syrian Christians and the Nayars became the "means of coercion." In contrast, lower castes and Dalits became dependent in one way or another on the temples and landowners. Lower-caste-based occupations, such as oil pressing for the Vaniyans, coconut harvesting for the Ezhavas, or agricultural slave labor for Pulayas and Parayas, were debased. Since the Syrian Christians folded themselves into the hierarchical caste system yet, with their Eastern Christian traditions, remained a separate religion from Hinduism, the Syrian Christians are often described as "Hindu in culture, Christian in religion, and Oriental in worship."[27]

There are many different denominations of Christians who fall under the label "Syrian Christians." But to study the Syrian Christian community is to study a community where the intricacies of these denominational differences are often glossed over, misrepresented, and misunderstood.[28] Over the years, I've frustratingly tried to find sources that document the numerous denominational divisions between Christians and the number of Christians within each denomination. I believe that such documentation is necessary because the divisions between Christians mark lived caste and class boundaries and can help explain the enormous political power of certain Christian denominations. But histories of denominational differences are often partial as each denomination seeks to legitimize itself over another. Demographics within denominations can be self-inflated by churches. On a national level, Christians are often lumped together as a homogeneous religious minority within states.[29] This is despite the fact that the state of Kerala recognizes Latin Christians and Dalit Christians as Other Backward Classes (OBCs) and separates these Christians from the upper-caste Syrian Christian denominations.[30] There are references to "Roman Catholics" in the state of Kerala, especially in the media's understanding of "the Church," but this combines the upper-caste Syrian Christian Catholics with lower-caste Latin Catholics. Sometimes this is problematic, especially because of the obvious caste differences between the Syrian Christian Catholics and the Latin Catholics. And yet at other times this lumping together is justified as there is often a call for Catholics to unite across rites, especially in regard to minority rights in education.

SYRIAN CHRISTIANITY: A HISTORY

The Syrian Christians pride themselves on being one of the earliest groups of Christians in the world and are intensely proud of their St. Thomas apostolic tradition. According to their oral history, St. Thomas chanced upon one hundred Namboodiris taking a ritual bath and throwing water into the air as an offering to the gods. St. Thomas told the Brahmins that their gods were rejecting the offering because the water fell back down to Earth. Taking water in his hands, St. Thomas threw it into the air, where the droplets were suspended before finally falling to his feet as flowers. The Brahmins, impressed by this miracle, immediately asked to be baptized.[31] St. Thomas reportedly performed other miracles as well, such as removing a heavy log on a beach at the behest of a local king and bringing forth a freshwater spring on the top of the Malayattoor mountain. Today the Catholic Church recognizes St. Thomas's evangelical mission in India and his martyrdom outside the city of Chennai.

Whether St. Thomas came to Kerala and converted Brahmins to Christianity has always been a matter of dispute among scholars because there is little documentation of the community in its early years.[32] Further, St. Thomas's arrival in Kerala predates Brahmin migration to the region by roughly seven hundred years. Despite this scholarly doubt, the St. Thomas origin story, the oral history of the community (*margum kali*), St. Thomas churches and prayer sites (now popular pilgrimage sites), the St. Thomas cross (figure 1.1) and portraits of St. Thomas (prominently displayed in Syrian Christian houses and churches), St. Thomas's feast day celebrations, the Eastern Christian traditions, the Aramaic language, and Aramaic names still given to Syrian Christian children at baptism are all a large part of the community's identity. The St. Thomas apostolic traditions give credence to the stories of St. Thomas's visit and are given as evidence of an early Christian community in the region. I take the St. Thomas origin story as a given because it is how the community and much of the wider Kerala society understands the Syrian Christians, and I do not engage in debates over whether or not St. Thomas came to the region and converted Brahmins.[33]

Aside from oral tradition, historical records do report that in the year 345 CE, a group of Christians from the Middle East traveled to Kerala and

FIGURE 1.1. St. Thomas cross, 2015. Photograph by the author.

assimilated into the existing St. Thomas Christian fold.[34] These Christians are called Knanayan Christians because they trace their lineage to seventy Christian families that arrived in Kerala from the Middle East under the leadership of a man named Thomas Cana. The arrival of the Knanaya is significant because it created ties between the Syrian Christian Church and the Chaldean Church in the Middle East that lasted for centuries. In some histories, the Knanaya are referred to as the "Southists," to distinguish them from the descendants of the original St. Thomas converts, called the "Northists," namely because the Knanayan Christians are said to have settled in an area a little south of the existing community of Syrian Christians.[35] Other histories describe the Northist/Southist division as one that divides two factions of Knanaya.[36] Although the Knanaya do not have the same apostolic origin story, they are considered part of the Syrian Christian faiths. The majority of Knanayan Christians are Catholic in denomination.[37]

In 1498, Vasco da Gama sailed around the tip of Africa and hit the Kerala coast, paving the way for Portuguese missionaries. In 1544 and 1549, the

Portuguese missionary St. Francis Xavier converted tens of thousands of Mukkuvars, a fisher caste, to Catholicism. This mass conversion was based in part on a military agreement between the King of Venad and the Portuguese, which shifted the Mukkuvar community from royalty-based patronage to a church-based one.[38] These converts and their descendants are known as Latin Christians, and are not considered to be part of the Syrian Christian community because of their difference in caste and their difference in Catholic rite. Even though the Latin Christians are Catholic like some Syrian Christian denominations, and even though they have been upwardly mobile in terms of socioeconomic class, to this day marriage between the communities is not encouraged.

At first the Portuguese worked with the Syrian Christians, but they soon began to object to certain customs within the community, including ones that were more (upper-caste) Hindu in nature. Also, because of the community's ties to the Chaldean Church, the Syrian Christians were deemed to be part of the Nestorian Heresy by the Portuguese authority. In 1599, the Portuguese attempted to Latinize the Syrian Christians in a historical event known as the Synod of Diamper (Udayamperoor). In 1653, the majority of the Syrian Christians rebelled against the Latinization efforts in the *coonen kurisha*, or crooked-cross oath, so named because the Syrian Christians tied a rope around the cross of a church and held on to it as they recited an oath to reject the dictates of the Portuguese Church. This act, however, split the Syrian Christians into two groups, the *puthankutukar*, or new Christians, who participated in the *coonen kurisha*, and the *pazhaykuttukar*, or old Christians, who did not take part in the oath.

Today the new Christians are conglomerately called Jakoba because after 1665 they began to follow the teachings of Jacobus Zanzalus.[39] They are also known as Syrian Orthodox Christians. They number 977,000, or 15.9 percent of Kerala's Christian population.[40] In 1889, because of the influence of the Anglican Church, a small group preached for reform within the Jakoba and splintered into a separate denomination known as the Marthoma. The Marthoma community is quite small. Its members number 405,000, or only 6.6 percent of the Christian population in Kerala.[41] In the early twentieth century, the Jakoba divided into two more factions with differing hierarchal structures, the Malankara Orthodox Christians (the Methran faction) and the Jacobite Syrian Orthodox Christians (the Bava faction).[42] Even though the two factions are identical in liturgy, efforts to unite these two groups have repeatedly failed. In 1926, another small minority of Jakoba attempted to reunite with Rome. A separate Catholic faction, known as the

Syro-Malankara rite, was then created that is Roman Catholic in doctrine and jurisdiction yet Jakoba in liturgy.

The old Christians who did not take part in the 1653 *coonen kurisha* oath are known today as the Syro-Malabar Catholics and are now the largest group of Syrian Christians in the state of Kerala.[43] There are more than 2 million Syro-Malabar Catholics (38.2 percent of Kerala's Christian population).[44] The Syro-Malabar Catholics were under the authority of foreign Carmelite bishops for centuries and were granted indigenous bishops only in 1896. In 1992, the Syro-Malabar Church became a major archiepiscopal *sui juris* church and is recognized by the Vatican as an Eastern rite of Catholicism.[45]

In this book, I focus primarily on the Syro-Malabar Catholics, the most numerous and arguably the most politically powerful of the Syrian Christian denominations. The Syro-Malabar Catholics have routinely protested under the banner of minority rights even as their political interests often differ widely from those of other minorities in the state, including linguistic minorities, lower-caste and Dalit Christians, Muslims, and tribals. Syro-Malabar Catholic traditions, especially ones that concern women's roles and domesticity, are often the ones that dictate what is considered dominant minority culture. There are few critical historical or ethnographic studies on the Syro-Malabar Catholics, which is curious, given their numbers, their influence in the arena of education, and their prominent role in defining minority rights in India.[46] The dearth of critical scholarship on the Syro-Malabar Catholics is countered by the plethora of studies by theologians and scholars from within the Syro-Malabar Catholic faith. But these studies often provide a detailed theological or liturgical analysis rather than an examination of political or sexual economy.[47]

The Syro-Malabar Catholics, the Knanayan Christians, the Methran and Bava factions of the Jakoba, the Marthoma, and the Syro-Malankara Catholics are united under the banner of Syrian Christianity. Together they constitute a very strong political and economic force in Kerala.[48] Since the shared upper-caste and middle-class status of the Syrian Christians often unites them politically, I refer to the larger group name, Syrian Christians, throughout the book. Whenever it is necessary to distinguish between the denominations, I have used the proper denominational name. Figure 1.2 gives a clearer picture of the major denominations and demographics of the Syrian Christians.

Western missionaries have, generally speaking, not exactly attracted the Syrian Christian faithful away from Syrian Christianity. Rather, the impact of Western missionaries has historically led to the fractionation of Syrian

Syrian Christians 52 CE

Knanayan Christians 345 CE
population: 83,100

Syro-Malabar Catholics 1653 CE
population: 2,345,911

Jakoba 1653 CE

Marthoma 1869 CE
population: 405,089

Malankara Orthodox (Methran Faction) 1911 CE
population: 493,858

Jacobite Syrian Orthodox (Bava Faction) 1911 CE
population: 482,762

Syro-Malankara Catholics 1926 CE
population: 465,207

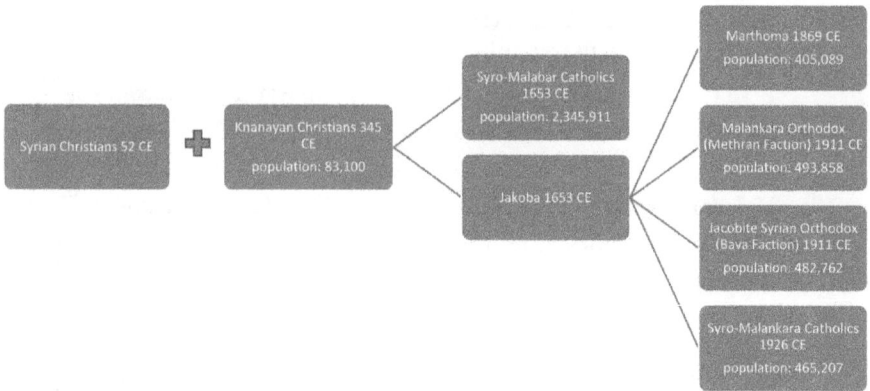

FIGURE 1.2. The major denominations and demographics of Syrian Christians. Sources: Zachariah, *The Syrian Christians of Kerala*, 52; and Zachariah, "Denominations," 29.

Christians into their current denominations.[49] Western missionaries were much more successful in converting lower-caste Hindus and Muslims to Protestant Christianity, and their influence led to the proliferation of Protestant Christian churches in the region. Protestant Christians fall into many denominations, such as Anglican, Kerala Brethren, and many independent Pentecostal churches. In this book, I touch on Protestant Christians in relation to the politics and traditions of the Syrian Christians.

Because Christians are such a significant minority in Kerala, and because the caste divisions between Christians are so pronounced, the state of Kerala offers many insights into conventional readings of minority communities. However, Kerala is often viewed as different from the rest of India, especially because of its remarkable turn from one of the most caste-stratified areas of India to its contemporary status as a "development model." I turn now to a brief discussion of this historical shift and contextualize politics and Christian minority rights in the state.

SOCIAL REFORMS AND THE CHRISTIAN CONGRESS PARTY

In the late nineteenth to mid-twentieth centuries, Kerala experienced a massive social upheaval that steered the state from being one of the most backward and caste-divided societies in India to being almost fully literate and ranking high on the United Nations' development index. This reform was not brought about by middle-class educated elites but from the bottom up. For example, one of the most influential reform leaders of Kerala, Sri Narayana Guru, fought for social justice in and through his caste status.

As an Ezhava, Narayana was barred from entering Hindu temples. Narayana built the Shiva temple near Varkala and shrines throughout Kerala, allowing Ezhava and other lower castes to worship. When questioned about the right to consecrate temples, he famously responded that he was consecrating the Ezhava Shiva and not the Brahmin Shiva. His writings and teachings of "one caste, one religion, and one God for man" inspired millions throughout Kerala. Other social reforms included agitations for the right for lower-caste women to wear the upper-caste Hindu breast cloth, rights to travel on roads, temple entry, and calls for intercaste dining. In only a few short decades, caste discrimination, as manifested through distance pollution and temple-based feudal labor, came to be seen as a mere relic of an embarrassing past.

A large part of the 180-degree turn in society was the increasing cultural importance of education to all castes and religions. The influence of British Christian missionaries in this regard was profound. Although Kerala already had many Christians, in the mid-nineteenth century there was a higher density of Protestant missionaries in Kerala than in any other part of India.[50] They came to Kerala in an attempt to reform the Syrian Christians, who were seen as "souls ripe for the Protestant picking."[51] But the missionaries fared much better in converting lower-caste Hindus and Dalits, many from the Nadar, Ezhava, Pulaya, and Paraya castes. The missionaries provided schools for their newly converted Christians. But these schools were seen as a space for conversions and were resented by upper-caste Hindus.[52] Upper-caste Hindus appealed to the government for their own schools, free from missionary involvement. An ironic consequence of missionary involvement in education was that Kerala's upper castes, once holding a monopoly on education and "ritually superior knowledge," ended up accepting universal education.[53]

The demands for education from all castes resulted in a strain on the government's budget. Without enough funds to meet the demand for education, the Travancore government turned to private education. It was the Syrian Christian community that began to open many of the private schools through grants-in-aid, or government grants to private institutions set up specifically for education. In 1865, Father Kuriakos Elias Chavara—an influential Syro-Malabar Catholic priest and now a canonized saint—issued a pastoral letter stating that all churches should be accompanied by an educational institution. So started a process whereby almost every Syro-Malabar Catholic church in Kerala now additionally supports a private school. These schools are known as *pallikudams*—literally, with the church. Between 1882 and 1887, the number of schools under Catholic management rose from ten to over a thousand.[54] Literacy rates skyrocketed in only a few short decades.

Rising literacy rates led to the founding of political newspapers and communal groups. Kerala has only 3.5 percent of India's population, but 8.5 percent of the daily newspapers in India are published in Malayalam.[55] At the turn of the twentieth century, reading rooms became popular; they served tea, provided newspapers, and functioned as meeting places where politics could be discussed.[56] The rise of print culture in Kerala made it possible for different groups to articulate their different points of view.[57] The early twentieth century was thus marked by the founding of communal groups in Kerala. The Ezhava caste organized the Sri Narayana Dharma Paripalana Yogam (SNDP) in 1903 and dedicated the organization to the advancement of Ezhavas and the promotion of Sri Narayana Guru's teachings. The Nair Service Society was created in 1914 and played a key role in bringing about the Nair Act of 1925, which abolished matrilineal inheritance.[58] The Keraliya Catholic Mahajana Sabha, formed in 1918, later became the All Kerala Catholic Congress, the mouthpiece for the Syro-Malabar Catholic community. The organization centered its activities on *Deepika*, a newspaper that remains the daily for Syro-Malabar Catholics in Kerala today.[59]

In the princely state of Travancore, in southern Kerala, agriculture and property ownership also underwent massive change during this time of social reform. The British introduced cash crops to Kerala in the nineteenth century—coffee in the 1830s, tea in the 1880s, and rubber in the 1890s.[60] In 1865, the Pattom Proclamation granted full landownership rights, which allowed for the unrestricted transfer of properties. This move commercialized agriculture and led to a flurry of land sales and transfers. There were also many subsidies given to people for the reclamation of "waste land"— jungle and wetlands—and these subsidies led to an increase in cultivatable land. The Kottayam district experienced a 50 percent increase in cultivatable land in the early twentieth century.[61] Syrian Christians and Ezhavas became a new force in cash crop agriculture. While the upward mobility was a bit more uneven for the Ezhava community, Syrian Christians were well positioned to "advance their claims as loyal, industrious wealth producers" in Travancore.[62]

As landowners with interests in the private school industry, the Syrian Christians found a political voice in the Kerala Pradesh Congress Committee (KPCC), so much so that the Congress Party in Kerala is often called the Christian Congress Party.[63] The opposition party, the Communist Party of India, Marxist, or CPI(M), was very successful in organizing tenants and agricultural laborers. Since Kerala statehood in 1956, the KPCC-led coalition party (the United Democratic Front, or UDF) and the CPI(M)-led coalition party (the Left Democratic Front, or LDF) have traded state ministries.

In 1957, Kerala became one of the first places in the world to democratically elect a communist government in the state's first elections. The first Communist ministry initiated wide-reaching reforms, such as the 1958 Agrarian Relations Bill, which fixed ceilings on landownership, and the 1958 Kerala Education Bill, which sought to reform the corruption in teaching positions, salaries, and student fees in schools. Upper-caste opposition to these bills brought the state to a standstill in the summer of 1959 during the statewide strike known as the *vimochana samaram* (see chapter 4). It was the first but not the last political clash between the Christian Congress Party and the CPI(M) since Kerala statehood.

Syrian Christians had an advantage in organizing politically compared to other religions because of the extensive network of churches and, for Syrian Catholics, the hierarchical organizing structure of parish, diocese, and archdiocese. During the 1959 protest, churches become organizing sites, and village priests used the pulpit to consolidate vote banks. Today the Syrian Christian clergy remain outspoken opponents of communist reforms, especially in education. The Syro-Malabar Catholic community is oftentimes advised on issues concerning minority rights and education through pastoral letters written by archbishops, which are read out to congregations on a parish level almost every Sunday.

From its dramatic turnaround in caste practices to the widespread cultural acceptance of education, Kerala has been examined as a kind of social reform puzzle. Some have attributed social reform to the long history of Christianity in the region, some to communism, and some to the supposed high status of women because of Nayar matrilineal inheritance. I would argue that instead of looking for the source of the reforms, we should focus on situating Kerala's social reforms in the history of Kerala itself. From the eighth century to the early twentieth century, Kerala's upper castes amassed power based on race and caste hierarchies, patriarchal privileges, and land rights—a trifecta assemblage of power that was supported by an array of social relationships between groups that have historically held landed and casted privileges. This power did not magically disappear in the latter half of the twentieth century. But for many scholars who look to Kerala as an exception, it may be difficult to see this power, given Kerala's remarkable statistics, which supposedly point to a utopian egalitarian society. It is therefore the problems and paradoxes associated with Kerala's development model in post-Independence India that I focus on next.

THE KERALA MODEL OF DEVELOPMENT
AND THE GENDER PARADOX

Kerala hits the radar of many today because of the Kerala model of development. The Kerala model has been heavily referenced by notable scholars such as Amartya Sen, Jean Drèze, and Martha Nussbaum.[64] The Kerala model is the state's supposed high standards of well-being gleaned from development indicators despite low levels of economic development (table 1.1). These development indicators include low fertility rates, low infant mortality rates, high literacy rates (especially for women), and a population where women outnumber men. Kerala's statistics are on a par with numbers from developed nations in the Global North, and so Kerala has been labeled as a model that nation-states in the Global South could emulate. Kerala has been called a "baby friendly" state by the World Health Organization because more than 95 percent of all births in Kerala are in hospitals, and because the male-to-female population ratio indicates that female feticide and female infanticide are not practiced in the state.[65] Scholarship on development indicators has noted a correlation between low fertility rates and higher literacy rates in developed countries.[66] Kerala's low fertility rates and high literacy rates reflect this correlation. Not only are fertility rates in Kerala lower than in most other Indian states, the highest fertility rates are found in an age group that is older than in most other states (that is, in most Indian states the highest fertility rates are found in people between the ages of twenty and twenty-four, but in Kerala the highest fertility rates are found in people between the ages of twenty-five and twenty-nine). Further, the average age of marriage for females is higher in the state of Kerala than in the rest of India. These statistics indicate that women are delaying marriage and childbirth, presumably in order to obtain higher education, or possibly to enter the workforce.

However, while development indicators are high in Kerala, so are rates of mediflation (increased expenditures on health care), unemployment, and alcoholism. Kerala's suicide rate is twice the national average, and the state has the highest number of family murders/suicides in India.[67] Full access to education was and continues to be divided on class and caste lines.[68] The Kerala model itself relies on statistical data that homogenizes the entire Kerala population. When this data is disaggregated, disparities start to come

TABLE 1.1. Comparative Development Indicators in Kerala and in India as a Whole

Indicator	Kerala	India
Birthrate[a]	14.8	22.1
Female-to-male ratio[b]	1,084	940
Infant mortality rate[c]	14	44
Literacy rate[d]	Male: 96.02 Female: 91.98	Male: 82.14 Female: 65.46
Total fertility rate[e]	1.65	2.3
Female age at marriage[f]	22.6 years	21.2 years

[a] Expressed as the number of live births per 1,000 population; see A. Sathiya Susuman, Siaka Lougue, and Madusudana Battala, "Female Literacy, Fertility Decline, and Life Expectancy in Kerala, India: An Analysis from Census of India 2011," *Journal of Asian and African Studies* 51, no. 1, (2014): 35.

[b] Expressed as number of females to males per 1,000 population; see Census of India, "Gender Composition of the Population: Provisional Population Totals—India," accessed 27 November 2017, http://censusindia.gov.in/2011-prov-results/data_files/india/Final_PPT_2011_chapter5.pdf, 81–83.

[c] Expressed as number of infant deaths per 1,000 live births; see Susuman, Lougue, and Battala. "Female Literacy," 39.

[d] Expressed as percentage of total population; see Census of India, "State of Literacy," accessed 4 June 2012, http://censusindia.gov.in/2011-prov-results/data_files/india/Final_PPT_2011_chapter6.pdf, 101, 108.

[e] Expressed as the average number of children born to a woman throughout her lifetime; see Susuman, Lougue, and Battala, "Female Literacy," 37.

[f] Census of India, "Population Composition," 27, accessed 27 November 2017, www.census india.gov.in/vital_statistics/SRS_Report/9Chap%202%20-%202011.pdf.

through. For example, Muslims in the state rank the lowest on the Human Development Index, and their median per capita income is 15 percent below the state average.[69] The Kerala model therefore represents a particular stratum of society and tends to ignore communities that don't fit into the model.[70] When the marginalized are so erased, they can be blamed for Kerala's "dystopia" against the normative utopia the Kerala model represents.[71] In other words, the Kerala model serves the interests of the privileged and the creamy layer of marginalized populations. Jocelyn Chua has thus rightly found that the Kerala exceptionalism story is compelling but is "authored and authorized by elites."[72]

Feminists have also critiqued the Kerala model for the gender paradox it presents, which is to say the discrepancies between, on the one hand, the supposedly high levels of well-being that literacy rates, fertility rates, and the like should have produced for Kerala women and, on the other, women's actual experiences in Kerala society.[73] Women, despite being educated, remain excluded from the political realm and tend to distance themselves from "public-political" power in Kerala.[74] Violence against women is widespread. According to the National Crime Records Bureau (NCRB), in 2012 Kerala had the highest crime rate in the nation and the third highest violent crime rate in India.[75] Kerala also has a higher rate of violence against women than Delhi, the city that was branded the rape capital of India after the notorious atrocity in 2012.[76] From 1993 to 2008, violence against Kerala women increased a staggering 338 percent, and more than 90 percent of women feel unsafe while traveling on Kerala roads after sunset.[77]

To be clear, these statistics are sometimes misleading because some Indian states do not gather statistics or may under-report. Kerala tends to gather and record statistics quite rigorously, perhaps because interest in the Kerala model demands proper upkeep of the statistics machine. However, qualitative research supports the prevalence of violence against women in the state.[78] Qualitative evidence also suggests that education becomes an element for a better match on the marriage market rather than a tool for women's empowerment.[79] As a symptom of this, although women in Kerala are educated, the female workforce participation rate is low.[80] In the Kerala model, many of these gender paradoxes are ignored in favor of statistics like the male-to-female population ratio and women's literacy rates, which are held up to indicate women's high status. The familiar move to paint Kerala as exceptional erases the realities of women in the state, who face struggles against gender- and caste-based violence and patriarchal religious norms similar to those of women in other areas of South Asia. In the next chapter, I examine this gender paradox through the lens of clothing, both as a means of regulating bodies and as a means of protesting against such regulation.

2   Clothes Reading

Communal and Secular Clothing "Choices" and Women's Mobility in Kerala

TO UNDERSTAND THE EFFECTS OF EARLY TWENTIETH-CENTURY social reform movements, and to grasp how regulation and resistance function in postcolonial India, it is necessary to critically examine a period of history when women's communal clothing was reformed and "secular choices" emerged. As J. Devika argues, "When the history of dress-reform is written someday, it will reveal not only the smooth acceptance of specifically male and female codes of dress (as opposed to the many different dress codes signifying one's position in the *jati*-hierarchy), but a whole series of moves and counter-moves, reversals and re-deployments, reinforcements and withdrawals. Resistance will have to be conceived of as much more flexible and contextual."[1] Especially in light of the history of "God's own country," this chapter focuses on the "counter-moves, reversals, re-deployments, reinforcements, and withdrawals" embedded in "choice" of clothing. It is not enough merely to document social reform. It is also necessary to conduct a specific analysis of the larger forces that dictated how and why communal clothing was used, why it was abandoned, and why the sari has entrenched itself as the professional dress of choice among Kerala women today.

Clothes are often perceived as the outward projection of an individual's acceptance of a group's ideology.[2] By wearing the clothing of a group, members nonverbally communicate social homogeneity to each other, and to outsiders. It is clothing's proximity to the body that gives it special potential for such elaboration.[3] Clothing is so tied to the body that, in many instances, an individual's choice to change clothes is read as the shedding of a former self and a move toward a new and different way of being.[4] But the "choice" of embodied belonging can often be prescribed. Feminist scholars on religion and dress have correctly noted that women's clothes are often tied to patriarchal religious moves to control women's sexuality.[5] Thus, for women, proper feminine behavior is enacted through the donning of religious clothing. In order for women to remain adherent not only to religious norms but

FIGURE 2.1. N. J. Mariakutty,
Syro-Malabar Catholic woman,
1968. Photograph by Thomas
Matthew Theempalangad.

also to gender norms defined by (male members of) the community, religion-based clothing often becomes something that women subscribe to. Therefore, this chapter is attentive to the ways in which clothing is an embodied practice that may not always be a willed choice. Arguably, nowhere is the relation between dress, gender, and group belonging so fittingly illustrated as in the state of Kerala, India.

From the nineteenth century until the early twentieth century, all women in Kerala wore particular communal garments that distinguished them on the basis of class, caste, race, and religion from women in other communities.[6] This special dress made women in the community easily identifiable (figure 2.1).[7] Consider this report from an elderly Syrian Christian woman, Mary Kutty: "When we were walking long distances to church in our distinctive dress, everyone knew we were Christian women. Our white clothing made us stand out as Christians and made the Christians of the village feel like they belonged to a religious family."[8] For Mary Kutty, the white dress of Syrian Christian women engendered a sense of religious belonging. What is left unsaid in her romance of community is how the women's communal garments differentiated them bodily, spatially, and ideologically from social "others." As we will see, clothing can be used to project communal norms, but it can also be used to protest the social exclusion and inequalities that are embedded in the ascendancy of dominant culture. In this chapter, I draw upon photographs as well as these oral sources to discuss embodied acts of belonging through not only communal-based clothing but also secular clothing practices.

COMMUNAL DRESS AND WOMEN'S MOBILITY
IN THE EARLY TWENTIETH CENTURY

The Syrian Christian communal dress is a three-piece garment. The first piece of clothing, the *thuni*, is an unstitched white cloth (indeed, "cloth" is the literal translation of *thuni*) wrapped around the waist to cover the bottom half of the body. The end of the *thuni* is folded into pleats so that it resembles a fanned tail (figure 2.2).

The second piece of clothing is the *chatta*. In the early nineteenth century, Syrian Christian women wore a short white jacket known as the *kuppayam*. That jacket eventually gave way to the *chatta*, a V-neck top with sleeves extending to the wrists. Over generations, however, the *chatta*'s sleeves were shortened, and by the early twentieth century the *chatta* with sleeves extending to just above the elbow had become the norm; today, most of the elderly women who still wear the *chatta* have sleeves of this length. The *chatta* and the fan-tailed *thuni* together were called the *chatta* and *thuni* (figure 2.3).

An unstitched white or cream-colored cloth known as the *kavani* completes the garment. For a brief time in the early 1930s, colored and patterned *kavanis* were available. But, as eighty-seven-year-old Threshamma explained to me, "Nobody wanted those colored *kavanis* because the *set* [cream with gold border] was always fashionable. It was our tradition to have white."[9]

The white color of the *chatta* and *thuni* gave the Syrian Christians a direct link to Brahminism. The sixty-four rituals of the *Sankara Smriti* included prescriptions for the Namboodiri Brahmins of Kerala to wear white clothing and not to wash their own clothes. As a result, Namboodiri women's communal clothing consisted of a white or cream-colored garment known as the *rouka*, which was an unstitched cloth tied at the breasts. Upper-caste Nayar women wore a *mundu* that was virtually identical to the Syrian Christian *thuni* except for not having a fanned tail. Nayar women also wore a cloth across the breasts and over the shoulder, known as the breast cloth. This style was almost indistinguishable from the Syrian Christian *kavani*.

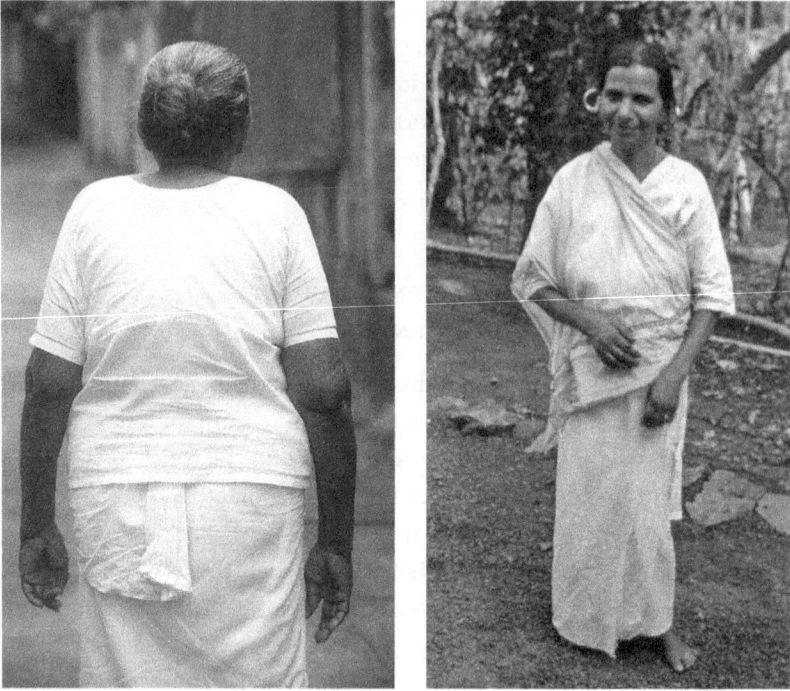

FIGURE 2.2 (left). Fanned tail of the Syrian Christian *thuni*, 2017. Photograph by Serin George.

FIGURE 2.3 (right). *Chatta* and *thuni* with *kavani*, Vellaplamuryil, 1968. Photograph by Thomas Matthew Theempalangad.

The *mundum-neryathum* dress of the Nayars developed later and consisted of a set of two cloths, one tied at the waist in the style of the *mundu*, and the other wrapped and tied over the breasts, without a blouse. This style was famously depicted in Maharaja Ravi Varma's painting *There Comes Papa* (figure 2.4). The *mundum-neryathum* became the basis for the *set mundu* and for today's *set sari*, a cream-colored *sari* with a gold *kasavu* border. Even today the *set* sari is showcased as Kerala's specific regional wear, an example of how primacy is given to Hindu upper-caste cultural norms. The white *chatta* and *thuni*, in its similarity to Hindu upper-caste women's clothing, thus marked an embodied symbiotic relationship between upper-caste Christians and upper-caste Hindus in Kerala.

The white clothing of Kerala's upper-caste women also signaled an Aryan racial identity. According to the Parashuram creation story of Kerala, the land was given to Arya Brahmins. Women from the Nayar caste entered into marriages with Arya Brahmins, and in this way the entire caste gained

FIGURE 2.4. Raja Ravi Varma, *There Comes Papa*, 1893. Oil on canvas. Kowdiar Palace, Thiruvananthapuram, India.

a particular claim to Aryan-ness. The Syrian Christians, as Brahmin converts, also claim Aryan racial roots. There is more to say about the connections between upper-caste identity, colorism, and Aryan racial purity (see chapter 3), but suffice it to say for now that there is a link between white clothing, Arya Brahmins, and the assumption that all of Kerala's upper castes are fair-skinned.[10] It is my conviction that the whiteness of their clothing literally reflected the belief that Kerala's upper-castes were racially fair-skinned Aryans and could thus be differentiated from lower-caste and Dalit Dravidians.

The Namboodiri *rouka*, the *mundum-neryathum*, the Nayar *mundu* and breast cloth, and the Syrian Christian *thuni* and *kavani* were all garments made from a seamless cloth. This gave each of the garments yet another relation to an upper-caste identity because unstitched clothing was considered to be impermeable and to hold fewer pollutants than stitched clothing.[11] In contrast, stitched clothing was seen as impure and was associated

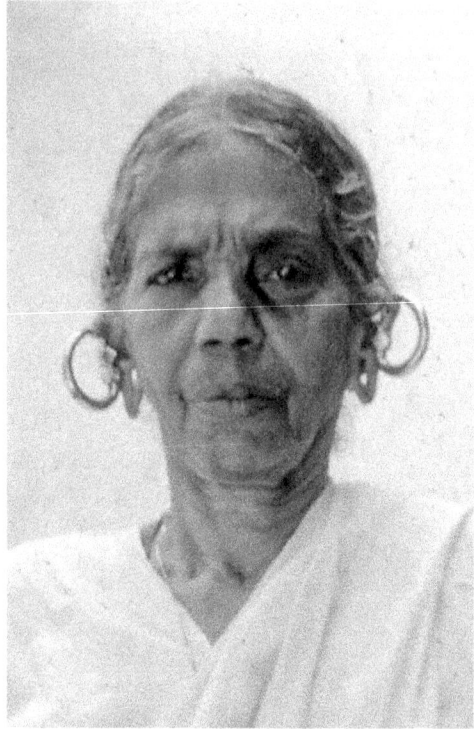

FIGURE 2.5. Elongated bored
lobes of Peramma, a Syro-
Malabar Catholic woman, 1982.
Photograph by Thomas Matthew
Theempalangad.

with Islam. The Hindu/Muslim difference embedded in the stitched/
unstitched dichotomy was not absolute. Hindus did wear stitched clothing
prior to Muslim migration to India.[12] But linking Muslims to stitched clothing became a way for Hindus to preserve their embodied difference from
Muslims.[13] By the late nineteenth century, stitched clothing was seen as
defiling, especially in religious contexts. To this day, many temples in Kerala
require devotees to wear an unstitched *mundu* in order to enter.

The symbiotic embodied relationship between upper-caste Hindus and
the Syrian Christians was also reflected in the practice of ear boring and in
use of gold ornamentation. In the late nineteenth century and into the early
twentieth century, Nayar and Syrian Christian women elongated their
earlobes as a sign of beauty (figure 2.5). Indeed, the ear boring of the Syrian
Christians was so similar to that of the Nayar caste that Syrian Christians
used thorns from the same species of lime tree that was used for the ear
boring ceremony in the Nayar community. As one elderly Syrian Christian
woman told me, "The Nayars had a big ceremony where they would take the
thorn and bore the ear. We didn't have a ceremony, but we took the thorn
from that particular lime tree. It was very sharp and could bore a large hole.

FIGURE 2.6. Mariamma Ampalathumkal in *chatta* and *thuni* (left) and Aleyamma Thekkekuttu in *chatta* and *thuni* with *kunniku* earrings (right), 2008. Photograph by the author.

The longer your ears were, the more beautiful you were considered to be. My own grandmother's fell almost to her shoulders."[14]

Syrian Christian women also wore the unique *kunniku*, large hollow gold hooped earrings that pierced the top of the ear (figure 2.6). A gold chain dangling from the ears, known as the *motheeshu* or the *vaaleeku*, was worn by Syrian Christian women alone.[15] Nayar and Namboodiri women wore gold earrings and different sorts of necklaces, including the *kashamallu*, the *nagapadam*, and the *cherutali*. The use of gold united the upper castes because it was a status symbol, a mark of feminine beauty and upper-class luxury.

The embodied nature of clothing reflected Syrian Christians' differentiation from and similarities to other communities. On the one hand, the uniqueness of the *thuni*'s fanned tail and the distinctive *kunniku* earrings set Syrian Christian women apart as members of a Christian religion. On the other hand, the whiteness of the communal garment, the unstitched *thuni* and *kavani*, and the use of gold ornaments tied the community to Kerala's upper-caste Aryan Hindus. Syrian Christians functioned as both a separate and an integrated community in Kerala—again, "Hindu in culture, Christian in religion, and Oriental in worship."[16] The *chatta* and *thuni* embodied the dual nature of their social standing as both similar to and distinct from other communities in Kerala.

Across all groups, communal clothing was specifically worn by women, and it marked embodied gendered norms as well as communal norms. It was not until Syrian Christian women donned the *chatta* and *thuni* that the gendered nature of clothing took effect. In the early twentieth century and into the 1940s in villages, most Syrian Christian female toddlers wore the *kumpala*, which consisted of leaves from the areca nut tree strung together to cover the pelvic region. They then graduated to a small towel, a *thorthu*, tied around the waist; this was worn without gender distinction by boys as well. In the mid-twentieth century, girls from wealthier families could wear the *pavadu* (skirt) and a blouse. And as teenagers, they could wear the half sari, which consisted of a skirt, blouse, and breast cloth folded in the shape of a *sari pallu*. But in the early twentieth century, no such clothing choices were available. Syrian Christian women went straight from the *thorthu* to the *chatta* and *thuni*. Women of this earlier generation were commonly educated through grade school and would have worn the *thorthu* to school. After schooling, girls were to stay at home, learn domestic duties, and marry soon afterward. At this time, young women switched from wearing the *thorthu* to the *chatta* and *thuni*. Chinamma, a Syrian Christian woman who married in 1937, explained, "I never wore a *pavadu* and blouse, because it was too expensive. It was only 4 chakram for a *chatta* and *thuni*.[17] I wore a *thorthu* until my mother had me do housework in *chatta* and *thuni*. At twelve years old, I had to cook breakfast, start the food preparation for lunch and dinner, and sweep before going to school. After I finished with school, I got married in *chatta* and *thuni*. I was the only one here in my husband's house during the day, so my days were filled with housework, and housework is done in *chatta* and *thuni*."[18]

Achamma, a Syrian Christian woman in her late eighties, also spoke of the link between the *chatta* and *thuni*, domesticity, and marriage: "In those days, all we had was *chatta* and *thuni*. Before that, they just wore a *thorthu* with nothing on top. Boys and girls all went to school with a *thorthu*. It was quite a sight because both boys and girls were the same. Then, sometimes as young as thirteen years old, women would get married. This was the time that we would wear the *chatta* and *mundu*."[19] Indeed, the *chatta* and *thuni* was often given at marriage as part of a girl's dowry, an indication of its relation to married domesticity.

Because the *chatta* and *thuni* was enmeshed with domestic life, it was sexualized and signaled a girl's coming of age. This is illustrated in the

Malayalam film *Kolangal*. The movie centers on a young Syrian Christian woman named Kunjamma in central Travancore in the 1940s and 1950s. After her mother gives her a *chatta* and *thuni* for Christmas and tells her that she should wear only the *chatta* and *thuni* from now on, Kunjamma immediately becomes a sexualized object. The first day she wears the *chatta* and *thuni*, she fends off a proposal for marriage from the ferryman, Paili. Kallavarkey, the toddy-drinking landlord, vows that he'll marry no other but Kunjamma soon after she appears in the village wearing the *chatta* and *thuni*. And Cheriyan, the ribbon vendor, gives her a necklace and states his intention of asking her parents for her hand in marriage. When the villagers begin to speculate that Kunjamma has a relationship with Cheriyan, her life spins out of control. With the sudden death of Kunjamma's father, her mother marries her off to the drunk and abusive Kallavarkey. The plot of this tragic film is set the moment that Kunjamma is treated as a sexual object, an event that is itself encapsulated in her wearing the *chatta* and *thuni*. Kunjamma's experiences highlight the relation between dress and the production of a specific sort of morality defined by upper-caste privilege and restrictions on women's mobility.

In early twentieth-century Kerala, daily life was highly structured in gendered spaces for upper-caste women. Separate huts were common for Syrian Christian women when they menstruated. Houses were traditionally built with a welcoming area for visitors at the front. When male visitors stopped by, women were not allowed to enter the front of the house. This policing of women's movements was especially pronounced after marriage. Syrian Christian mothers-in-law would separate their sons from their new brides, sometimes for years, and prohibited any kind of sexual contact. This separation is described in a charming story by Lalithambika Antherjanam that was published in 1937, "In the Moonlight." The story revolves around a fifteen-year-old girl, Annamma, married for six months to the sixteen-year-old boy Avuda. His mother, who wears the traditional gold hooped *kunniku* earrings at the top of her ears, separates the newlyweds: "Theirs was a household that adhered very rigidly to the Catholic custom of not allowing newlyweds to meet or to talk to each other."[20] Avuda, following his mother's wishes, avoids contact with Annamma so fiercely that she eventually runs back to the house where she was born and grew up. Two years later, Avuda starts to miss the girl, and he walks all night in the moonlight to her family's house to take her back. Readers can perceive this short story's happy ending only if they are aware of the sex segregation and moral policing of young Syrian Christian brides that were prevalent at the time in which the story is set.

In real life, the policing of a newly married woman was not so romantic. By monitoring when, where, and with whom Syrian Christian women could have contact, families sought to prevent potential extramarital sexual encounters and to regulate the conjugal relationships of their sons and daughters-in-law. Many of the elderly Syrian Christian women I spoke with had been confined to the home, under constant surveillance, and they felt resentful and trapped after marriage. An example is Mariamma, who was ninety-two when I interviewed her in 2008:

> I couldn't go anywhere. Women couldn't go anywhere. When they said, "Don't go," I didn't go, because I would face such abuse here. My in-laws wouldn't let me go anywhere after marriage, not even to my younger sisters' marriages, because it would reflect badly on the family. . . . If we needed water, I wouldn't tell anyone. I had to hurry and gather the water and come straight back home and hope that no one had seen me go. Every Sunday I could go to church, but my husband would say, "You can only go if you ask me for permission." The minute you tell them you are going, they will say, "The second mass ends, you should be home."[21]

Mariamma's recollection of how her movements were policed reveals the cult of true womanhood, defined in terms of a woman's piety, purity, submissiveness, and domesticity.[22] Mariamma's husband, neighbors, and the surrounding society shaped every aspect of her new role as wife, whether that meant her going to church (piety), sustaining her body (purity), or asking permission to leave the home (submissiveness and domesticity). The distinctive white and cream-colored clothing of Kerala's upper castes was easily recognizable in the public sphere and aided in socially stigmatizing any upper-caste married woman who transgressed the boundaries of true womanhood. Mariamma recounted that as a child, before donning the chatta and thuni, she had enjoyed much more freedom of movement.[23] Indeed, many of my research participants discussed the chatta and thuni in narratives that were inseparable from their experiences of being policed by their husbands and in-laws.

Nor was this restriction of mobility limited to women in the Syrian Christian community. The Sankara Smriti declared that Brahmin women must not look at men other than their own husbands, and if they were to leave the house, they had to be accompanied by a servant and to cover their faces with a palm-leaf umbrella. In the late nineteenth century and into the early twentieth century, Namboodiri women (anterjanams, who lived

FIGURE 2.7. Thara, a Pulaya
bare-breasted woman in
soiled clothing, 1968. Photograph by Thomas Matthew
Theempalangad.

inside) had, upon reaching puberty, come to be known as *asuryampasyakal*,
or those who should never see the sun; needless to say, they had to follow
strict rules of seclusion.[24] During the same period, Nayar women were not
free to leave the family property unless they had permission from the matriarch, and they were segregated from men after the *thali* (coming-of-age
ceremony).[25] In this way, limitations on upper-caste women's mobility
engendered a definition of morality that was bound to the home.

This definition of morality is further demonstrated in its relation to its
"other"—the presumed sexual availability of lower-caste and Dalit women.
In contrast to upper-caste women, many lower-caste and Dalit women had
no access to feminine moral identity, as defined through domesticity and
proximity to the home, since they were almost exclusively engaged as manual agricultural laborers in servitude to the landowning upper castes. They
often left the house and participated in manual labor with the men of their
communities. As in other parts of India, lower-caste and Dalit women were
read as sexually available because of their mobility in the public sphere and
their proximity to men.[26]

The clothing and ornamentation practices of Dalit and lower-caste
women embodied this moral distance from upper-caste Christian and

upper-caste Hindu women.[27] Certain lower-caste women served as washer-women for the upper castes. This labor made the clothing of the washer-women even more "polluted" because the dirt they encountered in the course of their work was understood to be transferred onto their clothing.[28] In some parts of Travancore, even into the 1940s, Dalits were not allowed to wear white clothes.[29] They wore a coarse, low-grade cloth and were pro-hibited from washing their clothes (figure 2.7).[30] The lower castes were not allowed to wear gold ornaments, and Dalits were forced to wear the *calla malla*, or stone necklace.[31] I would also argue that the literal dirtiness of their clothing reflected the assumed darkness and Dravidian-ness of the lower castes of Kerala. The separation between lower- and upper-caste women was therefore embodied in clothing and ornamentation "choices": the use of white and cream-colored clothing and gold jewelry signified the racial purity, wealth, and morality of Syrian Christians, Namboodiri Brah-mins, and Nayar women, while dirty clothes and the stone necklace symbol-ized the Dravidian-ness, pollution, and assumed sexual availability of Dalit and lower-caste women.

THE BREAST CLOTH MOVEMENT

One of the most striking and fascinating aspects of clothing, gender, and group belonging in Kerala was the practice of bare-breastedness. By the nine-teenth century, Brahmin pundits had interpreted Hindu *smritis* as justify-ing the practice of bare-breastedness and to explain upper-caste sexual ownership of non-Brahmin women. Therefore, Dalit and lower-caste men and women were not allowed to cover the upper half of their bodies in front of upper-caste males and females or in the presence of a deity.

As Kerala's creation story has it, the god Parashuram assigned lower-caste women to Brahmin men for the purpose of serving the men's sexual needs. And in 1891, in the *Report of the Malabar Marriage Commission*, the British connected this reading of sexual ownership to bare-breastedness: "There are probably several versions, but in substance the [creation story] contains a mythical account of how certain celestial damsels were brought from Indra's world by Parasu Rama to satisfy the sexual cravings of the [Kerala] Brahmins, and it recites how Parasu Rama at Vishabhadri (Trichur) pronounced his commandment to the women (not being of the Brahmin caste) to satisfy the desires of Brahm[i]ns, enjoining upon them to put off chastity and the cloth which covered their breasts, and declaring that pro-miscuous intercourse with three or four men in common was void of the

FIGURE 2.8. Bare-breasted Syrian Christian woman (seated), 1968. Photograph by Thomas Matthew Theempalangad.

least taint of sin."[32] This reading sutured covering with chastity, and the bare-breastedness of lower-caste women with promiscuity.

In actuality, though, many groups in Kerala, upper-caste Syrian Christian women among them, practiced bare-breastedness (figure 2.8). Uncovered breasts were a token of obeisance, and bare-breastedness was thought to be a sign of subservience to God.[33] Indeed, as Devika suggests, covering the female breasts was often associated with immodesty, since temple Devadasi dancers used cloth in eroticizing ways, to make the female body more desirable.[34] But the difference between upper-caste and lower-caste bare-breastedness was the *ability* to cover. Namboodiri, Nayar, and Syrian Christian women had the option of wearing the *rouka, mundum-neryathum*, breast cloth, *kavani*, or *chatta*, respectively. Yet under no circumstances were lower-caste and Dalit women allowed to cover their breasts, compelled as they were to signal their perpetual deference to the upper-castes. The clothing mandates were enforced by upper-caste Hindus who meted out extreme penalties for the most ordinary caste offenses committed by lower-caste people and Dalits.[35] In the case of clothing-related infractions, the most common punishments were public stripping of lower-caste and Dalit women and, when women of lower-caste and Dalit communities tried to cover their breasts, the looting and burning of lower-caste businesses and homes.

In the early nineteenth century, British missionaries working in Travancore converted thousands of Nadars, also known as Shanars, to Protestant Christianity. Under the protection of the British missionaries, the Nadars began to attend missionary schools, and they turned to trade and landownership. They were able to remove the oppressive taxes and the unjust *corvée* (unpaid labor, or labor compensated only with food or shelter) imposed on them by Kerala's upper castes. Under the new notions of female sexual morality promoted by the Christian missionaries, they also began to challenge the mandated bare-breastedness. The Breast Cloth Movement, or the movement for the right of lower-caste and Dalit women to cover their breasts, has been well documented by scholars.[36] The movement attests to the significance of clothing as an embodied act of belonging, and it reveals the systematic regulation of bodies in terms of caste, gender, and religious identificatory practices.

Nadar men and women, before their conversion, had worn a coarse cloth that covered only the lower half of the body, to the knee.[37] The British missionaries saw the ability of lower-caste women to cover their breasts as "a symbol of upward mobility through the idiom of modesty."[38] For the missionaries, covering the Nadar women was part of a larger discourse on gender, sexuality, and European subjecthood. European bourgeois sexuality was situated in the imperial landscape and, as Ann Stoler argues, the discursive regulation of sex, bodies, and sexuality was not charted in Europe alone but rather was articulated in and through the politics of race in the colonies.[39] As a symptom of this, there arose among European scholars a singular preoccupation with photographing and documenting the naked female native.[40] Studies on nakedness supported the colonial rhetoric that linked colonized people to sexual deviancy and, in relation, served to regulate British sexual norms. The colonial administration did not take an official stance on clothing native women in India, but the missionaries did.[41] Covering the native female body became a way to transform and civilize the colonized. Therefore, in Kerala, a shift occurred in the meaning of bare-breastedness for native women: whereas covering the breasts was once associated with the sexuality of temple dancers, lack of covering came to be considered sexually immoral.

In 1813, British Resident Colonel James Munro issued a circular order allowing converted Christian women to cover themselves with the Syrian Christian jacket, the *kuppayam*. On the basis of this order, the wives of British missionaries sewed loose jackets for converted Nadar women. But the Nadar converts overwhelmingly preferred the Hindu Nayar women's breast cloth to the Syrian Christian jacket. This led to clashes between Nadar converts and upper-caste Hindus. The upper-caste Hindus began publicly divesting Nadar women of the breast cloth; they also forced reconversions to Hinduism, and they burned chapels and homes. Upper-caste Hindus appealed to the Travancore Maharani, arguing that if lower-caste women used the upper-caste cloth, no distinction could be made between castes.[42]

Maharani Gowri Parvati Bai followed Resident Munro's circular with a proclamation in 1829 allowing converts to cover with the Syrian Christian jacket but explicitly forbidding them to wear the Nayar breast cloth.[43] The Breast Cloth Movement became highly volatile in 1858. Upper-caste Hindus understood specific parts of Queen Victoria's proclamation for direct rule to mean that the British could not interfere with any caste issue. They burned down Nadar homes, assuming they had impunity.[44] In December of that year, the Dewan of Travancore issued another proclamation, warning the Nadars to stop using the breast cloth, in view of the increased violence: "It has been brought to the notice of the Sirkar that some Shanar women have begun to wear upper-clothes in the fashion different from that hitherto customary and that this gives occasion to quarrels between Shanars and Sudras and other upper caste people. . . . Conduct in violation of old usages is not proper, and is punishable. This the Shanars should bear in mind, and shape their conduct accordingly."[45]

The British missionaries, too, tried to urge the Nadar converts to wear the Syrian Christian *kuppayam* instead of the breast cloth. In a letter to the British Resident in 1859, Reverend F. Baylis wrote, "I have also always told the Christian converts to be content with wearing the jacket, the use of which we have tried by every means to encourage, and I am happy to say that during last year about 600 of these jackets (which are not at all like the Rowkey worn by the Brahmin women) were made chiefly by the girls in our schools, and bought at the full cost of material by the women in our congregations."[46] Despite this, the Nadar converts continued to wear the Nayar breast cloth, and the Breast Cloth Movement spread to Nadar Hindu women and to women of the Ezhava caste. In 1865, the royal family issued another proclamation allowing both the Nadars and the Ezhavas the right to cover—but, again, not with the Nayar breast cloth.

The preference for the breast cloth over the *kuppayam* is a significant point for scholars of religion and caste that is hardly discussed in scholarship on the Breast Cloth Movement. The breast cloth signaled caste reform within the Hindu religion while it simultaneously normalized caste differences within Christianity. The conversion of lower-caste Hindus and Muslims to Christianity had not created a unified Christian community. Syrian Christians insisted that converts continue to be referred to by their Dalit caste names, and they worked to block Pulaya and Paraya Christian converts from enrolling in the Church Missionary Society college.[47] In the latter half of the eighteenth century, Syrian Christian priests, almost foreshadowing the Breast Cloth Movement's debates on embodied belonging, had strongly objected to Latin Catholic priests wearing Syrian Christian vestments. Their objections eventually led, in 1773, to the intervention of the Carmelites and a "compromise" that segregated Latin Catholic priests from Syro-Malabar Catholic priests in the seminaries.[48] The compromise also established that lower-caste priests would not be trained in the Eastern rites.[49] Therefore, the Breast Cloth Movement was not merely a "people's revolt" against Hindu caste; it was a revolt that reinforced caste boundaries within the Christian religion and set the Syrian Christian community farther apart from lower-caste Christian converts. While one aspect of social exclusion was challenged, another one was reinforced through embodied sartorial choices.

The Breast Cloth Movement eventually died down, especially because in the latter half of the nineteenth century and into the twentieth century Kerala's upper-caste Hindus were undergoing internal reforms. The Namboodiri community was facing a backlash from a younger generation of reformers bent on social change. The Namboodiri Yogakshema Sahba was founded in 1909 and specifically focused on reforming many of the patriarchal customs of the caste, including the seclusion of Namboodiri women. The Nayar community as well faced a backlash from young reformers who succeeded in abolishing the matrilineal system of inheritance.[50] Upper-caste opposition to lower-caste and Dalit use of the breast cloth began to ebb among this new generation of upper-caste reformers. By the early twentieth century, the practice of bare-breastedness was disappearing, and its disappearance signaled a shift from a backward to a more modern Kerala.

But shortly after the movement's eventual "success," women of all castes and religions suddenly abandoned their communal clothing and opted for the sari. By the 1950s, young Syrian Christian women throughout Kerala wore the sari alone; they never learned how to fold the fanned tail of the *chatta* and *thuni*, they rejected the custom of boring holes in their ears and elongating their earlobes, and they refused to pierce their upper ears for the *kunniku*. Photographs of this era of generational change are quite

FIGURE 2.9. Generational changes: mother-in-law in *chatta* and *thuni* (seated) and daughter-in-law in *sari* (standing), Vellaplamuryil, 1968. Photograph by Thomas Matthew Theempalangad.

striking. Figure 2.9, for example, shows a mother-in-law in *chatta* and *thuni* and *kunniku* while her daughter-in-law has opted for earrings and the *sari*. This abrupt generational change occurred in each and every Syrian Christian family in Kerala. Today the *chatta* and *thuni* and *kunniku* are only seen on Syrian Christian women who came of age before Indian independence. Communal dress is, quite literally, a dying tradition.

Curiously, while there is a wealth of scholarship on the Breast Cloth Movement, the change from communal dress to the sari has attracted little scholarly attention. The preoccupation with the Breast Cloth Movement among historians may be in line with the early orientalist obsessions with covering and uncovering the native woman's body. The fact that clothing has been viewed as a female issue, and marginalized as unscholarly, may also play into the lack of attention to this second sartorial change. Whatever the reason, the abandonment of communal dress that once proved to be so important for highlighting, combating, and sometimes even reifying social inequalities is particularly noteworthy because it denotes a reworking of power and resistance.

THE "SECULAR" SARI-CLAD SUBJECT

How were gendered and embodied divisions between peoples reenvisioned in postcolonial South India? One key to understanding this change is the move from communal clothing to the pan-Indian sari.

The *nivi*-style sari, with a petticoat, tight blouse, and unstitched fabric wound around the body, was popularized in India in the first half of the twentieth century. The lifting of British restrictions on Indian textile manufacturing after World War I engendered large-scale sari production at textile mills in Bombay.[51] Simultaneously, Bombay cinema began to project women wearing saris and made saris visible in a way never before possible.[52]

Kerala village women began to wear the sari in large numbers in the 1940s and into the 1950s, when fabrics finally made their way to isolated locales. According to the owner of a village textile shop that opened in 1952 near Kanjirapally, Kerala, saris were transported by boat from wholesale shops in Bombay all the way to the city of Kottayam. From there, buses were able to travel on newly constructed roads to villages in the region. While it took approximately a week to get the sari material, the demand was great enough to justify the cost of shipping. Even after a 1957 flood damaged all the store's goods, the store owner was able to rebuild, open an even larger store, and buy a sewing machine to create sari blouses on the premises with the new profits from sari sales.[53]

By adopting the pan-Indian sari, Kerala women were projecting Indian national belonging, especially because the sari was increasingly marketed as the national dress of India. As Caroline Osella and Filippo Osella argue, dress in India was "produced, performed, and read" through the opposition between Hindu and Muslim religious identities.[54] The sari therefore became India's national dress, over and against Muslim Pakistani dress. In postcolonial Pakistan, the opposite occurred: Muslim women's use of regionally specific attire, the sari, and Western styles disappeared because the *salwar kamize* became the embodiment of Pakistani-ness.[55] In its relational opposition to the Muslim *salwar kamise*, the Hindu sari became a token of Indian national belonging. But the Hindu-ness of the sari was masked through a promotion of secular citizenship. Take, for example, the experiences of two *chatta* and *thuni*–wearing grandmothers, Threshamma and Thangamma:

> Threshamma: For us, there was nothing but the *chatta* and *thuni* and
>   *kavani*. We didn't know the sari, because it didn't exist. But when we
>   saw it, we liked it, and we wished we could wear it, too, and wouldn't

have to wear this outdated dress. But it was too late for us because we
had already married in *chatta* and *thuni*.

Thangamma: Our daughters wore sari to school—side by side with Hindus,
Muslims and low-castes—all were the same in sari. They all belonged
to Mother India.[56]

While Threshamma and Thangamma were bound by dress to their communal identities, their daughters were free—free to leave the house, to
obtain an education alongside other religions and castes, and free to belong
to a "Mother India," over any caste- or religion-based identity.

Many elderly Syrian Christian women I interviewed stressed the importance of the sari's having first come to Kerala from outside the state. In my
fieldwork, I heard story after story of women leaving Kerala and coming
back in sari. For example, Threshamma told me this story of the first woman
in the village to wear the sari: "The first person to wear the sari in my village
was a woman named Chinamma. She married, and then her husband got
a job in Bangalore. A few years later she returned, and she wore the sari
to church. After she returned, she wore nothing but the sari. Never again
the *chatta*, because she had seen the city life. The sari was so beautiful
in comparison to the *chatta*! It was such a striking difference to see her in
church, next to all of us in our white *chattas*. We all wished we could wear
sari, too."[57] In so many of these narratives, the sari is urban and set against
village life. For example, Penamma was the first woman in her village to
wear the sari and began wearing it only after she had spent a few years in
the city of Ernakulam:

My husband was a professor, but his family was from a village called
Nedunkunam. My parents said, "We are sending you to a forest. They
are not civilized—you must have their costume." So we bought the *chatta*
and *thuni* and I came to Nedunkunam. But then my husband started
working in Ernakulam. When we lived in Ernakulam, I switched and
wore the sari. After some time, I came back to the village because my
father-in-law was ill, and he called for us. I wore sari in the village, and
I always wore shoes. I was the first one here to wear sari. I even wore a
bra! When I would walk to church, they all stared at me because I wore
a watch, shoes, and the sari. It was normal to see the sari in Ernakulam
because it was the city. But no one had seen the sari before in the village—
it was not here yet. I was the first to wear and bring the sari to this
village.[58]

The adoption of the sari was in step with Kerala's shedding of its communal past and its becoming a development model for India. Once cast as one of India's most backward states, Kerala now boasted an amazing growth in development indicators, including the dramatic rise in literacy rates. This narrative of progress, against the backwardness of Kerala's communal past, has become central to how Kerala is seen today, both in development discourse and by Malayalees themselves.[59] It was important that the sari came from outside because Kerala's caste-stratified society was seen as incapable of generating this change. Coming from outside, the sari signaled the coming of secular modernity to Kerala.

It is significant that the sari was adopted at a time when India was actively engaged in secular nation building. A commitment to secularism became essential to defining Indian nation-statehood and to proving India's ability for self-rule. Secularism provided a moral compass for the entire nation because it homogenized Indian peoples under a citizen-based identity, as opposed to a religious one. This egalitarian ideal was nice in theory. But the way Indian secularism was actualized led to a type of Hindu secularism, or majoritarian secularism, that casts Hinduism as a religion more aligned with secularity, and minority religions as forever bound by (patriarchal) religious practices.

In postcolonial India, Hindu laws were reformed and regulated. The 1955 Hindu Code Bill reformed Hindu personal law by legalizing intercaste marriages, legalizing divorce, and prohibiting polygamy.[60] A number of states passed legislation on temple entry for lower castes, and Hindu temples were brought under state jurisdiction, especially when it came to religious endowments. This regulation affects the Hindu religion in profound ways. In Kerala, for example, a special bench meets two days every week to hear temple-related matters alone.[61] While the state did intervene somewhat in Islam and Christianity, the vast majority of regulations since Independence have been to the Hindu religion.[62] This type of regulation marks a difference between how the Indian secular state treats the nonminority in comparison to minority religions, something that Rajeev Barghava has called the "principled distance" (not equidistance) of the state from religions.[63]

Because Hindu law was reformed, a common (mis)conception arose that it was secularized in comparison to Muslim and Christian personal law. This leads to Hinduism standing in for the progressive "secular" while minority religions stand in for the backward "religious." Indian secularism has thus been called "majoritarianism," and India a "Hindu-secular state."[64]

The idea that Hinduism was more progressive affected not only public perception of religious personal laws but also how the constitution was interpreted.[65] Interpretations of Article 30(1), for example, have narrowed the very definition of "minority" in regard to the schools that minorities establish and administer. This has caused Ranu Jain to argue that the courts have been tolerant rather than encouraging of minority religions.[66] Even the women's movement in India was affected by majoritarian secularism. Instead of critiquing the Hindu code, feminists within the women's movement focused on the patriarchal personal laws of minority communities.[67]

Nivedita Menon has argued that secularism served the purposes of India's elites and mediated a development discourse that relied on the creation of an unmarked citizen.[68] This unmarked citizen, I argue, was idealized in the sari-clad Syrian Christian woman, seemingly undifferentiated from other castes and religions as she once was in the *chatta* and *thuni*. Kocharotha, a seventy-nine-year-old Syrian Christian woman who wears the *chatta* and *thuni*, was quite vocal in her distaste for communal divisions and strongly related to me how she preferred an unmarked secular subject: "Now you cannot strictly tell if a woman is a Syrian Christian, because she wears either full sari or *churidar* and no more *chatta* and *thuni*. It won't come back—it has gone. Will anyone use it now? No, they won't! It won't ever come back, and why should it? We shouldn't know another's *jati* [caste] through clothing anyway. We should only be secular."[69] Since women from all communities started wearing the sari, one could no longer point to a woman in public and say, "She is a Syrian Christian woman," "She is a Namboodiri woman," or "She is a Nadar woman" but only "She is an Indian woman"—an unmarked modern citizen, idealized over a divisive religious past.

While I don't want to dismiss the Syrian Christian women who preferred the "secular" sari to the communal *chatta* and *thuni*, when placed within how secularism in the postcolonial nation-state functions, Kerala women's adoption of the "secular" sari was more truthfully an adoption of India's majoritarian secularism. As mentioned, upper-caste Hindu clothing was differentiated from Muslim clothing in the nineteenth century because it was unstitched and was assumed to hold fewer pollutants. For Syrian Christian women in Kerala, the unstitched sari was in direct line with the use of the unstitched *mundu* and *kavani* and the embodied claim to an upper-caste Hindu identity. Not only was the sari accepted, Syrian Christian women began wearing the *pottu* (*bindi*), previously only worn by Hindus. They also

FIGURE 2.10. Fisher women in *kaili*, 2006. Photograph by the author.

shunned the Syrian Christian gold hooped *kunniku* and, like Hindu women, began wearing earrings.

As in the past, when lower-caste women's soiled clothes were associated with manual labor, and upper-caste white garments with domesticity, the expensive fabrics and embellishments of saris represent the leisure of domestic life and the economic privileges of Kerala's more affluent upper-castes. Lower-caste agricultural laborers in Kerala continue to wear soiled clothing and the traditional work *mundu*, the *kaili* (figure 2.10), when engaging in jobs such as weeding.[70] One agricultural laborer, Anna, wears a sari to the homes of her employers but changes into a *kaili* to weed gardens and small farms: "I have only two saris. I wear them on the way to the houses I work for, but I change at the job's location. People would make fun of me if I tried to do work in a sari. For shame! This work is done by us in the *kaili*, not in saris! The sari makes a woman look respectable. That's why I wear the sari on the bus and only wear the *kaili* when I work."[71] For Kerala women, use of the *kaili* in public spaces is an embodiment of class- and caste-specific labor. Fisher-caste women in Kanyakumari have been banned from buses because of their "immodest" clothing, which, as Ajantha Subramanian has argued, signals the "entrenchment of caste-specific notions of bodily comportment among low-caste moderns."[72] Indeed, in a study on Dalit women in the Kollam district of Kerala, Dalit women reported being discriminated against on the basis of their clothing.[73]

The change to the sari shows how shifting notions of belonging, from communal belonging to national belonging, reworked overt demarcations of identity into implicit ones. The clothing practices that once privileged upper-caste Hindu connections did not disappear when the homogenized sari-clad subject became the ideal for Kerala women. As Nivedita Menon explains, the secular citizen was only seemingly unmarked because secularism itself was "Hindu, upper-casted, and modernized upper-class all along." These identitarian modes of belonging "simply functioned underground all the while we thought they were gone."[74] With this reworking of embodied belonging and exclusion came a revision of previous codes of female sexual morality. In the past, clothing was able to mark the transgressing female subject in the public sphere. Now, with a transformed public sphere, new forms of gendered controls emerged to reinforce the boundaries of good womanhood in postcolonial Kerala.

SEX SEGREGATION AND SEXUAL MORALITY

In Kerala, sari use coincided with the normalization of women's presence in the public sphere. As soon as demarcations of group belonging were pushed underground, with the advent of the sari, a revamped form of public social organizing became prevalent: women-only and men-only spaces (figures 2.11 and 2.12). As in other areas of South Asia, Kerala society today is quite striking in its adherence to heteronormative sex segregation. It is common to see the words *sthreekal/purushanmar* (women/men) in buses and on bus stops, demarcating where men and women should sit or stand. If signs are not present, gender separation is denoted by pairs of waiting sheds or benches with some sort of divider between them. Separate lines for men and women in banks, at ticket booths, and at political marches are typical. Also very striking is the sex segregation in Kerala that is self-imposed. At public events and in public spaces that are not labeled, women and men will choose to sit or stand with strangers of their respective genders. It is most often the case that husbands and wives will sit separately, as will daughters and fathers, sons and mothers.

Sex segregation is not unique to Kerala. In fact, I would argue that the prevalence of sex segregation in Kerala points to similarities between the intersections of caste-based and gender-based violence that feminists have discussed in other regions of South Asia.[75] Sex segregation in many regional contexts normalizes violence against women by painting gender-based violence as an unfortunate by-product of unbridled masculinity. Michael

FIGURE 2.11. Concrete divider at bus stop separating men from women, 2008. Photograph by the author.

Kimmel argues that a man must prove his masculinity to other men in sex-segregated spaces, and he calls masculinity a "homosocial enactment."[76] Kimmel's work on masculinity centers on the United States, but even though he stresses the cultural specificity of his research, I find his definition of masculinity useful in discussing sex-segregated spaces in South Asia. For Kimmel, violence is the single most evident marker of manhood, a manifestation of the desire to prove that one is not a "sissy."[77] When violence is so sutured to masculinity, sexual violence is often legitimized as the uncontrollable expression of maleness. It is the prevalence of sex-segregated spaces that normalizes violence against women and the harassment of women in mixed-gender public spaces.

In Kerala specifically, Caroline Osella and Filippo Osella have found that Kerala men see mixed-gender spaces as an opportunity to harass women.[78] Praveena Kodoth has found that the sexual morality of unmarried working women is often under scrutiny because of their mere presence in mixed-gender spaces.[79] Many research participants described the mixing of the genders with the word *nadikilla*, translating to both "an impossibility" and "not permitted." But insistence on sex segregation does nothing to interrogate gender-based violence. Rather, it takes the sexual predation of men

FIGURE 2.12. A Syro-Malabar church, 2015. Photograph by the author.

as a norm and is favored by many because it is seen to provide the only safety from gender-based violence for unaccompanied working women.

Night provides another element in the connections between sex segregation and justifications of gender-based violence because public space is male-dominated at night. In cities throughout Kerala, one can readily see upper-caste and middle-class women flooding public transportation between 5:00 p.m. and 7:00 p.m. in an effort to make it home before sunset. If a woman needs to be in the public space, a "good" woman would not travel far from the home or be without a male chaperone (father, brother, or husband). A woman transgressing these heteropatriarchal norms is seen to invite sexual violence or is viewed as a sex worker. Sex workers solicit after sundown in public spaces such as hotels, bus stations, and theaters. They are therefore positioned outside domestic space, and against the virtuous housewife.[80] It is not surprising that violence against sex workers is common in Kerala, with almost 80 percent of sex workers visiting drop-in centers reporting physical violence and mental illness.[81]

This association between sex work and male-dominated space at night has dire implications for lower-caste working women. Lower-caste women work in larger numbers than their upper-caste counterparts.[82] They tend to work at jobs that entail traveling long distances from their homes including such manual labor as fish vending, domestic work, weeding, and other small agricultural jobs.[83] For example, fisher-folk women travel largely by foot to places far away from their homes to sell fish door to door. In urban spaces, fisher-folk women set up roadside fish displays at bus stops and train stations late in the day. Because many fisher-folk women return to their own homes well after dark, they are forced to occupy a space associated with female sexual availability and sanctioned gender violence. Dalit women in Kerala's Kollam district were asked in a survey published in 2008 whether they felt it was safe to travel alone in Kerala; a large number of the women believed it was safe only for elderly women, because of the threat of sexual violence, and half the women surveyed believed that it was not safe to travel alone at any age.[84]

Again, these stereotypes of working-class women and the realities of violence against casted and classed women are not unique to Kerala. But because of the assumed high status of Kerala women, an assumption associated with Kerala's development model, it may be difficult to see that Kerala women face caste- and gender-based violence and threats of violence that are similar to caste- and gender-based threats and violence against women in other regions. Likewise, Kerala's image as a sort of utopia for women may make it difficult to tackle the very real issues—high rates of rape, sexual assault, and so-called Eve teasing (public sexual harassment of any unaccompanied women)—that are part and parcel of Kerala's gender paradox. Although violence against women cuts across economic lines and occurs in the home as well as on the streets, the dominant understanding of sexual violence and sexual morality has prevented Kerala police from viewing upper-caste and upper-class women as victims.[85] Conversely, it may prevent activists from understanding the agency of lower-caste and lower-class women outside a dominant rape script.[86]

The shift in dress from the *chatta* to the sari was accompanied by this change in gendered spatial arrangements, a change that redeployed previous ideas of female sexual morality predicated on controlling and monitoring upper-caste women's mobility. Increasingly, sari-wearing women were able to enter into public life alongside men and women of other castes and religions. But in many ways the shift did not signal an emancipation for women. Dress still marks aspects of belonging, just as women's mobility is still monitored and restricted in service to the brahmanical patriarchal order of Kerala's caste-stratified past.

DRESS TODAY: FROM *CHATTA* TO *CHURIDAR*

The August 2000 cover of the magazine *Kalakaumudi* featured an image that traced the evolution of women's dress in Kerala, from bare-breastedness to the *mundum-neryathum* to the *set* to the sari and the *churidar* (*salwar*

FIGURE 2.13. Evolution of dress shown on the cover of *Kala-kaumundi* magazine, August 27, 2000.

kamize) and, finally, to the immoral descent into Western clothing and an imagined future of bare-breastedness. In figure 2.13, the sari and the *churidar* both occupy the middle ground of Kerala's sartorial history, marking the most "moral" period in this social critique of Kerala's present-day moral disintegration. It is the relation between these two modest styles of dress that I turn to now.

It could be argued that the sari has been replaced in contemporary Kerala by the *churidar* (figures 2.14 and 2.15). The *churidar*, called the *salwar kamize* in North India, consists of a long *kurta*, drawstring pants, and a shawl. Not unlike what occurred in the change from the *chatta* and *thuni* to the sari, the *churidar* is replacing the sari in one generation. Even in South India, where women tend to wear saris in greater numbers than in North India, sari weavers are having trouble finding buyers because of the switch to the *churidar*.[87] Many younger women have no idea how to tuck and fold a sari properly, a situation that has led to the emergence of readymade saris, or saris with pleats stitched into the elastic waistband of a skirt so that one has only to slip the skirt on and throw the remaining fabric over the

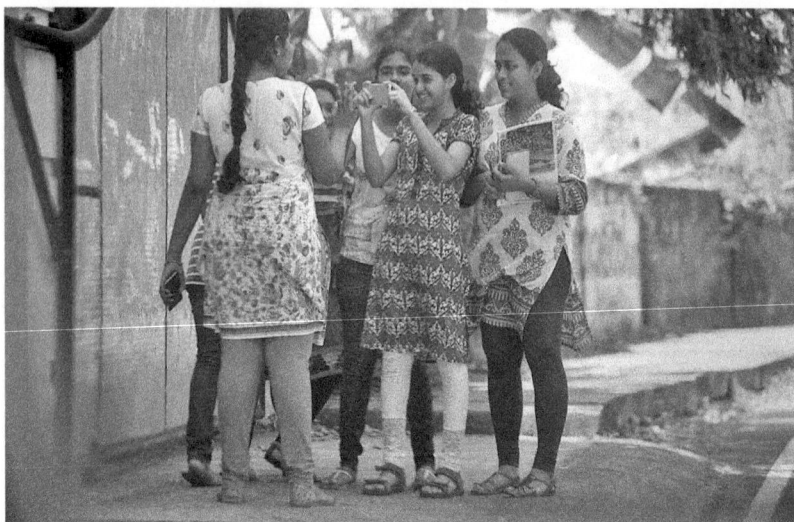

FIGURE 2.14. Young women in *churidar*, 2014. Photograph by Serin George.

shoulder. *Churidars* have even become a common school uniform for young ladies in Kerala.

Despite the *churidar*'s popularity, Hindu temples throughout Kerala have banned the use of the *churidar* within temples. According to Caroline Osella and Filippo Osella, the *churidar* is "scornfully referred to as 'Muslim dress' or even 'Pakistani dress' by older Hindu men."[88] If women come to a temple in Kerala wearing the *churidar*, they are asked to leave and are not allowed return unless they are wearing a *mundu*. At the popular Guruva-yur temple, outside the city of Thrissur, the official decision to allow women to wear the *churidar* into the temple led to public outrage. Soon after the temple's board reached this decision, in 2007, a writ petition was brought against the change. The petitioners' attorney argued that wearing the sari is a five-thousand-year-old tradition, and that the temple's board had no power to impose a restriction on that custom.[89] While this dispute over traditional dress was taking place in court, Guruvayur temple astrologers deemed the use of the *churidar* in the temple "inauspicious." The astrolo-gers said that "traditional dress" had to be maintained. On the basis of this reading, another writ petition was brought to the Kerala High Court. The court dismissed both petitions, with Justice Balakrishnan specifically ques-tioning the notion of traditional dress: "Do you know that women [in ear-lier times] were not allowed to cover the upper part of their body? It was

FIGURE 2.15. Young woman in *churidar* school uniform, 2015. Photograph by Serin George.

only after a revolution that they were allowed to cover the upper part of their body, so should we go back to that practice?"[90] However, devotees reported seeing a drastic decline in *churidar*-clad women at Guruvayur after the astrologers' reading. An aide to the head priest of the Guruvayur temple stated, "These days one can hardly find a woman in a *churidar* in the temple. This seems a voluntary change and no one can alter the centuries[-]old temple rules."[91]

The social policing of sartorial choice is not limited to the space of Hindu temples. It has infiltrated a number of other public institutions. In 2008, the Kerala government released an order allowing female government employees to wear *churidars*, but many women continue to wear the sari. When the state of Kerala issued a similar order allowing teachers in government schools to wear *churidars*, private schools, many of them under Syrian Christian management, continued to issue the sari as the dress code for their women teachers (figure 2.16). A former Syrian Christian teacher explained to me that Syrian Christian teachers shouldn't wear *churidars* because of their professional status. After all, she explained, teachers were not engaged in manual labor but professional work.[92]

Many of my Syrian Christian female research participants wore the *churidar* daily, but when they went to church or to religious functions they would switch to the sari, an indication of their continued reluctance to switch completely to the *churidar*. It remains Syrian Christian "tradition"

FIGURE 2.16. Kerala schoolteacher, 2015. Photograph by Serin George.

to wear a white sari for marriage and to be draped with a sari, the *mantra-kodi*, by the groom during the marriage ceremony. This invention of tradition is especially curious—first, because the sari is by no means part of Syrian Christian tradition; second, because the sari was embraced precisely because it came from outside and could not be tied to any of Kerala's traditions; and, third, because the sari as traditional Indian wear was an invented tradition engendered so recently in Indian history.

In my research, I attempted to find any similar narrative of resistance to the sari when it became popular in the mid-twentieth century, but without success. When interviewing three *chatta* and *thuni* wearers, I was finally told in exasperation, "No, no, no! There was no anger about the sari. Everyone liked the new dress. *We* all liked it, anyway. We were actually praying not to have to wear the *chatta* and *thuni*."[93] I have found no comparable writ petitions filed by men against the change from communal dress to the sari in the same spirit as the resistance to the *churidar*. Nor was I able to find any government orders allowing saris to be worn by women over communal dress. The Guruvayur temple could not provide any information on whether or not the temple had issued a formal resolution to allow women to wear saris into the temple, or whether there was any opposition to women wearing saris.[94] Rather, it appears that the sari was welcomed and considered respectable almost immediately. The *churidar*, by contrast, does not command that same professional quality in comparison to the sari.

Ritty Lukose has argued that the *churidar* offers a mode of protection for young women today by enabling them to enter into Kerala's public sphere in a way that is both demure and modern. For Lukose, young women's use of the *churidar* over the *pavadu* or Western dress "qualifies its own modernity" even as this option may not necessarily offer women a foolproof safeguard against sexual harassment or assault.[95] I would add to Lukose's argument that the continued insistence on the sari as professional wear over the *churidar* subsumes one type of demure modern under another, with the demure modern of the sari outranking the *churidar* in regard to female respectability.

Deeper analysis of what, exactly, constitutes the superiority of the sari's demure modernity reveals that the sari was part of the promotion of a modern secular citizen emerging after Independence. This modern secular citizen was implicitly marked as upper-class, Hindu, and upper-caste and was therefore accepted, in and through a reworked version of the familiar communal divisions of Kerala's backward past. The instant success of the sari reveals how powerful embodied differences, projected through women's clothing, continue to shape society as social "others" are regulated through the same systems of domination that characterized Kerala's caste divisions in colonial India. The reluctance to fully accept the *churidar* as professional wear can be attributed to the way in which the sari conveniently hides the workings of privilege within its very folds. From the *chatta* to the *churidar*, women's clothing continues to embody notions of who is included, who is excluded, and how embodied aspects of belonging police women's bodies, especially in the public sphere.

I have yet to discuss in-depth how race is an element of this embodiment. It may seem a stretch to equate the whiteness of upper-caste clothing to an Aryan racial identity, especially for South Asianists. This is because there is a constant denial that racialized discrimination even exists in India despite clear racial biases against African migrants, Northeast Indians, and South Indians.[96] For instance, in trying to deny that racism against Africans exists in India, former Bharatiya Janata Party parliamentarian Tarun Vijay stated, "If we were racist, why would we have all the entire south? . . . Why do we live with them if we are racist. We have black people around us."[97] As Duncan McDuie-Ra has argued, "A great deal of energy goes into strenuously denying that racism exists in India or upon recognizing that it may exist, stressing that it is not as bad as in other countries."[98] When racism is so denied, there are few frames of reference for us to discuss race in South Asian studies despite the associations between the whiteness of clothing and upper-caste identities, between upper-caste identities and the perceived fairness of skin, and between the perceived darkness of skin and certain caste-based occupations. In the next chapter, I further my analysis of embodiment by especially examining how racialized discrimination functions intersectionally and serves as yet another element of brahmanical patriarchal power.

3   Aryans and Dravidians

Syrian Christian Mythistories and
Intersectional Racialized Oppression

WHEN I BEGAN MY RESEARCH IN KERALA, I MET A NAMBOODIRI
Brahmin woman, Savatri, who became one of my most enthusiastic research
participants.

On the day we met, Savatri asked me, "Are you Namboodiri?"

"No," I answered, "I'm a St. Thomas Christian. I'm studying the history
of Christian women in Kerala."

"Oh," she said knowingly, "that explains it. You have such Aryan-looking
features, with fair skin and a nice *netti* (forehead), that I was sure you were
Namboodiri. But you know the St. Thomas Christians were once all Brahmins. That's why you look like us. Do you know that history? Write that
down for your *gaveshanum* (research). You Christians were Aryans when
you converted, not Dravidian like the Pulaya (Dalit) Christians."[1]

What amazes me about this exchange is how Savatri managed to articulate the relationship between Namboodiri Brahmins and Syrian Christians
through an intersectional understanding of a racial designation (Aryan),
perceived phenotypical differences (fair skin and shape of the forehead), a
religion (Hinduism/Syrian Christianity), and a caste (Brahmin) all at once.
It leads to an interesting understanding of how race functions in South Asia,
not necessarily as a recognized or identifiable social category but through
symbiotic assemblages between social identities that, when deconstructed,
reveal the inner workings of intersectional caste-, religious-, class-, color-,
and caste-based power dynamics.

"Race" is a loaded word, and when it comes to South Asian studies, it is
a completely overdetermined one, subsumed within particular modes of
scholarly inquiry. When we discuss race in South Asian studies, we often
get stuck in certain silos of identity—namely, linguistic difference (Indo-
Aryan versus Dravidian language trees), religious difference (Aryan as
Hindu, Muslim as Semite), caste difference (Dalit as Dravidian), or skin-
color difference (fair or dark). Rarely is class brought into the mix, even as
caste-based occupations have profound racial undertones that tie together

color, purity, and pollution with the work one's body is assumed to be best suited for.[2]

The problem with all these categories that discuss something on race is that they use unidirectional vectors of analysis and fail to capture the dynamics of how racialized differences are experienced and maintained from generation to generation. For example, the discussion of skin whitening and fairness becomes removed from the communal positioning of Hinduism as a religion founded by racially homogeneous Aryans. While skin whitening discusses race in terms of color, "Aryan" is used as a racial category that unites Indians through a religion. Rather than seeing color and religion as two separate articulations of race, I would argue, we need to contextualize calls for religious rights within discussions of color. As seen through Savatri's explanation of the relation between Syrian Christians and Namboodiri Brahmins, a working idea of Aryan-ness justifies certain social privileges to such a degree that they operate as natural hierarchies between peoples. It is this naturalness of race that should provide us with a starting point to discuss race with a multivariate analysis.

THE IMPOSSIBILITY OF RACE IN SOUTH ASIAN STUDIES

I want to be clear that it is not my intention to replace the term "race" with my own made-up, South Asian–specific term, nor is it my intention to prove that race exists in South Asia. I see attempts at proving the existence of race in South Asia to be futile because, as mentioned earlier, there will always be a siphoning off of one particular understanding of race into either caste, religion, color, or language. Rather, it is my intention to understand how the privileging of one understanding of racialized difference forecloses the possibility of understanding another as similarly formative and potentially even more oppressive—like cars colliding at an intersection and driving off without any accountability.[3]

One of the reasons why we cannot seem to discuss race in South Asian studies is that race is depicted as something that is foreign to South Asia. Either race is understood to have been imposed on the region by British colonialism or it is a problem located solely in other countries (the United States or South Africa), with a history that has little to do with South Asia.[4] The foreignness of racism is supported by the belief that *religion* is what divides the people of South Asia, and that *caste* is the hierarchal system that has led to institutionalized oppression. As a symptom of this, studies on race in India have primarily focused on Aryans and the Hindu religion, or

Dalit activism for international recognition of descent-based oppression.[5] Yet in India, caste and religion are themselves two overdetermined categories that have historically been mobilized, politicized, and understood as entirely specific to the nation-state. Some of the most brilliant work on South Asia and race today is actually located in transnational scholarship that examines race, migration, and social movements in global contexts.[6] However, this work somehow doesn't trickle down to area studies proper. This may be because of the nation-state specificity of caste for South Asianists over race. Kamala Visweswaran notes, "Scholarship on caste tends to remain entrenched within area studies, becoming difficult to track within African or South Asian diaspora studies, while scholarship on race also tends to be nation-bound, producing a Brazilian racial paradigm, or American or British racial paradigm, even within African diaspora studies."[7] Despite the most nuanced transnational studies on race, nation-state specificities only seem to further marginalize race as foreign to South Asia.

Even the usage of the terms "Aryan" and "Dravidian" is problematic in South Asian studies. Linguistic studies often use "Aryan" and "Dravidian" to discuss differences between North Indian and South Indian language trees. But usage of the terms is not seen as racial, and thus linguistic studies are separate from other studies on race in South Asia. Further, because of the sheer volume of work done on Tamil Nadu by comparison with studies of other South Indian states, and because of how work on Tamil Nadu stands in for work on South India, any sort of discussion of the term "Dravidian" outside the Tamil language experience is (yet again) overdetermined in South Asian studies. I would argue that the way in which "Dravidian" is invoked in Tamil politics is unique to South India. Bernard Bate, for example, in his work on Tamil oratory, has thoroughly discussed how modernity shaped a new democratic process in Tamil Nadu through the creation, in the 1940s, of *centamil*, a literary variety of ancient Tamil that is used in political speeches today, and that is separate from everyday spoken Tamil.[8] Malayalam has a divide between vernacular and oratory speech as well, but the division is entirely the opposite of the one that characterizes Tamil Dravidian oratory. The Malayalam oratory invoked by politicians, priests, and even news anchors is Sanskritized, a feature that indicates the primacy of Aryan-ness over Dravidian-ness.

In Kerala, "Aryan" signals both a Brahmin caste identity and lighter skin. In other words, "Aryan" and "Dravidian" are not just linguistic divisions but markers that intersect in profound ways with color and caste as well. But, to be fair, people do not walk around calling themselves "Aryans" or

"Dravidians" in the same way that people can self-identify in terms of caste or skin color. Here, I use the terms "Aryan" and "Dravidian" not because they denote distinct social categories but because they are the terms most readily available for moving through the existing literature on language, religion, gender, color, caste, and class in South Asian studies. I strategically deploy the terms "Aryan" and "Dravidian" to critique the way in which the study of difference in South Asia truncates a complex understanding of race and creates particular silos of marginalized identities that function to separate caste from religion, language from race, and feminine issues from political ones.

It is also not my intention to transplant an understanding of racial discrimination in the United States to India, or to compare race in the US context with caste in India. There are already many studies that compare race in the United States and caste in India, in an effort to highlight how forms of descent-based discrimination are similar to one another. Scholars have shown that neither caste nor race is biologically determined, and that both are socially constructed categories, which are relational, historically and culturally contingent, and shaped by other identities such as gender and class, and which operate at the everyday level as if they were natural, commonsense, inevitable divisions between peoples.[9] Racism and casteism have similar effects, including segregation, job discrimination, depictions of overly sexualized women (depictions that, all too often, are used as an excuse for sexual violence against Black and Dalit women), and depictions of violent men (depictions that, all too often, lead to profiling and "preemptive" violence against Black and Dalit men).[10] Feminists in India have used the term "brahmanical patriarchy" to discuss the intersections of casteism and patriarchy, in a way that is similar to Black feminists' use of the term "racist patriarchy" in the United States.[11] The similar struggles of both African Americans in the United States and Dalits in India led to Dalit groups in Maharashtra taking the name Dalit Panthers in 1972. There are also similarities between reservations for castes in India and affirmative action in the United States. The backlash against these programs (charges of "reverse racism" in the United States, and the anti–Mandal Commission protests in India) use a similar discourse of entitlement, and fear of the "other" taking "our" jobs, to incite political fervor against reformist policies. There are even attempts to bring out the solidarity between the freedom movement in India and the civil rights movement in the United States. Rather than comparing race and caste per se, these studies compare American racism with British imperialism and highlight leaders who traveled to India or to the United States and wrote or spoke about racial discrimination and/ or imperialism.[12]

Scholars have also shown that there are comparable differences between race in the United States and caste in India. Caste is seen as a Hindu practice. As a result, caste becomes endemic to India because "caste never redefines itself out of existence[;] it retains always its tether to Hinduism and so also to India."[13] While the "curse of Ham" narrative once justified slavery and racial divisions in the United States, the role of religion in race today is arguably not as evident in the United States.[14] This is especially visible in the very idea of a "postracial society" and "color blindness," phrases used in the United States that actively attempt (yet ultimately fail) to redefine race out of existence. Gyan Pandey argues that the political unity of Dalits in India was cultivated to establish their difference and to highlight their unique experiences of oppression, while in the United States, African Americans opted into the universality of American liberty. The political mobilizing of caste in India is therefore different from how race functions in American political contexts.[15] Intercaste marriages are also not comparable to interracial marriages, especially because of the common conception that arranged marriages in India have kept caste divisions the same from time immemorial. The category of mixed race makes sense in the United States, but there is not a concept of mixed caste in India (see chapter 5).

While these comparisons are helpful for understanding the limits of our current understandings of how caste and race function, the problem that I see with all these comparisons of (South Asian) caste and (US) race is that they end up reifying caste as distinctly South Asian and race as foreign to the region. As a result, we end up lacking an understanding of what we should do with these comparisons once they've been made and, at worst, run the risk of sliding a context-specific version of US definitions of race onto South Asia. I argue against mere comparisons of race/caste in South Asia and the United States and instead examine how racialized difference operates through assemblages of multiple oppressions. Can we understand Syrian Christian Aryan racial origin stories, the assumption that all lower-caste people in South India are Dravidian, and agricultural labor as an occupation best suited for dark-skinned bodies as interrelated issues operating at the intersections of religious difference, casteism, and classism in India today? How is the perceived sexual morality of fair women today in line with caste, religious, and class hierarchies generated during a previous age? How do our current understandings of racialized difference efface the intersecting oppressions faced by Dalit women by separating caste, class, color, and sexuality from one another? These are the questions I seek to answer in my examination of race in South Asia.

WHAT IS THIS "ARYAN" IN HINDU INDIA?

In October 2007, Andrew Symonds, an Australian cricket player of West Indian descent, was racially jeered by a Mumbai crowd that heckled him with monkey noises and gestures. Four spectators were detained and fined after pictures of the incident surfaced. The punishment for the Indian fans came only days after Symonds complained of a similar incident in Vadodara, without any action taken by the Indian Premier League. Vadodara's city police chief, C. P. Thakur, explained to reporters that the fans were most likely praying to the Hindu monkey god, Hanuman. He also stated, "Symonds mistook their chanting for racial abuse because he couldn't understand what [they were] saying. Obviously, he can't understand Gujarati and Hindi languages."[16] Two things are conflated here in the defense of the racism of the Indian fans: the Hindu religion and North Indian languages. This conflation is not so innocent, having resonance with the Aryan migration theory and how "Aryan" is understood both as a linguistic and religious difference in South Asia.

The very idea of Aryans in India begins with the Aryan migration theory. In colonial histories, the Aryans were depicted as a superior, fair-skinned, racially homogeneous group that came from Iran and migrated to both Europe and India. They supposedly excelled at statecraft in Europe, and they refined a distinct culture based on the Hindu texts, the *vedas*, in India. British colonization of India was justified as merely the second wave of Aryan migration, which would institute modern governance in the region and restore Hindu India to the glory of its Aryan past.

This story of Aryan migration, although used for political purposes during British colonization, is today supported by archaeological evidence. Comparisons between the culture of early Aryans and the first documented civilization in India, the Indus Valley civilization, point to evidence of Aryan migration. The writing of the earliest *veda*, the *rgveda* (1500 BCE), coincides with the gradual decline of the Indus Valley civilization, which flourished from roughly 2600 to 1700 BCE.[17] Archaeologists have noted a difference between the urban culture of the Indus Valley civilization and the pastoral Vedic civilization. Archaeological evidence of horses (the horse being an animal that figures prominently in the *vedas*) was not found in India until the decline of the Indus Valley civilization, which suggests that migrating Aryans brought the animal with them.[18]

The Aryan migration theory was further supported by linguistic studies on the Indo-European language tree. Sir William Jones first introduced the concept in 1786, at the Asiatic Society of Calcutta. Jones, a court judge, had learned Sanskrit in an effort to improve on Warren Hastings's *Gentoo Code*, a volume that outlined Hindu personal law.[19] In his study of Sanskrit, Jones recognized similarities between Sanskrit, Greek, Latin, and Persian and theorized that they derived from a now extinct proto-Aryan language. Latin and Greek, he said, were Western derivatives of this protolanguage, while Sanskrit and Persian developed over generations among Aryans who had migrated east. While speakers of a language need not be culturally or racially similar, early Indian linguistic scholarship equated speakers of a language with a distinguishable racial group, thus making linguistic scholarship paramount in the understanding of racial divisions between peoples in India. Today, while linguists may not discuss language in terms of race, they are in agreement about the Indo-European language group because of the similarities between certain words and the common syntax of modern languages within the Indo-European language tree.[20] The Indus Valley civilization's script has not yet been deciphered, but it is decidedly not the Sanskrit language of the *vedas*, which gives further scholarly credence to the Aryan migration theory in linguistic studies.

In colonial histories, migrating Aryans were racially differentiated from the native population of India, the Dravidians. Dravidian culture is characterized by the literature of the South Indian Sangam age, written from the third century BCE to the third century CE. Sangam literature suggests that Dravidian culture was much more egalitarian than Vedic culture, with a system of labor based on kinship instead of caste.[21] Nevertheless, the migrating Aryans were seen as superior because the Vedic culture gradually replaced the culture of the Sangam age. South Indian languages, known as Dravidian languages, actually have a non-Sanskrit base, as was discovered by Francis Whyte Ellis in 1816. Although Ellis's construction is now recognized as correct, Dravidian languages continued to be seen by colonial scholars as a "debased dialect derived from Sanskrit."[22] Hindu speakers of Dravidian languages could be religiously united with speakers of the Indo-European language group even as they were racially and culturally differentiated within India.

To explain the racialized difference between Aryans and Dravidians, the Aryan migration theory was modified into a theory of Aryan conquest. The *rgveda* discusses a division between two different *varnas* (colors), the *aryas* and *dasas*. *Varna* was therefore taken by European scholars to be a reference to skin pigmentation.[23] Max Müller, a nineteenth-century British scholar of Sanskrit and the *rgveda*, theorized that the *aryas* were light-skinned Aryans who conquered the *dasas*, or native darker-skinned Dravidians, of the Indus Valley. In their supposed conquest of the Indus Valley, the Aryans incorporated the Dravidians into the lower rungs of the caste system and pushed them south as the Aryans advanced from North India into South India.

There is no scholarly evidence to suggest that Aryan migration was a migration of conquest. Linguistic scholars today are in agreement that the *rgveda* has many borrowed Dravidian words, pointing to a culture of exchange between Aryan and Dravidian language speakers.[24] The interpretation of *aryas* and *dasas* as different in skin color may be a flawed reading and instead may refer to the knowledge of the *aryas* as being "light" over the "darkness" of the *dasas* knowledge.[25] Further, archaeological studies of Indus Valley ruins have not found any proof that urban centers were destroyed by conquering Aryans.[26] However, the Aryan conquest theory helped to explain caste in a way more familiar to colonists—through a discourse of race. As Romila Thapar explains, "Racial separateness required a demarcating feature and conquest became the mechanism by which caste hierarchy and inequalities could be explained as a form of racial segregation."[27]

It would appear, then, that the Aryan race was a construction of British imperialism, which privileged the Hindu religion and Aryan languages and peoples over Dravidians, and Thapar argues as much.[28] Peter Robb, in an edited collection, has also examined the question of whether race existed in South Asia prior to colonization.[29] It is true that the nineteenth century especially generated a plethora of studies on race in South Asia, under the guise of "race science." In an age when Western national identities were not a given but in a developing status, the notion of a European subject was racially stabilized through the body of the colonized.[30] Race in South Asia cannot be understood without being contextualized in the modern era.[31]

However, to view race as an invention of colonialism simplifies the social category of "Aryan" in India and masks how it continues to operate today in contemporary communal and caste-based politics. The Hindu Right, the academic left, Dalit groups, and minority groups have all taken up certain parts of the Aryan migration and Aryan conquest theory in present-day communal, caste, and rights-based activism. This confluence of political interests in the term "Aryan" shows both a vested interest in racial privilege and a wounded attachment to a politicized "minority" identity. These interests all center on the idea of racialized indigeneity and the question of who truly belongs to the Indian nation-state. Whether or not race was an invention of colonialism is really not so relevant to the question of how race functions today. In other words, rather than focusing on the question of where race came from, we should focus on how groups have aligned themselves with Aryan and Dravidian identities and why these identities have been used for specific political purposes.

INDIGENOUS TO INDIA: ARYAN CLAIMS, DALIT RIGHTS

The Hindu Right has tried to claim that the Aryans did not migrate to India but were indigenous to South Asia. If the authors of the Hindu Sanskrit texts were indigenous to India, then all others who migrated to South Asia at later dates—namely, Christians and Muslims—could be painted as racially different and foreign. The desire to prove Aryan indigeneity is part of the promotion of the Hindutva ideology, whereby only those who can claim India as their holy land and their homeland are considered "true" Indians. In 2002, the Hindu nationalist Bharatiya Janata Party attempted to change the National Council of Educational Research and Training (NCERT) history textbooks so that the Indus Valley civilization was renamed the Saraswati River Civilization, thus linking the peoples of the first Indian civilization to a Vedic culture and an Aryan race.[32] The Bharatiya Janata Party was able to whip up communal support for the changes because the new textbooks distanced the "indigenous" Aryan Hindus from "invading" Semite Muslims. This racialized religious difference is revealed by the terminology used to describe Hinduism in India: "Aryanization" and "Sanskritization" that ushered in the "golden age" of Vedic Hinduism, as opposed to the violent Muslim "invasions" and "conversions" that led to "medieval" India. Mona Bhan has found that the Hindu Right's construction of Aryan indigeneity has more recently used the Brogpa, a minority Buddhist community in Jammu and Kashmir, to further discredit the Aryan migration theory and tribal claims to indigeneity; as Bhan explains, "The RSS [Rashtriya Swayamsevak Sangh, a right-wing Hindu nationalist organization] promotes Brogpas as 'pure Aryans,' showcasing them as India's *mul nivasis*, or indigenous inhabitants, a political feat that is accompanied by disregarding the claims of many other 'non-Aryan' *adivasi* groups to indigeneity."[33]

Secular academics have argued against the Hindu Right's construction of Aryan indigeneity and instead supported the Aryan migration theory because of scholarly agreement from linguists, historians, and archaeolo-gists. However, arguments used to counter the Hindu Right separate and reify the category of religion into its own silo, distinct from caste and race. For example, the Syrian Christians are invoked as a community that is not foreign to India, since their conversion to Christianity in 52 CE predated Christianity in Europe.[34] The historical academic analysis of Christian indi-geneity falsely solidifies "Christians" as a unified group seemingly untainted by Aryan and Dravidian racial divides.

Simultaneously with the Hindu Right's attempt to claim Aryan indigene-ity, Dalit groups are attempting to use Dravidian indigeneity to bring caste into an international discussion of race and descent-based discrimination. The theory of Aryan conquest, popularized by Müller's reading of the *rgveda*, is used to prove present-day Dalit subordination by ancient Aryan domination. If the natives of India were Dravidian and were subjugated into the caste system by conquering Aryans, then Dalits "have a chronological priority in their identity with the land."[35] In Kerala, Dalit groups have used this narrative of "invading Aryans" to create a history in which Kerala's Dalit Dravidians were once rulers who were dispossessed of their lands, power, and knowledge by conquering Aryans.[36] On the basis of the notion that Aryans conquered and oppressed Dravidians, Dalit groups in India and entities such as Human Rights Watch began a movement for Dalits to be formally included in the United Nations' 2001 World Conference Against Racism (WCAR) in Durban, South Africa. The government of India opposed the inclusion of Dalits in the conference and claimed that because descent-based discrimination is defined in terms of race in article 1 of the United Nations' International Convention on the Elimination of Racial Discrimi-nation (ICERD), descent-based discrimination can only be about race.[37] In this argument, caste is not (and can never be) race. Further, the govern-ment of India argued that caste is an issue specific to the nation-state and should be addressed through internal mechanisms such as reservations, an endeavor that the Indian nation-state was already heavily invested in.[38]

International attention to caste as a form of descent-based discrimination with ties to racial discrimination is a relatively new phenomenon. Caste was previously seen by the United Nations as a problem that affected India alone. The Universal Declaration of Human Rights does not mention caste, nor does ICERD. With its post–World War II focus on civil and political rights, the United Nations has privileged certain communities of former European colonies in its understanding of racial discrimination.[39] Caste was explicitly referenced as a form of descent-based discrimination by ICERD only in 1996, when India's commitment to ICERD was reviewed by the United Nations.[40] Despite requests from the United Nations in 1996 and 1997, India did not permit the Special Rapporteur on Contemporary Forms of Racism and Racial Discrimination to visit India.[41] In January and February 2000, the treatment of Dalit women and children was also brought up by the Committee on the Rights of the Child and the Committee on the Elimination of Discrimination Against Women in the United Nations' review of India and the upholding of signed conventions. This increased attention from the United Nations on descent-based discrimination in India galvanized support for the inclusion of Dalit concerns at the WCAR. Despite international activism and pressure, key paragraphs concerning caste and "discrimination based on work and descent" were later erased from the final *Programme of Action* document that came out of the WCAR. This exclusion separated caste from race and, in essence, reified two ideas: first, that race is foreign to South Asia and, second, that caste is unique to the (Hindu) Indian nation-state.[42]

The politics of "Aryan" today shows many conflicting narratives and counternarratives that lead to single-vector scholarship on race in South Asia. Is "Aryan" a linguistic category? According to comparative linguistics between Indo-European and Dravidian languages and Sanskrit scholarship of the *vedas*, yes. But on a purely linguistic track, "Aryan" and "Dravidian" become hollowed-out, depoliticized placeholders, emptied of their racialized history and seemingly unsuitable for use in discussions of race in South Asia. Is "Aryan" merely a designation of a Hindu religion? In comparison to the culture of the Indus Valley civilization, which preceded the Hindu Vedic age, yes. But this understanding of "Aryan" as Hindu also supports the Hindutva ideology and has been used to paint minority religions as foreign and suspect. Is "Aryan" a caste identity that separates upper-caste Aryans from lower-caste Dravidians? For Dalit groups seeking international recognition of caste as a form of descent-based discrimination, yes. But this understanding of Aryan relies on an unfounded orientalist reading of the *rgveda* and the unsupported Aryan conquest theory.

"Aryan" and "Dravidian" in the context of South India, however, are terms that are operationalized in a very different manner than this North Indian conception of Aryan migration and conquest. Aryan not only signifies the Hindu religion but in Kerala is synonymous with the Namboodiri Brahmins and fair skin.

SYRIAN CHRISTIAN ORIGIN STORIES AND ARYAN-NESS

Breaking from South Asian studies' tendency to focus on North Indian history and politics, this section offers an analysis of particular Christian conversion stories and mythistories. By disengaging the Aryan identity from Hinduism and filling in the gaps in the literature on race in South India, we can better understand how religion intersects with color and caste on an everyday level in profound and problematic ways.

In discussions of race in Kerala, it is necessary to begin with the Parashuram creation story because it is so ubiquitous, and because it is steeped in racialized assumptions concerning the history of Aryan dominance in the region. As discussed in chapter 1, the land of Kerala was given to the Arya Brahmins (as were weapons and sexual ownership over bare-breasted Sudra women) by Parashuram to atone for his sin of killing the Kshatriyas twenty-one times over. The mythic origin of Kerala is understood by scholars as an explanation for Aryan migration and later Brahmin male dominance in Kerala, when society became caste-based and temple-oriented, sometime between the seventh and tenth centuries. There is no real consensus among historians as to the exact date of Brahmin migration to Kerala. However, most scholars agree that there was a gradual cultural shift from the Sangam age to the rise of temples and the emergence of the caste system.[43] The changes between the Sangam age and the emerging caste-based society are referred to by historians as the "Aryanization" of the region. There are similarities between Kerala's Namboodiris and the Tulu Brahmins of Karnataka, supporting the theory that Aryans migrated to Kerala from the north.[44] This separates the Namboodiri Brahmins from the Tamil Brahmins in Kerala, who migrated to the region prior to the British colonial period and later "dominated the bureaucracy" in Travancore.[45] Indeed, even though the Tamil Brahmins outnumbered Namboodiri Brahmins in Kerala, there was very little interaction between the castes.[46] There is even sometimes contempt toward Tamil Brahmins as some consider the Tamil Brahmins in Kerala to be Dravidian Brahmins against Kerala's Aryan Brahmins. Thus the story of Parashuram's ax throw becomes an important racial marker explaining the emergence of Kerala's caste divisions and temple-based occupational structure that tied all castes and religions to Kerala's Namboodiri Brahmins.

The Syrian Christian origin story is tied to the Parashuram story because, according to oral history, St. Thomas converted Hindu Brahmins to Christianity. It is not just caste that is explained through the story of the conversion of Brahmins to Christianity. Critical race theorists in the United

States have argued that race is a social process that results from human interaction, exists in relation to whiteness, and is part of a social fabric that shapes and is shaped by gender and class divides.[47] In the same vein, critical caste theory shows how caste is relational and part of a social fabric that encompasses other social categories, including race.[48] The way in which caste is imbricated with racialized difference can be seen in how my research participants slide together caste and race to separate the Syrian Christians from Dravidians, lower castes, lower classes, and Latin Christians:

> Mathai: Syrian Christians believe they were converted from Brahmins. If you ask any ordinary Catholic, they'll say "Yes, we were converted from Aryans." They will not give any proof—they will simply say they are Aryans. We believe we are converted Aryans because we are upper-class in Kerala. We believe we were converted from Namboodiris.[49]
>
> Markos: There are no *jatis* [castes]. There are only two *vargums* [tribes]: Dravidian and Aryan, with two languages and civilizations. From there, St. Thomas came to Kerala and converted Brahmins. That's how we Catholics came about. We Syrian Christians are Aryan.[50]
>
> Sarakutty: We are Nayar and Namboodiri converts. We are Aryan. We know because we are related to Hindus. We have lamps in our churches. We build our churches on the model of temples. Latin Christians have a different layout. Our cross is different from the cross used by Latin Christians.[51]

In each of these participants' explanation of Syrian Christian origins, one can see that Brahmin, Aryan, and Hindu identities and upper-class status are folded into one natural explanation of Syrian Christian identity formation. Mythic origin stories therefore work to explain and naturalize current caste, class, and racial norms of the Syrian Christian community.

Mythistories have naturalized perceived phenotypical differences between upper-caste Christians and lower-caste Dravidians as well. The Syrian Christians take pride in their supposed fair skin because it is seen as a status marker of their caste and religion, and proof of St. Thomas's conversion of Aryan Brahmins in the first century. The belief in the fairness of the community is supported by early ethnographic research on the Syrian Christians, which likened the features of Syrian Christians to those of the upper-caste Hindus in Kerala.[52] Even later scholarship on the Syrian Christians used biological markers to discuss the Syrian Christian–Dravidian divides. Take, for example, C. J. Fuller's explanation of Syrian Christian skin color, published in 1976: "Fair skin is required in order to pass as a Syrian because of the stereotyped belief of almost all Syrians that they are fair like the Nambudiris, considered to have the lightest skins in Kerala. In fact, most Syrians are relatively fair, especially when compared with the Harijan castes, the majority of whose members have typical 'Dravidian' features, including dark skins and woolly hair."[53]

As reported at the beginning of this chapter, one of my research participants, Savatri, noted that my features indicate the historical connection between Brahmins and Syrian Christians, and her comment is an important example of how assumed phenotypical differences between Syrian Christians and Dravidian "others" get solidified as "natural" in Kerala society. It is not just that the Syrian Christian community claims to have fair skin but also that scholarly and upper-caste acknowledgment of this "fact" fuels the continued reliance on biological notions of Syrian Christians' color difference from others.

Recall that the date of St. Thomas's arrival, 52 CE, predated Aryan migration and dominance in Kerala by some seven centuries. In the face of Western doubts about St. Thomas's visit to Kerala and the conversion of the so-called Brahmins, there are many online forums discussing Syrian Christian history in an effort to prove the origin stories of Syrian Christians. On these websites, many faithful resort to discussing race and biology. For instance, Nasrani.net publishes articles on the history of Syrian Christians in Kerala. In the comments section of an article titled "Subsequent Divisions and the Nasrani People," a commenter writes:

> We are believed to be Dravidians as South Indians, but I have been noticing a phenomenon that many Ammachis [grandmothers] and Appachans [grandfathers] of our families, at least one of them have some non Dravidian features like long face, being tall, different eye color (pucha kannu).
>
> I have seen families which their sons and daughters, some of them incredibly look black and some look very much fair. This is because their parents, one of them look dark or other look fair.
>
> Like Nidhin Olikara said, we all look same but when I stand close to that some people I noticed some of their hair seems brownish naturally and it also happened on me too. Also any dark color person among our community may not be a pure Dravidian.[54]

Comments such as this one, attesting to the lighter skin and non-Dravidian-ness of Syrian Christians, abound and help substantiate the "naturalness" of racialized differences. There is even a Syrian Christian group project trying to gather DNA data from Syrian Christians on the site FamilyTreeDNA.com. According to the project leaders, "This is an attempt to bring together the results of Syrian Christians of Kerala, India[,] to evaluate the results and check whether oral traditions and beliefs are in line with genealogical data."[55] Although there is no biological basis for race, the supposed fair skin of Syrian Christians, reportedly obtained by way of their Namboodiri origins, helps naturalize caste, religious, and color hierarchies in Kerala.

Mythistories of religious origins therefore tend to highlight phenotypical differences to prove one's privileged status over others today. This racial positioning even happens within castes. For example, the Knanayan Christians trace their history not to St. Thomas's conversion of the Brahmins but to the arrival of Thomas Cana and seventy-two Christian families from Jerusalem. Knanayan Christians claim to have lighter skin and lighter eyes than other Syrian Christians because of their Middle Eastern background. Strict endogamy within the Knanaya community bolsters the claim to fair skin as marriage within the caste/denomination is seen to have always produced lighter-skinned Knanaya offspring. Counter to this racialized history is an oral history within the Syro-Malabar Catholic community debunking the Knanayan Christian claim to fairer skin. According to this oral history, Thomas Cana chanced upon a Hindu washerwoman at a river. She begged him to stop his journey and help her find a necklace she had lost in the river. After Thomas found the necklace and helped the washerwoman put it back on, he went on his merry way. Upon his return home, Thomas Cana was surprised to find the washerwoman at his house. She explained to him that when he put the necklace around her neck, they had "tied the knot," the *talli-kettinu* ceremony. Because of this union between Thomas Cana and the lower-caste washerwoman, Syro-Malabar Catholics view the Knanaya as having darker skin. While both the Knanaya and Syro-Malabar Catholics are considered to be Syrian Christians and upper-caste, these two competing mythistories of racialized difference indicate how communities position themselves against each other vis-à-vis skin color.

Pheonotypical differences are exacerbated by the stigma associated with manual labor. Kerala's agricultural classes are assumed to be darker because they labor in the sun, while the upper castes were protected indoors as temple priests and landlords. Filippo Osella and Caroline Osella write that the "imperfect body" in Kerala is deemed to be a body with dark skin and curly hair, features commonly attributed to the agricultural laboring classes of Kerala; in turn, the imperfect body is associated with "bad luck" and negatively valued personality traits.[56] As discussed in chapter 2, working-class women in the public sphere are assumed to be sexually available, their bodies being intimately tied to the notion of the imperfect body. Moreover, the assumption that skin color produces bad luck justifies a particular type of racialized oppression for people with "dark" bodies who are employed as manual laborers.

ONE'S "FATE": DARK BODIES AND SEXUAL TRANSGRESSION

One day, after visiting a monastery in the Western Ghats, I was unable to make it home before sunset. I was lucky to catch the last bus to my village, over an hour away from the monastery. On a bus increasingly filled with men, the ticket collector and the bus driver asked me, "Who is your uncle? Where does he live? Why is he not here? Who were you meeting? For what reason? Why are you out at night? Why didn't you go home earlier? Why are you alone? What were you thinking?" At that point, Lucy, a working-class woman who was two years my senior and a vendor of fish, boarded the bus and was immediately ordered to sit next to me. She was carrying the large aluminum tub used to hold her fish, and she wore the workwoman's *kaili*, or patterned cloth tied around the waist like a skirt, and a sari blouse; I was carrying a purse and wore a sari. Sitting next to each other for the next hour, we were conspicuous both for being the only two women on the bus and for simultaneously displaying the embodied differences between women in Kerala. When I asked Lucy if she had ever been questioned about her uncle, her whereabouts, or her contacts with others when she was out alone, she laughed. "I often travel at night because I sell fish at sunset," she said. "Look at my dark skin. You are fair, and that is why these men are concerned. Some gents might come in here, and you and I might be in danger. We are both young, and traveling alone at night is always dangerous for young women. But if someone harassed me, would anyone do anything? It is my *vidhi* [fate] for being dark."[57]

Anna Lindberg discusses how jobs for women in Kerala's cashew factories depend on caste: the dirtiest job—shelling the cashews and removing the roasted nuts from the blackened shells—is done by the lowest castes; the next step up, peeling the brown skin from the cashews, is performed both by scheduled castes and by Ezhavas; Nayar women work exclusively in the grading section, separating the peeled white cashews.[58] Although Lindberg's analysis rests on caste as the basis for the division of labor, the fact that the lowest-caste employees work with the blackened shells, the middle castes with the brown skins, and the highest caste with the white cashews points to an understanding of color when it comes to the employment of certain castes. The whiteness of upper-caste women's clothing (see chapter 2) is another example of the embodied intersections between skin color and class. Recall that Dalit and agricultural laborers were forced to wear soiled clothing and the *calla malla* (stone necklace), while upper-caste Hindu and Christian women wore white clothing and gold ornaments. Labor, then, takes on embodied racialized differences, which only confirms assumptions regarding the differences between Aryan and Dravidian peoples.

Syrian Christians once held the esteemed racialized position of purifiers, which literally made them racially distinct from lower-caste Dravidians in Kerala. After the Brahmin rise to power, and the emergence of a temple-centered society, the purifying role of Syrian Christian males became especially important. The temple lamps used oils manufactured by lower-caste workers. By the ninth century, lamp oil made by the Vaniyan caste had become an important aspect of Kerala life, both in the temples and in households.[59] With growing caste divisions and rigid caste practices, oil manufactured by the lower-castes would not be touched by the upper-castes, whether in their households or in the temples. Almost every village that had a temple also had a Syrian Christian family that was given land in exchange for purifying the lamps. Even today, many Syrian Christian families begin their family history with a story of how they came to a particular region at the behest of a Namboodiri family.[60] This special purifying status of the Syrian Christians elevated their racial status over that of lower-caste laborers. In return, Syrian Christian landowners supported the Brahmanical patriarchal system.

During the late nineteenth and early twentieth centuries, Kerala's agricultural sector underwent a shift, and the role of purifier became obsolete. Upper-caste Syrian Christian women retreated to the domestic sphere or began to be employed in care-oriented work such as nursing and teaching.[61] In contrast, lower-caste women continued to be employed in casted agricultural jobs. The overall data today shows that the female workforce participation rate in Kerala is low. But new studies on women's work have shown that lower-income women work at higher rates than affluent women.[62] Lower-income jobs are typically those that require manual labor, such as fish vending, weeding, and coir work.[63] Women from affluent communities rarely take such jobs.[64] Three separate analyses of women's work in Kerala, by Mridul Eapen, Lakshmy Devi, and Aparna Mitra and Pooja Singh, suggest that the female workforce participation rate is low in Kerala because of a preference for "status employment" due to the education of women and high literacy rates.[65]

Yet what these studies fail to discuss is how jobs requiring manual labor are tied to colorism in the state. It is not just that these jobs lack status for educated women; such jobs also entail working in the sun for long periods without an umbrella, something extremely frowned upon for "fair" Syrian Christian women. For example, many Syrian Christian women garden and display their flower-gardening skills at the front of their houses. Often, the weeding and maintenance of the gardens, especially during the hot dry season in April and May, are done by lower-caste women. One day in April, when the temperature and humidity levels were particularly high, I visited a Syrian Christian house early in the morning where the auntie was gardening. "Let's go inside now," she said. "We don't want to be in the sun today." An hour later, a lower-caste woman came to the door, and the auntie directed her toward the remaining weeding tasks in the garden. "It's too hot," I protested. "No," the auntie said, "she is used to it. You see her dark skin? These people have always done this kind of work, so their bodies are more suited to it than ours."[66] It is not only that weeding is considered a job without status but also that this job is seen as better suited to perceived dark bodies.

The assumptions between work and color continue today in a variety of spaces. Take figure 3.1, which shows a still frame from *Manchadi 2*, a hugely popular children's show that presents animation, stories, and songs. This particular still, from late in the first decade of the 2000s, is from a song about umbrellas. The song describes the many uses for umbrellas: they can be used in the sun or in the rain; a grandfather uses an umbrella as a walking stick; workers attach umbrellas to their hats. The personified mice using the umbrellas to protect themselves from the sun are white, while the agricultural laborers using the umbrella hat are brown monkeys (and naked).

Feminist analyses of skin whitening have shown that fair skin acts as "symbolic capital that affects, if not determines, one's life chances," while dark skin acts as a social handicap.[67] This idea of social betterment through fair skin is reflected in numerous ads for skin-whitening cream in India, which imply that fair skin improves one's life chances economically. For instance, in a highly criticized ad for one brand of cream, Fair & Lovely, a young woman overhears her father complaining about not having any sons, and about his daughter's inability to help the family financially. After using Fair & Lovely, the young woman lands a job as an air hostess and becomes the apple of her father's eye. The theme of jumping class boundaries is also

FIGURE 3.1. Still from *Manchadi 2*, "Umbrellas." Source: Hibiscus Digital Media Pvt. Ltd., *Manchadi 2*.

apparent in ads for men's skin-whitening products. A commercial for Fair & Lovely Men's Active depicts an actor on a movie set who performs a motorcycle stunt only to be swapped out for a fair-skinned actor after the stunt is performed. After using the skin-whitening cream, the stuntman again performs the motorcycle scene and takes off his helmet, and the director tells the cameraman to keep rolling as the stuntman now becomes the film's leading man.[68] The message of these ads points to the importance of skin color in India and to how, if one can improve one's skin color, one can gain the symbolic capital to lead a better life, especially economically.

For women, economic security is closely linked to marriage, and fairness has become a particularly important element in this regard. Calls for fair-skinned brides in matrimonials abound. Particularly for Syrian Christian women, who traditionally do not inherit land but rather are given a dowry at the time of marriage, securing a husband through an arranged marriage is especially important to securing a sound economic future.[69] Thus, according to Amali Philips, skin color is "sexualized, feminized and moralized" in the context of marriage, and the *pennukannal*, or Syrian Christian bride-viewing ritual, plays a large role in Syrian Christian marriage, in part because of this link between fairness and life chances.[70] In the *pennukannal* ritual, the prospective groom and his family visit the prospective bride's parents. Sometime during the visit, the prospective bride serves the prospective groom and his family tea and sweets, thus allowing her beauty and the fairness of her skin to be viewed. Her skin color can be the basis for a proposal of marriage—or for rejection.[71]

A number of sanctioned rituals are performed to maintain the fairness of the community. In seventeenth-century Kerala, the intensely racialized *mannapedi* and *pulapedi* customs were observed. If an upper-caste woman, during the evening of a particular day, was seen by a lower-caste man, or was touched by a stick or stone thrown by a lower-caste man, she was excommunicated from her caste and claimed by that lower-caste man.[72] *Mannapedi* and *pulapedi* literally translate to "fear of the Mannam" and "fear of the Pulaya," both Dalit castes in Kerala. Most histories describe this custom as a night of extreme lawlessness that was meant to bolster the numbers of the slave castes. *Mannapedi* and *pulapedi* were abolished in 1696 by Unni Kerala Varma. Nevertheless, we should not separate the legacy of this custom from the "fear of dark bodies" paradigm that associates sexual excess and predatory behavior with dark bodies. Other rituals that were centered on color, such as rituals surrounding pregnancy and birth, are still practiced in the Syrian Christian community. For example, during pregnancy a Syrian Christian woman takes ayurvedic medicines, drinks milk mixed with gold flaked off the girl's mother's wedding ring, and is covered with a paste of green turmeric and bitter gourd juice, all to ensure that the child will have fair skin.[73] In a practice similar to that of the expectant mother who drinks milk with flaked gold, the baby, once born, is given honey with gold flakes, to be ensured of growing up with fair skin. Other rituals, such as the use of communal clothing as a marker of Syrian Christian status, have been redefined and redeployed through other aspects of identity, but these colorism rituals continue to be practiced as a matter of "tradition."

The intersection between fairness and a girl's marriageability produces a version of female morality centered on gendered forms of control that police the movements of upper-caste women and also make them always already suspect of sexual transgressions. On four different occasions, I was told a virtually identical story about dark skin and "fate" that involved assumptions about illicit unions between fair Syrian Christian women and dark lower-caste men.

The first story involved a woman who was known in the village to be a victim of domestic violence. Varghese, a man who matter-of-factly explained to me his knowledge of the situation, said that the woman's husband was beating her because she was having an affair. "How do you know?" I asked. "Her second child is very dark," he told me.[74]

The second story involved women in a women's church group meeting, *mathrajothies*. After a meeting, three women stayed behind and began gossiping about a fourth, who had left promptly at the meeting's conclusion. "What exactly did she do?" I asked. "She is having an affair with a lower-caste man who works on the land," I was told. "How do you know?" I asked. "Her husband works in the Gulf and is not always at home. You see how all of her children are dark, and she is very fair? It has happened because of her relationship with that laborer."

The third story involved a woman who was very fair and had many fair children, with the exception of one boy. According to the woman's extended family, she had become pregnant with this particular child after she had a fight with her husband and moved back to her parents' house. There, it was rumored, she had an affair with a laborer. Although the woman often declared this narrative false and insisted that her husband had come to visit her at her parents' house, the darker-skinner son was shunned by the extended family, and even by his own father, because of his skin color.[75]

I heard the fourth story when I visited a Syrian Christian family whose son had just finished an important academic exam. The family boasted about his test results and compared him to another dark youth in the neighborhood. I was asked whether I knew why the children of one particular family had never done well in school. The reason, I was told, was *kudumbhathil pirannathe alla* (they are not of good lineage).[76] The phrase *kudumbhathil pirannathe alla* is used only with disgust and contempt. It literally translates to "not born within the family."

In three of these stories, a woman who has a dark child is seen to deserve a fate of spousal abuse or social ostracism and is blamed for the fall of the entire family because of an alleged sexual transgression. The only proof of the alleged transgression is the color of her offspring, which makes colored bodies always already marked as a perpetual site of deviance.

The fate of those who conduct illicit unions, and the relation between class, color, and sexual politics, are depicted in Arundhati Roy's Man Booker Prize–winning novel *The God of Small Things*. The story is set in Kerala in the 1960s and revolves around a sexual relationship between Velutha, a Dalit Christian man from the Paravan caste, and Ammu, a Syrian Christian woman from a *modalali* (landlord) family. Velutha is described as a "rice Christian," so named because Dalit Hindus who converted to Christianity received a small amount of money and rice from the British

Christian missionaries. Velutha's very name depicts his color in its irony: "He was called Velutha—which means White in Malayalam—because he was so black."[77] Ammu is described as having smooth brown skin and shining shoulders.[78] In the past, Velutha's family has worked for Ammu's Syrian Christian family, delivering coconuts they had picked from her family's trees. When Velutha was fourteen years old, the matriarch of the family, Mammachi, convinced his father to send him to a Dalit school. Velutha became a carpenter, and now he builds furniture and fixes equipment in the Ammu's family's pickle-bottling factory. Velutha and Ammu's love affair coincides with the accidental drowning of Ammu's niece, Sophie Mol. When Velutha's father confesses to Mammachi that he has seen evidence of his son's affair with Ammu, Velutha is arrested, accused of raping Ammu and murdering Sophie Mol, and beaten to death in police custody. Ammu's two children are removed from her care, she is forced out of the family house, and she dies alone only a few years later. The Church refuses to bury Ammu's body, and her children are forever emotionally and psychologically scarred.

Priests in Kerala urged Syrian Christians not to read Roy's novel, and a Syrian Christian lawyer, Sabu Thomas, brought an obscenity case specifically against the last chapter, which narrates the sexual encounter between Velutha and Ammu; Thomas said of that chapter that "it deeply hurts the Syrian Christian community on whom is the novel based."[79] Outside Kerala, reviews and criticism of the book often discuss Ammu and Velutha's liaison as an intercaste relationship. But, through the transgressions of the characters, the reader sees how the intersections of classism, colorism, casteism, and patriarchy lead to a particular fate for the dark body of Velutha that goes beyond caste discrimination. In the novel, Velutha's family is depicted as having tried to escape caste persecution through conversion to Christianity. Velutha himself transgresses class boundaries by rejecting the type of work to which Dalits are considered best suited—agricultural labor—and becomes a skilled carpenter. When Mammachi hires him to take care of the factory maintenance, "It caused a great deal of resentment among the other Touchable factory workers because, according to them, Paravans were not *meant* to be carpenters."[80] Velutha joins the Communist Party, which as the novel highlights, is comprised of lower-classed laborers and ideologically driven by class inequalities in Kerala. Velutha's father is afraid for him because of the way he walks, holds his head, and offers suggestions, which "could (and would, and indeed, *should*) be construed as insolence."[81] As for Ammu, her sexual transgression taints her entire family. Ammu is seen to deserve her fate because she chooses to have sex with a dark man. But Velutha's fate is inextricably linked with his being a Dravidian, Dalit, lower-class rice Christian; his dark body is the body of difference that acts as the marker of the transgression itself.

In *The God of Small Things*, we see the definite divisions between two different Christian minorities in the state of Kerala—the rice Christians and the Syrian Christians. We see Ammu's Syrian Christian family called a *modalali* family during a Communist Party rally, where Velutha is spotted carrying a red flag. "Christians," in other words, are not united politically. The class divisions between minority communities, and the ways in which economic interests separate Christians from each other politically, require much more context and analysis (see chapter 4).

How do we define race in South Asia? While this question seems to be an important one, I would argue that it diverts us from asking the more immediate questions about the effects of racialized oppressions on bodies in South Asia. Further, this question prevents us from discussing the intersections that shape racialized differences because it forces us to discuss race through particular and overdetermined frames. In essence, this question is a trap. If I attempt to define race in South Asia, I will have to explain a version of race through and against understandings of race in other nation-state contexts, such as race in the United States, an endeavor that will only further alienate race as foreign to the region of South Asia. If I attempt to discuss a definition through a South Asia–specific understanding of religion, class, caste, or color, I run the risk of a unidirectional analysis of race by focusing more on one of these social categories than on another. The question, then, should not be about how we define race but rather what is at stake when we refuse to understand the intersectional aspects of racialized oppressions in South Asia. Only by approaching race in this way can we truly examine the complexities in play when we are working across the boundaries of identity politics and against the idea of an inherent fate for being dark.

4 Who Are the Minorities?

Gender, Minority Rights Protesting,
and the 1959 Liberation Struggle

IN 1958, THANU PILLAI, AN ASSEMBLYMAN IN THE KERALA LEGIS-
lative Assembly, voiced the following poignant questions in regard to
Kerala's minorities:

> In regard to the minorities, who are the minorities? In one place they say,
> Christians and Muslims and Anglo Indians (who are also Christians) are
> minorities. Then, who are the known majorities? Hindus. That is a very
> comprehensive term. There is more difference between certain sections
> of Hindus and certain other sections than there [are] differences between
> Hindus as a whole and the Christians. All these things, evidently, were
> not brought to the notice of the Supreme Court. Anyway, Sir, we have to
> accept this, and how can minorities be defined? Should there be a defi-
> nition? The amendments tabled by government do not contain any defi-
> nition in regard to minorities. Some of the non-official amendments,
> however, try to define that. We have to consider very carefully whether
> "minorities" can be satisfactorily defined. If the minorities are taken to
> be the Christians and the Muslims and the Anglo Indians, what are the
> sections that are left out? The Hindus. We all know that there is nothing
> more elastic [or] more comprehensive and more heterogeneous than the
> Hindus.[1]

As discussed in this book's introduction, numerical subordination can
lead to political disenfranchisement and the erasure of minority culture.
For this reason, minority communities are often understood to be vulnerable communities. But with caste, class, and racial privilege, the Syrian
Christians are not exactly a vulnerable minority community even as they
are numerically subordinate to the Hindu majority. As Pillai suggests, there
may be more similarities between (upper-caste) Hindus and (Syrian) Christians than there are between Hindus as a group. Conversely, there may be
more differences between minority groups than between the Hindu

majority and particular religious minorities. These dynamics quite often lead to the ascendancy of privileged minority concerns under the banner of "minority rights." Pillai's question concerning the definition of "minority" is therefore entangled in a web of confusion over how to protect a politically and culturally subordinate minority population from the tyranny of the majority while ensuring that the minority rights of the privileged few do not stand in for the homogenized whole.

The bill that prompted Pillai's question on defining minorities was the Kerala Education Bill. The KEB was introduced by the Communist-led state government in 1957 and was vehemently opposed by the Syrian Christian community because it instituted new government regulations on private schools, which affected the community's economic interests in the education sector. In response to the passage of the KEB, the Syrian Christians teamed up with other communal groups and organized a massive statewide strike, closing down schools, businesses, and public transportation. The protest, known in Malayalam as the *vimochana samaram*, or liberation struggle, lasted for over two months and brought the entire state to a complete standstill. In all, 177,850 people were arrested, 1,937 were physically wounded, and 15 were killed during the *vimochana samaram*.[2] On 31 July 1959, the central government responded to the lawlessness and instituted "president's rule," dismissing the elected Communist ministry. New elections were held in 1960, with the Kerala Pradesh Congress Committee emerging with a majority. Under the new ministry, the KEB was amended, and a key provision concerning the appointment of teachers was suspended.[3]

The *vimochana samaram* received extraordinary media attention. The *New York Times* published over sixty articles on the protest. The protest was rumored to have been funded in part by the Central Intelligence Agency.[4] In India, the *vimochana samaram* invoked discussions concerning the workings of India's democracy and fears over whether it was possible for elected state governments to be taken down merely by public protest. It also animated questions over who gets to count as vulnerable and enjoy state-sponsored protections in secular India.

While there have been studies on the first Communist ministry in Kerala and the protests against the KEB, there is a noticeable lack of scholarship on gender and minority women's participation despite their large numbers and important role in the protest.[5] J. Devika has suggested that an analysis of postcolonial Kerala should look at the tensions between, on the one hand, community identities that begin to dominate the political landscape and, on the other, emerging gender identities.[6] In this chapter, I therefore examine the concept of minority rights, minority culture, and the *vimochana samaram* protest through a feminist lens. In my analysis, I show how it is often gender roles and expectations that act as the fulcrum for defining group difference, rather than mere population totals that separate the majority from the minority. When groups protest for their minority rights, differing and competing definitions of womanhood and, indeed, women's rights can be engendered among minority groups, preventing feminist solidarity between minority communities. What interests me is not merely *if* women benefit from the struggle for minority rights but *which women* are in a position to benefit and *what sort* of benefit it is. As Devika further argues, "Today the feminist movement in [Kerala] can ignore the deep divide between 'embourgeoisfied' women and those who have been excluded from that category only at its peril. Nor can it afford to disregard the fact that patriarchies are built upon not just coercion but also upon consent, upon a certain shared privilege. And it may be that this 'embourgeoisfied' Womanhood, which has certainly spread far beyond the propertied classes since the 1930s, is precisely what is celebrated as the beating heart of the much admired "Kerala Model."[7] In my analysis of "embourgeoisfied Womanhood" in postcolonial Kerala, I draw out the gendered elements of what constitutes minority culture, and I question what the calls for minority rights actually set out to protect.

It is the secular protection of religious minorities under Article 30(1) that I particularly focus on in this chapter. Article 30(1) states that both religious and linguistic minorities shall have the right to establish and administer educational institutions of their choice. The constitutional article is seen to protect religious minorities because a minority educational institution can ensure that the culture of a minority community is passed on to the next generation through education. Minority schools therefore claim to be run for the benefit of the minority community.

The Indian constitution itself does not provide a definition for "minority," but the Supreme Court has narrowed the definition in its rulings concerning minorities and education. There remains a deep suspicion of religious minorities who would misuse Article 30(1) for the benefit of their own community by admitting only minority students or granting positions solely to minority teachers in minority schools. This fear of so-called reverse discrimination came out in the *T. M. A. Pai Foundation v. State of Karnataka* ruling when the bench stated:

Secularism and equality being two of the basic features of the Constitution, Article 30(1) ensures protection to the linguistic and religious
minorities, thereby preserving the secularism of the country. . . . Any law
or rule or regulation that would put the educational institutions run by
the minorities at a disadvantage when compared to the institutions run
by the others will have to be struck down. At the same time, there also
cannot be any reverse discrimination. . . . In other words, the essence of
Article 30(1) is to ensure equal treatment between the majority and the
minority institutions. No one type or category of institution should be
disfavoured or, for that matter, receive more favourable treatment than
another. Laws of the land, including rules and regulations, must apply
equally to the majority institutions as well as to the minority institutions.[8]

For Syrian Christians specifically, Article 30(1) has become a key element
of minority rights–based activism, from their protests over the KEB to the
present day. Looking at "Christian" protest, I ask these questions: What does
it mean for the class-, caste-, and race-privileged Syrian Christian community to mobilize politically to protect rights guaranteed by Article 30(1)? And
how do conventional understandings of vulnerability and secular protections mask gendered power dynamics at play in minority rights struggles?

KERALA'S EDUCATIONAL CULTURE

Any discussion of minority rights in Kerala is inherently a discussion about
religious minority rights in education. While there are a number of linguistic
minorities and Adivasis in Kerala, activism for other minority group rights
is overshadowed by the right of religious minorities to establish and administer their own schools. This one-dimensional view of minority rights is bol-
stered by a history of the politicization of education in the state. Robin Jeffrey
has argued that Malayalees' first encounter with government and public
politics is through schools.[9] I would add to Jeffrey's assessment that Malayalees' first encounter with the government and public politics is embedded
in existing communal hierarchies in education. These hierarchies are the
reason why education is so political in the overpoliticized state of Kerala.

Kerala is well known for its long history of universal education and for
having the highest literacy rates in the country.[10] But the educational landscape of Kerala was stratified from the very beginning. Travancore Maharani Gowri Parvati Bai's 1817 Rescript for universal education was actually

influenced by British Resident James Munro, who needed educated workers for the colonial administration.[11] Munro was also called "the father of the Christian mission," and he actively encouraged government support of missionary work, even advocating for British clergymen to be appointed as judges. With the support of Munro, British missionaries established a number of schools for Christian converts. Upper-caste Hindus viewed the Christian missionary schools as a threat to the traditional social order and as a conversion tactic. The Travancore government responded to upper-caste pressure by establishing segregated government schools.[12] In 1907, the Travancore government granted universal admission to schools, but this order was not enforced. Hindus of the Nayar caste went so far as to set fire to schools that tried to admit Pulaya children.[13] Syrian Christians blocked the admission of Dalit Christians into CMS College and instead advocated for Dalits to be trained in trades like carpentry or blacksmithing.[14] Both early missionary and government schools hired teachers from among the upper castes, which led to inherent caste divisions and biases between upper-caste teachers and lower-caste students.[15] The legacy of this divide continues today as class and caste disparities are pronounced, especially in the divides between government and private education, in access to high-quality English-medium education, and in access to higher education.[16]

Early on, the Syrian Christians positioned themselves as a community that was willing to invest in private education in the state. The Syrian Christians were an upper-caste community that transitioned quite easily from the temple- and caste-based occupational structure to the emerging capitalist society in the late nineteenth and early twentieth centuries. The Syrian Christians were able to take the investment risk in private education in addition to other investment risks, such as those involved in banking and in cultivation of rubber trees. But it was education that was so closely tied to the Syrian Christian churches. By the time of Kerala statehood, almost 70 percent of corporate private managements were Christian.[17] In addition, 65 percent of the primary and secondary schools were run by private management, and over three million students attended private schools.[18] The ratio of government schools to private schools in 1957 was 2:7.[19]

The rise in Christian-managed private educational institutions was helped by the state grant-in-aid policy, which gave private schools financial aid when they were unable to meet the salaries for teachers and/or to cover maintenance costs. After a government inspection of a school, the grant-in-aid was usually received by a private institution. The state policy of grant-in-aid increased the number of private schools from 20 in 1875 to 1,908 in

1910.[20] The privatization of education helped the state government meet the public demand for education. But the private school industry was largely unregulated. The 1951 Private Secondary School Scheme attempted to standardize grant-in-aid amounts. However, as Jeffrey has argued, these regulations were only grafted onto the already established missionary/private school system.[21] By the late 1950s, education accounted for one-third of the state budget.[22] Fees for students not covered by fee concessions were grossly uneven, especially in private schools. Teaching salaries were extremely low, but with a rising educated population and a lack of professional jobs, teaching positions were coveted. Jobs were auctioned off to the highest bidder, and bribes and nepotism for teaching positions prevailed.

In 1957, the Communist-led coalition government stepped in to reform the system with the Kerala Education Bill. The bill replaced the different regulatory structures (or lack of structures) in the princely states of Travancore and Cochin, and in Malabar under the Madras presidency, with a uniform structure in the newly formed state of Kerala. The bill was authored by the education minister, Joseph Mundassery. Mundassery himself was raised in a Syrian Christian family but was excommunicated for writing *Professor*, a novel chronicling the plight of teachers in the state. Because of his excommunication, Mundassery was denied burial in a Catholic cemetery. Mundassery was also fired from his job at St. Thomas College in Trichur.[23] Mundassery's bill proposed that teaching appointments to government and aided schools be made on a communal rotation from a government list. Teachers were to be paid directly by the government. In addition, certain provisions were included to acquire private aided schools, in an effort to guard against what the state called the "mismanagement of schools." An advisory board with elected local educational authorities was also proposed to assist the state education department. Private school teachers largely supported reform to level the playing field and increase salaries. According to Ausep, a teacher at the time, "I received 50 rupees at that time in salary. That was what we were living on! When we moved here in 1962, we were making 79 rupees in salary because of the changes."[24]

States across India were introducing similar bills in a move toward the standardization and regulation of education. In a 15 June 1957 meeting with the state, the central government suggested to the Kerala government that the KEB could be patterned after the 1956 Andhra Educational Institutions Bill, which passed the state legislature with little controversy.[25] Despite the need for the bill and the passing of similar bills in states across India, the KEB was met with resistance, especially from the Syrian Christian community.

Deshabhimani, a Communist newspaper, published a cartoon in August 1957 that illustrated public response to the bill in Kerala. The left panel of the cartoon is titled "Andhra Bill" and the placard says "No raise in teachers' salaries, government schools will be nationalized." The crowd responds to the Andhra Bill, saying, "Hai, one good bill!" In the right panel, the "Kerala Bill" placard is held by Joseph Mundassery and reads, "Teachers' salaries increased, schools will not be nationalized," to which the crowd angrily hops about shouting, "Attack, attack!"[26]

Even before the introduction of the KEB, any move to regulate education was continually met by strong political opposition from the Christian managements, the All Kerala Catholic Congress, Christian communal newspapers such as the widely read *Deepika*, and Syrian Christian priests and bishops. In 1945, when the Dewan of Travancore, C. P. Ramaswami Aiyar, called for the nationalization of primary schools, Bishop James Kalacherry issued a pastoral letter to the Syro-Malabar Catholic faithful asking them to "fight with their purses and with the spiritual sword."[27] The orders to arrest Bishop Kalacherry after he refused to withdraw the letter resulted in statewide rallies by Catholics; 16 September 1945 was declared Education Day, and a massive letter-writing campaign to the Travancore Maharaja ensued. Largely because of this opposition, the primary schools were not nationalized.

In the same way, the Syrian Christians organized quite fiercely against the KEB. Of particular importance to the Syrian Christian managements was how the minority rights of the community under Article 30(1) were under attack in the KEB. Christian managements specifically invoked Article 30(1) against the KEB's clauses 14 and 15, which outlined provisions for the takeover of an aided school in case of mismanagement, and clause 11, which concerned the proposed government list of teachers. These clauses, the managements claimed, gave the government too much control over minority schools and interfered with their constitutional right of autonomous school administration. In many ways, the history of caste and class hierarchies that characterized Kerala's educational history shaped the emerging debates over the KEB. These debates centered on Article 30(1), on what minority institutions were, and on how secularism could legitimately protect the vulnerable and not unduly aid the privileged.

MINORITY RIGHTS: DEBATING THE KERALA EDUCATION BILL

The KEB has become one of the most widely mentioned bills concerning minorities since its introduction in the Kerala Legislative Assembly in 1957.

All the most prominent Supreme Court rulings on minority rights, including *T. M. A. Pai v. the State of Karnataka* (2002), *Unni Krishnan v. State of Andhra Pradesh* (1993), *St. Stephen's College v. University of Delhi* (1992), and *Ahmedabad St. Xavier's College Society v. State of Gujarat* (1974), reference the KEB.[28] In Kerala, it was one of the most controversial bills introduced by the Communist ministry.[29] Over the course of two years, *The Hindu* reported that 650 KEB rules were tabled, 260 rules were moved and discussed, and 120 were accepted during the debates.[30] In the Legislative Assembly's 1957 second session alone, 310 amendments were made to the bill.[31]

The protest over the bill started immediately upon its introduction to the Kerala Legislative Assembly and continued for two years. On 11 June 1957, the minister of home affairs, Govind Ballabh Pant, wrote to Kerala's chief minister, E. M. S. Namboodiripad, informing Namboodiripad that he and the prime minister had received a number of telegrams from Catholic organizations protesting the KEB.[32] Namboodiripad responded by acknowledging that his office had received similar communications, but the letters were merely part of an agitation sponsored by the Catholic Church: "The Catholic Church has developed a sort of vested interest in the management of schools. They oppose any measure that seeks to curtail their unrestricted right over the management of Schools. They have developed a theory of . . . 'religious groups having the right to run their own schools as they please' to which of course they add the condition that the government should finance them. It is only under these circumstances, they argue, that the educational institutions can be made to permeate the 'religious atmosphere.'"[33]

The opposition to the bill in the Assembly was led by Syrian Christian politicians from the Kerala Pradesh Congress Committee, such as P. T. Chacko, E. P. Paulose, T. A. Thomman, and Joseph Chazhikadan. Chacko, representing Vazhoor in the Christian-heavy Kottayam district, was often quoted, and his speeches and amendments were discussed at length in the *Malayala Manorama* and *Deepika* newspapers.[34] The rise in literacy rates across the state and the constant reporting made the particulars of the bill well known across the Syrian Christian community. When the bill was referred to a select committee in July 1957, thousands of Syrian Christians came to testify, but only thirty-eight of them were selected.[35] The central government was flooded with form telegrams from Syrian Christians who were denied an opportunity to present evidence to the select committee.[36]

The targeted opposition to the bill placed the central government in an awkward position. Kerala was one of the only newly formed states *not* to elect the Congress Party to power after Indian Independence. If the

Congress-led central government supported the Christian KPCC opposition to the KEB, the central government could be seen as favoring the Congress Party in Kerala. If the central government showed unfettered support for the bill, it could alienate the KPCC base and minorities within the state and in India as a whole. As early as December 1957, the attorney general, M. C. Setalvad, reviewed the bill and stated that it allowed for unguided power capable of "arbitrary and discriminatory exercise" that could affect the rights guaranteed to minorities under Article 30(1).[37] Setalvad recommended that the KEB be examined by the Supreme Court.[38]

During a four-month correspondence in 1957 between Kerala Chief Minister E. M. S. Namboodiripad and the central government, Namboodiripad outlined the Communist ministry's position on minority institutions with the KEB: if the cost of education had to be met in any part by the state, then the state should have the right to regulate schools, within reason. This wouldn't bar minorities from establishing and administering their own schools under Article 30(1). However, it did require creating a state-supported definition of minority institutions that was predicated on the choice of either receiving a grant or operating as an unaided institution. This definition could discriminate against unaided minority schools that might choose in the future to receive state aid.

The Syrian Christians argued that religion was not a choice but a way of being that preceded the state. They latched onto the theoretical basis for Article 30(1) as a secular protection that would allow minority communities to pass on their unique and distinct culture through their educational institutions. In this reasoning, minority schools were for the benefit of the minority community, and the government had no right to interfere with the management of minority schools. Such interference would be an affront to a Christian way of life. In May 1959, Syro-Malabar Catholic Archbishop Mathew Kavukatt stated, "Catholic parents are bound to send their children to Catholic schools, in which a distinctly Catholic atmosphere is maintained. Hence arises the duty and right of Catholic parents to have schools of their own."[39]

The appointment of teachers on a rotating communal basis also threatened this idea of a minority way of life as only Christian managements—and, through them, Christian teachers—could shape the minority education of Christian students. In a writ petition against the bill, Archbishop Kavukatt and Bishop Vallopilly charged that the KEB was "a threat to the existence of the Christian community as a religious minority."[40] Thus the Syrian

Christians held that minority rights cannot be about choosing to operate as a minority school but must be about preserving the tradition of a minority way of life that could be passed on only by religious minorities themselves.

The KEB passed the legislature under strong dissent in 1958. Immediately, the governor sent the KEB to the president under Article 200 of the Indian constitution. In turn, the president sent the KEB to the Supreme Court to ensure that the bill did not interfere with Article 30(1). The Supreme Court struck down some of the most controversial parts of the bill, especially directing the Kerala Assembly to make changes to ensure that unaided minority schools would not be barred from future aid. But the Supreme Court also decided that if a school was aided, the government had the right to regulate the school, within reason. The KEB was sent back to the Kerala Legislative Assembly for revisions as per the opinion of the Supreme Court. Two years after it was introduced, the KEB was primed to go into effect on 1 June 1959.

In all the discussion over minorities and the KEB, nothing is mentioned as to what is actually being protected by Article 30(1)—only that the bill infringed upon this article. The Syrian Christian argument that minority schools were for the benefit of the minority community rested on the assumption that minority managements are the authentic and legitimate authorities over what constitutes "minority culture," and it masked the upper-caste and masculine power inherent in defining that culture. The definition of "Christian culture" is evident in the concurrent debates over another bill, the Kerala Dowry Prohibition Bill. Syrian Christians asked for exemption from the DPB on the basis of their customs enshrined in Christian personal law. As Anna Lindberg has argued, the codification of religious customs in Christian personal law was an "identity making process" for the Syrian Christians, one in which patriarchal controls over women were strengthened.[41] It is through the debates on this bill that we can see how gender roles and expectations act as markers for defining minority culture rather than any numeric difference between Hindus, Muslims, and Christians.

MINORITY CULTURE: DEBATING DOWRY PROHIBITION

The following excerpt is taken from the debates over the 1958 Kerala Dowry Prohibition Bill:

K. O. Aishabai: I am in favor of this bill. I am against dowry. Many years ago, I was one of the leaders of a women's organization that was against *stridhanam* [dowry]. I can say, in that same spirit, I support this bill. Other women's organizations in India have tried to bring a bill against dowry to the central government. But the Indian government took the bill out, because they wanted to bring a bill to parliament themselves. Now, the Kerala government has brought this bill. It will be an example to other states in the union. All Indian women will be thankful, and I am happy to be a part of it.

K. T. Achuthan: Do you know that they already passed a bill against dowry in Andhra Pradesh?

K. O. Aishabai: I didn't say that a bill didn't pass in Andhra. I just said that this particular bill could be an example. Today, we bring this bill for consideration.

Joseph Chazhikadan: Don't you think that there will be an increase in the number of weddings if this bill passes?

K. O. Aishabai: Marriage will happen or not happen with or without this bill. You are an elder member here. Perhaps there is something wrong with your head. I could remove the disorder that you seem to be afflicted with to help you change your opinion.

Joseph Chazhikadan: I asked out of interest . . .

K. O. Aishabai: I'm saying, ordinarily, when a girl is born, it is considered a bad thing. We believe it's a curse when there are a lot of girls in a family. This is because of *stridhanam*. In our country, dowry is the real curse. It's shameful. Women should be glorified, especially as mothers. But you look down on women. We have to change that and look upon women with pride. We need to take a stand. This bill is important for change. Secondly, men should be ashamed. Especially for Christian men, this should be shameful. Today, marriage is about property. But marriage is sacred. It is sacred for Christians, Muslims and Hindus. The ceremony shows that sacredness. But with dowry— fighting for dowry will destroy family life. In the Christian community, there is no such thing as annulments. In Muslim communities, when there is not enough dowry it leads to problems. There is a case in Kozhikode that a girl was married and didn't bring enough dowry. The family fought for more, and the girl was caught in the middle of both her husband and natal family. She committed suicide in front of a train. We have to think about how many lives were lost to *stridhanam*.[42]

Assemblywoman K. O. Aishabai's comments came in response to numerous points brought up by Syrian Christian assemblymen. Dowry prohibition bills were being introduced in other states in India at this time, and it was clear that the Indian nation-state was about to pass a nationwide bill prohibiting dowry. But in Kerala, the DPB was hotly contested, especially because dowry was part of Christian personal law, which was itself an extension of so-called Christian culture. The Syrian Christian assemblymen were in favor of excluding Christians from the reach of the DPB. In essence, this meant that the Syrian Christians were in favor of keeping dowry, something that Aishabai found "shameful."

The debates over the DPB were not exactly aimed at curtailing the social practice of dowry in Kerala. For many members of the Kerala Assembly, a law prohibiting dowry would do little to change the social custom. In fact, excessive dowry, which wives had little control over, had been on the rise among the educated classes in Kerala.[43] Assemblymen questioned whether a law alone could stop dowry.[44] They also argued that even if a law were passed, dowry would continue under "clandestine practices."[45] It seems the need for the bill was more to mark the arrival of Kerala into secular modernity. Part of this, of course, was the understanding that secular modernity provided women with an alternative to religion and patriarchal religious customs such as dowry. As Law Minister V. R. Krishna Iyer stated during the debates, "People should be alert to modern opinions. The world is moving fast. . . . Political exigencies should not prevail in matters of social progress."[46] The bill was debated, circulated for public opinion, debated again, and sent to a select committee that was to report to the Assembly in September 1959. The bill was never passed during the first ministry's tenure. Two years later, India passed the Dowry Prohibition Act. What is interesting about this debate is not whether the law could change the social practice of dowry but how the Syrian Christian community opposed the bill on the basis of what they called their Christian culture.

Assemblywoman K. O. Aishabai's comments on the DPB use both the words *stridhanam* and dowry. *Stridhanam* and dowry are terms that are technically synonymous, referring to money or property the bride brings with her to the groom's family at the time of marriage. But for Syrian Christians, *stridhanam* is often the preferred term because it refers to a woman's inheritance or "share" in the natal property.[47]

In 1912, the *Report of the Christian Community* was compiled to inquire into the customs of many denominations of Christians in Travancore. The report used the term *stridhanam* and described it as the sole form of inheritance for Christian women.[48] Unlike the Nayars and Mappila Muslims in Kerala, the Syrian Christians were patrilineal and practiced dowry. Patrilineal inheritance and dowry are offered as proof of Syrian Christians' Brahmin roots, as the Namboodiri Brahmins of Kerala were also patrilineal and had dowry. For Syro-Malabar Catholics specifically, the dowry is fixed by the families and announced at the bride's church during the engagement. One-tenth of the dowry goes to the Church. The engagement itself is possible only if both bride and groom have completed religious instruction in the faith. In contrast, intercaste and interfaith "love" marriages often do not involve the fixing of an amount by the families or an announcement of the dowry at the church. Marriage within the faith and caste was obligatory for women in order for them to have some kind of economic security.

One of the reasons behind compiling the 1912 *Report of the Christian Community* was to outline the plight of widows and unmarried Christian women, as "Christian tradition" had almost no provisions for women outside marriage; the report found that unmarried and widowed Christian women faced "lifelong misery" as they were left to the mercy of their brothers who only had a moral obligation to help and not a legal one.[49] Despite being a Christian woman's share, women did not (and do not) necessarily have any control over their *stridhanam*. In the report, the bridegroom is described as the "guardian" or "trustee" of the bride's *stridhanam*, especially in regard to gifted money and property.[50] And although *stridhanam* amounts were rising, most *stridhanam* amounts were (and continue to be), significantly less than the male heirs' share.[51] Nevertheless, without *stridhanam*, Christian women would have been destitute.

The "Christian tradition" of dowry was codified in the 1916 Travancore Christian Succession Act (TCSA), which drew from definitions of inheritance outlined in the report. As per the TCSA, women from the Christian community could inherit one-quarter of the familial property if the father died without leaving a will stating otherwise, or 5,000 rupees, whichever was less. If a Christian woman received dowry, she would forfeit all her claims to the family property. In 1958, Syrian Christian politicians invoked the TCSA to explain why Christians should be exempted from the DPB. For example, Legislative Assemblyman E. P. Poulose drew on the TCSA to argue for keeping the current practice of dowry:

> According to the law as affecting Christians, the property continues to be in the possession of the father till all the members of the family become majors and are in a position to look after their affairs. . . . But as it is the

daughter will [forgo] her share in the family properties once dowry is accepted, and in the middle-class families, the dowry exceeds the actual share of the woman, when the family properties are divided in the ratio of one to four between the daughters and sons. So in the interests of the women, it is better to continue the present system.[52]

Rather than being explicitly pro-dowry, the Syrian Christian assemblymen argued that Christian use of *stridhanam* was part of Syrian Christians' personal laws, which provided women with a substantial share. And since personal laws tend to be an "essential identifier" for minority religions, Syrian Christian Congress Party members defended *stridhanam* via their personal laws.[53]

The TCSA was in effect from 1916 until 1986, when it was finally replaced by the Indian Succession Act, after the Supreme Court ruling in the Mary Roy case. Mary Roy is the mother of Arundhati Roy, activist and author of *The God of Small Things*. The Mary Roy case was a bit of a sensation in Kerala. Mary Roy did not receive dowry from her family, because she married outside the religious community. She later divorced and moved into a family house in Tamil Nadu. After Mary Roy's father's death, her brother tried to evict her from that house. Since her father had left no will, Roy brought a case to the Kerala courts and challenged the Travancore Christian Succession Act on the grounds that it violated her right to equality. Mary Roy lost the case but went on to appeal the verdict along with two other Syrian Christian women in comparable circumstances. The Supreme Court ruled in favor of Mary Roy and two Syrian Christian women and repealed the Travancore Christian Succession Act. Because of this court case, Syrian Christian women in Kerala are now entitled to an equal share of their natal family's property if their father leaves no will stating otherwise.[54]

However, Mary Roy did not receive support from the Syrian Christian community in her fight for inheritance rights.[55] Moreover, women in the community do not actively exercise their property rights.[56] Even before the Mary Roy case, Syrian Christian women rarely fought for one-quarter of the family property or the 5000 rupees (whichever was less) that they were entitled to under the TCSA, and instead they would marry within the caste and faith and receive *stridhanam* as their share. Even to this day, Syrian Christian women view fighting for property as against Christian tradition and akin to being a bad daughter or sister.[57] In fact, when the TCSA was overturned, in 1986, the Church helped families draft wills to disinherit women.[58] There was even an attempt to repeal the ruling in the Assembly, with the introduction of the Travancore Cochin Christian Succession (Revival and Validation) Bill in 1995.[59]

In the 1958 debates, a key part of the discussion about the DPB centered not on the effects of the practice of dowry but on how dowry and Christian personal laws ensured the economic prosperity of the Syrian Christian community. During the debates, Congress Party member T. A. Thomman stated to his fellow assemblymen, "I think you will concede that the Christians are the most politically and economically forward community in the state. . . . I do not think that the Dowry system or the succession among the Christians stand in any way against their economic progress. . . . The system of inheritance has much to do with the economic progress of the community."[60] Or, in the words of M. C. Abraham, "For years, *stridhanam* has been a Christian tradition, and because of that, the community never became poor. Actually, over the years, Christians have risen in socio-economic status."[61] Pillai, himself not a Christian but a member of the Praja Socialist Party in coalition with the KPCC, also spoke of the links between dowry and Syrian Christian prosperity: "We find[,] so far as I am able to see, unanimity of opposition from our Christian friends here. . . . The Syrian Christian community of Travancore-Cochin . . . has been the most flourishing community in the State and they feel that it is their Succession laws, their Family laws[,] that have been of considerable help to them in securing for themselves that flourishing economic position."[62] In these comments, one sees how the economic prosperity of the community was tied to *stridhanam* while the "culture" of curtailing women's property rights, and of making economic dependence on husbands compulsory for Syrian Christian women, was not discussed in the debates, nor was the fact that a tenth of the *stridhanam* went to the Church (which had vested economic interests in the education sector that would be affected by the KEB).

The continued references to the flourishing status of the Syrian Christian community play into what Uma Chakravarti outlines as the most sustaining feature of brahmanical patriarchy: the caste hierarchies engendered through the endogamous union which function to maintain group status:

> Since the central function of marriage is to procreate, it is the children
> born of such a normative marriage who maintain and reproduce the
> social order. Both the hierarchical relations of caste and the immortality
> of the male line as well as the ancestors thus rest on marriage practices.
> Thus caste and kinship become inseparable; marriages mediate between
> *vansas*/lines and maintain the internal purity of castes in the larger system

of caste hierarchy. . . . Through marriage alliances, the status of the kin
group is believed to be maintained, strengthened, or weakened. . . . The
term "brahmanical patriarchy" is a useful way to isolate this unique
structure of patriarchy, by now dominant in many parts of India. It is
a set of rules and institutions in which caste and gender are linked, each
shaping the other[,] and where women are crucial in maintaining the
boundaries between castes.[63]

I quote Chakravarti's work at length because it illustrates the importance
of the endogamous union to maintaining the status of the kin/caste group.
Since *stridhanam* is given only when a marriage takes place within the caste
and faith, the Syrian Christian defense of dowry is a defense of the literal
reproduction of caste, class, and religious hierarchies. This is why the
debates on the Kerala Dowry Prohibition Bill kept returning to economic
prosperity and status of the community in Kerala society. Syrian Christian
opposition to the DPB was not merely an altruistic attempt by male politicians to save the only means of inheritance for Syrian Christian women; it
was also resistance to attempts to fiddle with a system that ensured the
reproduction of the entire community's status. The "culture" that is in need
of protection through the continuation of the dowry system is a culture that
protects the endogamous union, which itself ensures that brahmanical
patriarchal power is reproduced.

There arose from the debates over the DPB another important question
involving minority culture—namely, whose minority culture is this?
Throughout the debate, the term "Christians" was used interchangeably
with "Syrian Christians," and there does not seem to have been a voice for
lower-caste Christians. Only once was this point brought up in the debates.
On 1 March 1958, V. R. Krishna Iyer asked a Knanayan Christian assemblyman, Joseph Chazhikadan, "Is there only this section of the Christian community to represent the whole of the State? . . . I do not understand why
these pleadings are made under the guise of religion by one community."[64]
And yet the Syrian Christian traditions became projected onto the entire
Christian minority in the state, and their traditions were seen as the most
influential, and the most in need of protection. Archbishop Mathew Kavukatt wrote a pastoral letter in September 1958, stating that the Syrian Christians were "a lot more tradition-bound than other Christians."[65] Even in
the 1912 report, where all these so-called Christian traditions stem from,
the influence of the Syrian Christians is felt. Of the testimony received
by the select committee, 722 statements were from Syrian Christians, and

only 263 were collected from other Christians in the state.[66] This ascendancy
of Syrian Christian patriarchal interests over and against those of other
minority groups allowed for the homogenization of minority cultures and
for the projection of the interests of the most dominant Christians, both
economically and politically, as representative of all Christians.

While the protests against the KEB centered on the rights of minorities
under Article 30(1), the "culture" that was to be reproduced was revealed in
the defense of the DPB. In turn, this created a very narrow view of vulnerability and struggles for minority rights. I now turn to the so-called liberation struggle, or statewide strike, that was initiated after the passage of
the KEB to oust the Communist government from power. Keeping in
mind the ways in which "Christian culture" was and continues to be bound
to brahmanical patriarchal power, I especially examine how women from
different minority communities participated in and were affected by this
protest for minority rights.

"CHRISTIAN" WOMEN IN THE LIBERATION STRUGGLE

After the passage of the KEB, mobilization began for the overthrow of
the state government. The *vimochana samaram* was a statewide strike, organized by an interreligious coalition of the Nair Service Society (NSS), the
Syrian Christians (arguably led by the Syro-Malabar Catholics), and the
Muslim League, in an effort to remove the Communist ministry from
power.[67] The NSS, originally behind the KEB, joined forces with the Syrian
Christians because of another Communist-introduced bill, the Agrarian
Relations Act (ARA). The ARA sought to impose ceilings on landownership
that would have adversely affected the landowning Nayars and the Syrian
Christians. In response to the ARA, the NSS reversed its support of the KEB
and joined forces with the Syrian Christians, to pressure the central government into instituting "president's rule" in the state. The interreligious alliance gave the impression that all Hindus, Muslims, and Christians were
united in their lack of confidence in the Communist-led state government,
when in fact the interreligious alliance largely represented upper-caste and
middle-class economic interests in education and agriculture.

The protest itself was multipronged, but a key element was the decision
to shut down all private schools in the state. This was decided in a meeting
between Christian and Nayar school managers on 20 March 1959.[68] By May,
Syrian Christian managements across denominations were announcing that
their private schools would be shut down until the Communist ministry

was dismissed.[69] The state government attempted to curb the protest by delaying the start of the school year. But this did not stop the forced closures of the schools.

Schoolchildren were integral to the shutting down of the schools across the state. Student leaders led hundreds of schoolchildren wearing the *pala thoppi*, a hat made from palm leaves, from school to school, shouting slogans along the way. According to one student organizer, Yohinan, if the front line of students was arrested by the police, the next line of students would step up and take their place.[70] Paulose, a high school student at the time of the protests, also described to me how students were integral to the school shutdowns: "We'd go from school to school and call the leaders. Then all the kids would jump out. The last one we went to was Assumption College under Father P. C. Mathew. St. Peter's high school kids came there with us to try and close the college. But to go in—we were scared because the priest might dismiss us. Assumption College had a huge gate that was barred. Some of the kids climbed it while shouting slogans until [the management] had no choice but to close the school."[71] In Malabar, two hundred schools that tried to remain open were forcibly closed by students on the first day of the protest, and by 15 June all Malabar schools decided to close.[72]

Not only were schools shut down; public transportation was also brought to a standstill. Villages in Kerala were increasingly relying on buses for the transportation of goods and people. As part of the second five-year plan in Kerala, the government had set out to build 180 bridges and construct 1,500 miles of village roads.[73] By the late 1950s, Kerala had 150 vehicles per 100,000 people, while India as a whole had only 89 vehicles per 100,000 people.[74] The transportation department was offering passenger service on 301 routes covering 5,795 miles.[75] Sit-ins were staged across roads in Kerala to prevent transportation via public and private vehicles (figure 4.1).

Again, the central government was placed in a difficult position. Prime Minister Jawaharlal Nehru assured the Communist state government that the central government did not support any undemocratic behavior on the part of Kerala Congress Party members. The central government publically forbade KPCC members to protest under the Congress organization but allowed individual Congress members to participate in the agitation if they so wished. Kerala Chief Minister E. M. S. Namboodiripad frustratingly stated, "The Congress organization is trying to have it both ways—it wants to whip up and support the Nair-Catholic communal agitation against us, and on the other hand, it does not want to displease the large mass of people belonging to the backward communities. Is this a principled stand . . . which

FIGURE 4.1. Liberation
struggle, 1959. Photograph
© Marilyn Silverstone/
Magnum Photos.

[Indira] Gandhi claims her organization is taking, or is it an opportunistic
alliance with anybody who may be useful in attacking the Communists?"[76]
Nehru visited Kerala on 22 June 1959. He was met by thousands of protesters
in Thiruvananthapuram. Nehru suggested that the implementation of the
KEB be suspended.

In an effort to paralyze the government, Syro-Malabar Catholics, organized by the village churches, picketed by the thousands in front of the
collectorate and education offices in Kottayam, the secretariat and Legislative Assembly in Thiruvananthapuram, and police stations and government
buildings throughout the state. Christian protesters would gather at village
churches each morning to be bused into larger cities for coordinated picket-
ing and sit-ins.[77] Bishops issued pastoral letters throughout the *samaram*,
inciting Christians to protest and to protect their minority rights. In a
pastoral letter issued by sixteen Catholic bishops on 7 May, the clergy wrote,
"Let us be inspired by the words of the Divine: 'Blessed are those who are
tortured in the cause of justice, for theirs is the Kingdom of God.' And in

the end darkness is gathering around us. But we should not be frightened. This is darkness before dawn. Every member of our society is responsible to protect our rights and institutions."[78] Pastoral letters, as it turned out, were quite effective in organizing the Syro-Malabar Catholics, as Ausep, one of my research participants recounted: "We can't justify anything, but I took part in the protest because the bishops told me to. At that time, we would believe anything the bishops told us. . . . We didn't know about democracy. We were ruled by kings before statehood, and that's all we knew. And the pope was a king, and the bishop was king to us. That was our mentality at that time. They made us believe that the Marxists were against God."[79] The Syro-Malabar Catholics, backed by pastoral letters urging the faithful to protest, became a leading force in the *vimochana samaram.*

There was a special call for women to participate in the protest. In early June, out of more than 100,000 arrested, 42,745 were women.[80] From June through July 1959, over forty-five articles were written in the *Malayala Manorama* newspaper on women protesters.[81] For Syrian Christians, it was something new and entirely different to see women protesting in such numbers, with the Church's approval. One participant in the protest, Scaria, recounted to me how his sister had became active in the *samaram*, explaining that it "was a mass movement, and women took part. They were important in fund collections because they would go door to door for us. My sister, twenty-two years old at the time, would go from house to house every day with two female friends, traveling alone by boat! That would never have happened before."[82]

Their participation in the protest was lauded by the community. P. T. Chacko, the Syrian Christian politician mentioned earlier, stated that women in Kerala were the spark that lit the fire that would burn the Communist ministry down.[83] Syrian Christian women such as R. V. Thomas and Chinamma Chandy led the picket lines, were invited to give lectures at women's meetings, and spoke to the press as representatives of the women protesters.

While women were able to leave home to protest in the *samaram*, in many ways what the protest engendered was not necessarily the emancipation of minority women but a reinscription of patriarchal and caste power through the glorification of the upper-caste mother. Devika argues that in the early twentieth century, old ideologies of gender were selectively incorporated into new definitions of respectable behavior for the modern Malayalee woman.[84] The importance of reproduction for maintaining the rigid caste hierarchies of Kerala's caste-stratified past merged with new scripts that allowed women to enter the public sphere through controlled, moral sexual behavior. Motherhood was a key element in this understanding of morality. By the mid-twentieth century (especially in rural areas) the idea of the "modern woman" solidified as the norm and was exemplified in the sari-clad mother of the nuclear family charged with the moral upbringing of a reasonable number of children.[85]

During the *vimochana samaram*, it was minority women protesters' bodily capacity as reproducers of the community that was highlighted over any benefits they would stand to receive through struggles for minority rights. Chinamma Chandy declared to other women protesters, "We cannot stand this kind of tyranny against our children who we give milk. If we don't protest, the communists will control our lives."[86] On 26 June, *Malayala Manorama* ran a story on the women protesters that highlighted their courage, titled "Women Declare 'Our Children Will Know We Are Courageous.'"[87] *Deepika* published a picture of a *kunniku*-wearing Syrian Christian woman holding a baby and described the women protesters of Ankamali as heroic with "babies in arms."[88] This sentiment was also picked up by a political cartoonist at the height of the protest. The cartoon, published in *Malayala Manorama* on 30 July 1959, is set in the women's ward of the jail. A protesting mother runs into a cell with a baby in her arms, saying to the police looking on in surprise, "I have four more kids at home. Bring them, because we're living here till *Onam* [late August/early September]."

Spending months in jail away from home was by no means acceptable for any Kerala woman. It became normalized during the *vimochana samaram* precisely because it was within the bounds of the patriarchal disciplinary regime, which sanctioned women's political participation when the role of the mother was glorified. This channeling of motherhood works in service to Brahmanical patriarchy. Chakravarti argues that the caste system requires reproduction to be regulated in order for an idea of caste purity to be secured, and when reproduction is so regulated, motherhood becomes idealized, and mothers become worthy of worship.[89] The irony is that Syrian Christian women, despite being so very active in the *vimochana samaram*, did not become active in politics after their participation in the protest. In fact, they were largely shut out of "Christian" politics and continue to be underrepresented to this day—part of a "pattern of exclusion from the political [that] continues to characterize women's unequal citizenship in Kerala."[90]

In addition, not all women could access the figure of the ideal woman protester. In many ways, the experiences of "embourgeoisfied" Syrian

Christian mothers were set against the experiences of lower-class Syrian Christians and lower-caste Christian women. The divisions between Christians in the *vimochana samaram* are not overtly evident in news reports from the period, but such divisions do surface in recollections of the use of violence, and of the experience of violence during the protest.

One of the most evident differences between the various Christian protesters was the makeup of a paramilitary group known as the Christophers. Father Vadakkan, a Syro-Malabar Catholic priest, fashioned the Christophers "from the poorest sections of the Christian community exclusively. Even in the heat of the Liberation Struggle they remained a force separate from the middle classes in the movement."[91] The Communist ministry alleged that the Christophers were trained in the use of *lathis* (clubs), ropes for beating, choppers, and daggers.[92] The Communist ministry also accused the Christophers of stockpiling weapons, carrying concealed weapons to protests, and creating situations in which the police would have no choice but to open fire.[93] In the Ernakulam district alone, the Communist ministry estimated there were 28,000 Christian Christopher volunteers.[94] The doings of the Christophers were covert, and there is little mention of them in the news media during the *samaram*. Many Syro-Malabar Catholics I interviewed who participated in the *samaram* recalled Father Vadakkan and the Christophers, but none of the participants I interviewed belonged to the organization themselves, nor did any of their friends or family members. Some participants I interviewed noted that the Christophers differed in caste and class status from the more newsworthy "dominant" Syrian Christian protesters. For instance, Kurien, a member of the Kerala Students Union in 1959, said to me, "The Christophers? I think they were Latin Christians. They were from the coast, I believe. No one in our [Syro-Malabar] Church was part of that group. I think they were low-caste."[95]

Not only were lower-caste and lower-class Christians painted as perpetrators of violence; they were also victims of violence during the protest. In Ankamali on 13 June 1959, police fired forty-two rounds into a crowd of protesters, alleging that the mob was throwing stones and becoming increasingly violent; 7 died in the shootings. The crowd at Ankamali was 95 percent Syrian Christian, but 70 percent of these Christians were peasants and did not own land.[96] On 15 June there were police shootings that resulted in the deaths of five people at Pulluvila and Kochuveli, both villages near Thiruvananthapuram and composed chiefly of Latin Christian fisherfolk.[97] And on 4 July a protest at a fishing village led to the arrests of 2,949 people, 1,844 of them women.[98] The police fired shots at the crowd, killing 5.

Among those killed was a fisherwoman named Flory, a pregnant mother of five who was reportedly standing by a well and breastfeeding when hit by one of the bullets. The Ankamali shootings and Flory's death became rallying points during the *vimochana samaram*. Participants in the protest shared with me chants they remembered that combined the tragedies of Ankamali and Flory's death into one violent event:

> As it was getting dark in the evening,
> our husbands still not at home,
> the government cremated
> the pregnant woman named Flory.
> Know that we will demand
> justice for every drop of blood that was shed.[99]

> In the deadly fields of Ankamali,
> you who cremated
> the pregnant woman named Flory—
> expect no forgiveness from us.[100]

In these chants, the references to cremation establish a symbolic division between the Hindu majority and the minority Christians, who are supposed to be buried at death. The claim that Flory was cremated instead of buried makes the injustice of Flory's death an injustice inflicted on all Christians by virtue of their shared traditions. Flory's death, then, seemingly takes on a communal dimension, which paints all Christians as subordinated minorities with traditions that were infringed on by the state.

However, the victims of the Ankamali shootings, the protesters of the fishing village, and Flory did not match the image of class privilege of the dominant minority identity that emerges from the debates over the KEB and DPB. Indeed, even though Latin Christians and Syrian Christians are both buried at death and not cremated, their cemeteries are caste segregated from one another to this day. Again and again I asked Syro-Malabar Catholic middle-class women participants about the violence during the protests whether they had been afraid of being beaten and arrested, or whether they themselves had encountered any violence at the hands of the police. Not one of the Syro-Malabar Catholic women I interviewed who participated in some way in the *samaram* had faced any sort of violence. Take the experiences of Achamma: "I picketed and I stayed in jail for six days! I went with another politically minded female friend to Kottayam and picketed the collector. Then the police asked us, "Who should we arrest?' We gave our names because we were girls and they wouldn't harm us. I wasn't scared, because the jail was full of people, and we'd sing songs at night. For us, it was fun!"[101]

This is not to say that "embourgeoisfied" Syrian Christian women did not face any violence, as there may very well be accounts of this. Rather, I am concerned about the narrative that arises about "Christian" women and "acceptable" protest. The experience of Flory, a member of the fisher caste, is offset by that of protesters such as Achamma, who represented Kerala's "dominant Christian" women. In this there arise two separate scripts for women, especially when it comes to struggles for the rights of minorities. Fifty years after the *vimochana samaram*, these codes of conduct continue to shape communal politics, sexual morality, and social movements in Kerala.

In her work on sexual politics and sex workers in Kerala, Navaneetha Mokkil Maruthur describes two protests that occurred in front of the secretariat in Thiruvananthapuram in 2008.[102] The first protest was a night vigil staged by Dalit men and women in order to raise awareness about Chengara, a struggle for land rights. The media filmed Dalit women smoking and described the protest as a "masala" protest, condemning the behavior of the Dalit women as immoral. In response, on International Women's Day, women representing the feminist organization All India Democratic Women's Association (AIDWA) appeared at the secretariat with brooms, to protest the immorality of the night vigil by staging "a ritual cleansing."[103] The media's fixation on the "moral" behavior of Dalit women diverted attention from the Chengara struggle.[104] In addition, the fixation on the "masala" protest highlighted the narrow parameters set for "embourgeoisfied" women in the public sphere, parameters within which domesticity and morality shape political participation in rights-based movements.[105]

In a similar vein, Swapna Mukhopadhyay's closing contribution to an edited volume on Kerala women presents images of women in Kerala in 2006. Two of the photos show women protesting in very different ways. In the first photo, women fish vendors march with fists to their foreheads and fists in the air. In the second photo, middle-class women sit quietly in chairs. Of these two strikingly different photographs, Mukhopadhyay writes, "Some of [these photographs] bring [into] sharp focus how women are divided by class and culture ... between the unfettered anger of activist fish vendors involved in a public protest and the genteel and socially proper machinations of middle class service women participating in a demon-stration."[106] The social preference for the genteel or moral behavior of "embourgeoisfied" women is emblematic of a longer trend concerning women's protest in the state. Indeed, in June 1959, a headline in *Malayala Manorama* had invoked the very symbol of moral domesticity—the broom— that was used identically almost fifty years later in AIDWA's response to the so-called masala protest of Dalit women.[107]

It would be very easy to read minority women's experiences in India as subordinated, but what becomes harder to see is what sort of minority women we are talking about, what benefits they reap from minority rights struggles, and at whose expense. "Respectable behavior" continues to define differences between women, with significant repercussions for the struggles of the minority populations whom secular policies enacted in postcolonial India were intended to protect. It is clear from the legacy of the *vimochana samaram* that differing gendered codes of conduct make feminist solidarity *between* castes and classes and *among* minority populations virtually impossible. We must refuse to sit comfortably with a simplistic labeling of "minority rights." To return to Pillai's question at the beginning of this chapter, "In regard to the minorities, who are the minorities? . . . What are the sections that are left out?"[108]

5 A Life without Religion

Textbooks, Morality, and Protesting
across Religious Divides

IN JULY 2008, K. M. MANI, A FORMER CHIEF MINISTER OF KERALA, spoke at a protest organized by the Kerala Catholic Bishops Council (KCBC). He referenced the events of the *vimochana samaram*, powerfully reminding the Communist-led state coalition government that the actions taken by the Communists in 1957 were met by strong opposition from the populace. According to Mani, any antireligious move by the current government would have "serious consequences."[1]

The 2008 protest was organized to express the Church's demands for the withdrawal of a government-issued seventh-standard (seventh-grade) social science textbook—a textbook that included this story, titled "Mathamillatha Jeevan":

> After seating the parents, who had come with their ward, in the chairs before him, the headmaster began filling the application form.
>
> "Son, what's your name?"
>
> "Jeevan."
>
> "Good, nice name. Father's name?"
>
> "Anwar Rasheed."
>
> "Mother's name?"
>
> "Lakshmi Devi."
>
> The headmaster raised his head, looked at the parents and asked "Which religion should we write?"
>
> "None. Write that there is no religion."
>
> "Caste?"
>
> "The same."
>
> The headmaster leaned back in his chair and asked a little gravely "What if he feels the need for a religion when he grows up?"
>
> "Let him choose his religion when he feels so."[2]

The names of Jeevan's parents in this story imply an interfaith marriage: "Lakshmi Devi" is a Hindu woman's name, and "Anwar Rasheed" is a Muslim man's name. The very title, "Mathamillatha Jeevan," gives clues to why this particular story became a minority rights issue. *Matham* translates to "religion," while *illatha* is a negative suffix meaning "without." *Jeevan* is the boy's name in the story, but *Jeevan* is also the Malayalam word for "life." The title can therefore be correctly translated as either "Jeevan, the Boy without Religion" or "A Life without Religion." The alleged antireligious sentiment in this story became the focal point of a minority rights protest against the textbook—a second *vimochana samaram*. Like the first *vimochana samaram*, the second *vimochana samaram* protest invoked Article 30(1) of the Indian constitution and had widespread participation from Christians, Muslims, and Hindus. The intricacies of the protest against the textbook in Kerala, especially when read against other agitations for minority rights, help highlight the factors necessary to making a second *vimochana samaram* possible.

In chapter 4, I explored dominant minority culture and how protesting for minority rights can reveal separate struggles for minority communities and different experiences of women's activism within minority communities. In this chapter, I ask a slightly different question: What does it take to politically mobilize across group boundaries? I work against the idea that lower-class or lower-caste minorities are duped into the politics serving upper-caste Christians and instead look at how a unified definition of morality forms and contributes to political protest across religious and caste lines.

A MORAL EDUCATION: RELIGION AND SECULARISM IN INDIAN TEXTBOOKS

Textbook content is a hot-button communal issue in South Asia.[3] Religion is supposed to provide us with a path to live a moral life because it is considered to be the place where morality is established. In an effort to cultivate morally conscious citizens, textbooks usually have some sort of "moral" or "value" component. Religion and morality become almost interchangeable in debates over this moral content. During the *vimochana samaram*, a joint pastoral letter was issued by Kerala bishops, stating that it is "the sacred duty of Catholic schools to teach the children they educate religion and morality, because educational institutions must exert a healthy influence over the young."[4] In fact, one of the most widely dispersed pamphlets during the *vimochana samaram* was titled *The True Color of Textbooks*, and it whipped up communal support for the protest by playing off fears that the Communist-supported government textbooks contained atheistic views of history. The right to morally educate children thus resonates with the rights of religious groups.

In India, textbooks take on a particular sort of communal politicization because of the importance of textbooks in the Indian educational system. Exams, including the all-important class X and class XII exams, are shaped by the content of the textbooks that are published by the National Council of Educational Research and Training. NCERT was created in 1961, and in the late 1960s it issued its first set of textbooks. While NCERT standardized the curriculum, it forced teachers to teach to the textbook, and it limited freedom and innovation in the classroom. It also led to a specific sort of student learning that has been critiqued because it encourages students to memorize facts and cram for exams. This "textbook culture" is pervasive in both government and private schools.[5] While private schools do not have to use NCERT textbooks, exam-based learning leads to the replication of content in privately published textbooks. Thus both private and government schools in India are equally impacted by NCERT curriculum frameworks.

NCERT has issued three curriculum frameworks (referred to as set one, set two, and set three), all amidst controversies over religion and morality in textbook content. The first curriculum framework was created after a United Nations Educational, Scientific, and Cultural Organization (UNESCO) review of textbooks in 1961. Romila Thapar, the noted Jawaharlal Nehru University (JNU) historian who reviewed the textbook situation for UNESCO, found the textbooks reflective of an outdated colonial viewpoint on Indian history.[6] Colonial histories tended to present a linear narrative of Indian history, which started with the Hindu Vedic age (often glorified as the "golden age" of Indian civilization), cut short by waves of Muslim invasions that led to India's medieval period. Such a portrayal of Indian history supported a divide-and-rule colonial policy whereby the Hindu age was separated from the Muslim period. In colonial histories, the arrival of the British signaled the rebirth of Indian civilization and a reclaiming of India from despots. This colonial viewpoint created an up-down-up narrative of Indian history, one that started "up" with the Hindu Vedic age and was followed by a "downward" movement into India's Muslim medieval period and ending on another progressive "up," with a second wave of Aryan migration to the subcontinent (the British). The up-down-up historical narrative is a particular political move that promotes a specific reading of history to legitimize politics in the present.[7] Such a narrative is seductive because both the cause of civilization's decline in the past and the solution for society's uplift in the present can be easily located.

But for many Indian historians, history writing required a much more objective and scientific approach. After Indian Independence, history writing was becoming professionalized, with the expansion of higher education and the appearance of such respected peer-reviewed journals and presses as Oxford India, SAGE, and Orient Longman.[8] Postcolonial India witnessed the emergence of "high powered historians" who were educated in this system, writing largely in English and concentrated in urban North India (New Delhi).[9] After the UNESCO review, NCERT contacted Thapar and other "high powered historians" to write new history textbooks.

As mentioned earlier, the postcolonial nation-state adopted numerous secular policies intimately tied to nation building. One component of this was the promotion of history textbooks that conveyed a secular message of "unity in diversity." In an article reflecting on the first set of textbooks, Thapar explains that her generation was imprinted with nationalism, and textbook writing became a sort of national cause.[10] In an effort to decolonize textbooks, religion and "golden age" periodizations were downplayed in favor of socioeconomic explanations of conflicts.[11] Moments of religious tolerance were celebrated, and Congress Party nationalism was given a privileged place in Indian history.[12] With the wounds of Partition still open, the writers of the first set of NCERT textbooks presented a secular and democratic outlook, which was idealized as politically and morally superior to the divisive religious past.[13]

While professional history writing set out to correct communal versions of Indian history, it did not erase these histories from existence. As Partha Chatterjee explains, regional and sectarian "old social histories" were displaced to areas outside the academy, where they continued to flourish in the "domain of the popular," especially in the vernacular languages.[14] A great example of this can be seen in the highly literate state of Kerala, where there are a number of communal printing presses publishing in Malayalam that have widespread readership.[15] Practically every religious community and political entity has its own Malayalam-language newspaper, like *Deepika* for Syro-Malabar Catholics or *Desabhimani* for Communist supporters. There are also communal printing presses publishing countless pamphlets and books. For example, St. Joseph's Orphanage Press and Bookstall, in Changanacherry, publishes *Madyastan*, a monthly in Malayalam that includes pastoral letters, issues of importance to Syro-Malabar Catholics, and the monthly schedules for Syro-Malabar Catholic archbishops. The bookstall sells a number of books that have become real gems for my research. One in particular—an edited collection on the Syrian Christians, Namboodiris, Jews, and Sangam literature, that I bought at the bookstall and that was published by the Syro-Malabar Church's Liturgical Research Center—is based on the proceedings of a seminar, and many PhDs and theologians contributed to the collection. But whether the volume constitutes "professional history writing" is debatable, since many of the contributions are flavored with communal biases or were edited in such a way as to appeal to a Syro-Malabar Catholic audience.[16] Volumes like that one do indeed enjoy circulation within the community and even among scholars, but in an entirely separate realm from what comes out of such presses as Oxford India, SAGE, and Orient Longman. In other words, the division between the histories of the ivory tower and the domain of the popular is a deep and salient one and allows for old social histories to continue to shape perceptions of what constitutes moral textbook content in India today.

From NCERT's inception, different regions pressured the states and the central government for revisions to the NCERT textbooks, to reflect their specific versions of Indian history. When NCERT textbooks were translated into vernacular languages and local content was injected, the content of the NCERT textbooks was profoundly affected. As Neelandri Bhattacharya explains, "If the national sought to homogenize, erasing the particular and the local in an effort to produce the trans-local, vernacularization reinscribed the particular on to the homogenous national, producing a hybrid text which reflected a range of conflicting pressures within society."[17]

The conflicting pressures are not just regional but also communal in nature. Most vocal on this issue has been the Hindu Right. The Hindu Right rejected NCERT's secular version of history textbooks, promoting instead an up-down-up narrative of Indian history that was remarkably similar to the colonial histories NCERT had set out to replace. Instead of elevating the arrival of the British as a progressive return of the golden age, Hindutva ideology portrays Hindu nationalism as the force that will reinstate India's past glory. In post-Emergency,[18] the Janata Party attempted to ban set one of the NCERT's curriculum textbooks, claiming that they were biased, soft on Muslim invasions, and not appreciative of Hindu civilization.[19] The Janata Party fell before the books were officially banned. But in the early 1990s, after the Bharatiya Janata Party won elections in Uttar Pradesh and other states, textbooks were modified to reflect the up-down-up communal reading of Indian history at the state level. An expert committee was then formed by

NCERT to examine state textbooks. The committee found the Uttar Pradesh textbooks in particular to be so communal that the committee recommended withdrawal of the textbooks.[20]

In 1999, under the BJP-led central government, a new NCERT curriculum was put forth by the newly appointed NCERT director, J. S. Rajput. Under Rajput's direction, NCERT began modifying the set one textbooks and deleting a number of passages. The deletions included the removal of textbook content that suggested that the Aryans were not indigenous to India, which, as discussed in chapter 3, established a racial difference between Hindus, who were portrayed as racially indigenous to India, and Muslims, who were depicted as racially foreign. Also deleted were passages that portrayed Brahmanical Hinduism in an unfavorable light and passages from Thapar's history textbooks on ancient India which suggested that the upper castes did eat beef on occasion. The revisions to the textbooks were accompanied by a number of changes to academic boards. A new president and twelve new members were brought onto the Indian Council of Social Science Research, eighteen new members were appointed to the Indian Council of Historical Research, and a new president and secretary were appointed to the University Grants Commission, which then allocated 1.5 million rupees for teaching Vedic astrology in colleges in India.[21]

In the state of California, in 2005, similar deletions and changes to history textbooks were made in keeping with the recommendations of the Hindu Education Foundation in a ten-page memorandum to the State of California Department of Education. Ninety-one edits were ratified by the California Curriculum Commission, including deletions on the caste system and the unequal treatment of women within Hinduism. This was followed by a letter to the commission from Michael Witzel, a South Asianist from Harvard University, asking the board to reject the edits. The letter was cosigned by a number of South Asian academics, including Romila Thapar. The controversy was finally taken to the California courts, where most of the communal edits were eventually rejected.[22]

The BJP's win in 2014 indicates that there may be changes to NCERT textbooks in India yet again. In the state of Gujarat, nine new textbooks were written for grades one through twelve. Eight out of these nine textbooks were written by Dina Nath Batra, who was key in forcing Penguin India to withdraw Wendy Doniger's book *The Hindus: An Alternative History* from the Indian market.[23] Doniger's book became a communal flashpoint because it provides a non-brahmanical view of Hinduism and especially examines Hindu texts from the perspectives of animals, women, and lower castes. Batra was also a key figure in removing two other books from the Indian market that were supposedly "hurtful to Hindu religious sentiments."[24] There is also yet another textbook controversy brewing in the state of California, reminiscent of debates that occurred in 2005. In 2016, the #DontEraseIndia campaign was launched to protest the replacement of "India" with "South Asia" in California textbooks.[25] The Hindu American Foundation has also expressed a desire to remove casteism from California social studies textbooks.[26]

In India, the communal textbook changes made in 1999 set off a firestorm among secular academic historians. Textbook authors claimed that since they were not consulted, the changes to set one textbooks amounted to copyright infringement. Academic historians wrote numerous op-ed pieces in prominent English-language forums especially questioning the scholarly basis for the changes to the textbooks and the credentials of those who had participated in the changes: "NCERT has not been able to name a single well-known nationally and internationally recognized historian who is associated with the changes sought to be made in the syllabus. . . . There is not a single historian whose name has been given as the author of these books, and many newspaper reports in recent days have suggested that NCERT seems to be having trouble finding willing authors from among historians."[27]

Because of the "prominent public presence" of historians in India, the controversy over set two textbooks, most certainly played a role in their discontinuation.[28] Set two textbooks were used only for a few months, and many non-BJP states did not use the curriculum framework at all.[29] The next elections, in 2004, put the Congress Party back in power in the central government, and a new NCERT director, Krishna Kumar, was named.

In 2005, a curriculum framework written by an entirely new group of academic historians was launched. The writers deviated from set one *and* set two textbooks. In both set one and set two, the contributions of Dalits and women to Indian history were noticeably lacking, and both sets were largely uncritical of the nation-state and modernity.[30] The writers of set three textbooks emphasized the need to include regional histories and specific histories of subaltern communities. They also brought in a transnational focus that problematized the idea of the nation.[31]

The set three textbooks were also not without controversy. Many academic historians who were opposed to the set two textbooks wanted a return to set one. A focus on the local, it was argued, was irrational because "local knowledge is heavily burdened with superstition, social prejudices, and casteism and communalism."[32] In questioning the need for the changes in set three, Thapar wrote, "Local conditions and surroundings can be more purposefully studied if they are also seen in the context of a larger national perspective. A 'national' framework assumes this perspective."[33] Two seminars were organized to discuss the merits of the 2005 curriculum, and the papers presented at the seminars were published later that year.[34] Nevertheless, the new national curriculum framework went forward. States were to base their textbooks on the national curriculum framework and were also to add state-specific issues to account for India's cultural and regional diversity.

In Kerala, NCERT's set three textbooks were implemented in 2007 under the Left Democratic Front, a coalition government led by the Communist Party of India (Marxist). Before the regional content was written, the state government elicited public opinion through a number of forums. I spoke with the education minister, M. A. Baby, who had overseen the implementation of the textbooks, and who described the wide range of people involved in making the state curriculum framework: "We wanted the stakeholders to make their contributions involving this curriculum framework. So school-level discussions were there. Ground *panchayat* [village council]–level discussions were there, district *panchayat* organized discussions—so our idea was to take points from everybody. We don't want to conceal anything from anybody. So after having had a very detailed discussion, in which over a hundred thousand people participated—that is the statistics, we brought so many—we reframed the draft state curriculum framework. And it was on the basis of that curriculum framework that this textbook was created."[35]

The content itself was prepared by teachers and underwent analysis by a curriculum steering committee. After the curriculum was approved, final textbooks were prepared in a series of workshops. Since the steering committee had no problems with any of the content, the textbooks were released.[36]

Chapter 2 of the seventh-standard textbook dealt with caste and religion in Kerala and in India. In addition to the "Mathamillatha Jeevan" story, an excerpt from a 1924 Kerala school admissions ledger featuring upper-caste names was reproduced to teach students about caste discrimination. Descriptive paragraphs on the Breast Cloth Movement, the Vaikam Satyagraha, and the Guruvayur Satyagraha were included as a way to discuss caste movements in Kerala.[37] Vakkom Moulavi, a Muslim leader who fought for literacy within the community and especially for Muslim women's education, added a Kerala-specific Muslim component to the lesson. The chapter also included a portion from Jawaharlal Nehru's will requesting that no religious ritual be performed after his death, and excerpts from the Mahabharata, the Bible, and Hadith. The teacher's handbook instructed teachers to facilitate discussion in the classroom by comparing monetary success in life to a religious-filled life.[38] The lesson for the chapter includes questions such as, "Which caste is most likely to be affected by a tsunami?" to teach students that just as natural disasters do not discriminate by caste, so too should Kerala society be caste-blind.

It was the "Mathamillatha Jeevan" story in this chapter 2 that sparked the most controversy. Opponents claimed that the story was atheistic and told children to "not believe in God."[39] In a well-organized protest invoking comparisons to the *vimochana samaram*, Christian churches, the Congress Party, the BJP, the Nair Service Society, and Muslim groups joined forces and called for the withdrawal of the textbook. While many prominent educationalists—including Rohit Dhankar, who was involved in the 2005 curriculum design—supported the message of tolerance in "Mathamillatha Jeevan," the alleged antireligious content and the demand for moral education united all religions in Kerala to mobilize against the textbook.[40]

THE 2008 TEXTBOOK PROTEST:
A SECOND *VIMOCHANA SAMARAM*

The second *vimochana samaram* revealed the secular/communal duality in textbooks, whereby old social histories and the desire for religious/moral content continue to politicize textbooks, despite the best secular intentions of their writers.[41] It occurred in the summer of 2008, when Christians, Muslims, and Hindus united in a successful protest against the alleged antireligious sentiment in Kerala's seventh-standard social science textbook (figure 5.1). The student wing of the Congress Party, the Kerala Student Union (KSU), called for numerous *hartals* (strikes) against the textbook, one of which forced the Kerala University to postpone all examinations.[42] T. Siddique, state president of the Youth Congress, staged a highly publicized hunger strike against the textbook. In the Kerala Legislative Assembly, the United Democratic Front (UDF), a coalition led by the Kerala Pradesh Congress Committee, attempted walkouts to protest the "insensitive attitude" of the government toward Siddique's fast.[43] The KSU violently disrupted teachers' cluster meetings in Thiruvananthapuram and refused to meet with education minister Baby until the textbook was withdrawn.[44] The

FIGURE 5.1. Protesters from St. Mary's Church, 2008. Photograph by the author.

Nair Service Society and Christian churches joined forces under the Aided Schools' Managements' Coordination Committee.[45] They refused to negotiate with the state government and called not only for full withdrawal of the seventh-standard textbook but also for the removal of class one, class three, and class five textbooks.[46] On the other side, the Communist Party's college wing, the Student Federation of India, staged counterdemonstrations and *hartals* in favor of the "secular" message of "Mathamillatha Jeevan." The protesters often clashed with each other and with the police. For example, on 26 June 2008, protesting pro-Left government employees met with BJP antitextbook protesters in front of Thiruvananthapuram's secretariat. Stones were thrown and landed on a tent where antitextbook KSU protesters were sitting, which led to more fighting between groups and police involvement. Later in the afternoon, the Communist youth organization, the Democratic Youth Federation India, staged a march to protest the morning attack, which erupted into even more street violence between all groups. On that day alone, over twenty protesters and policemen were injured in the fighting.[47]

In the Muslim-majority district of Malappuram, over fourteen thousand books were seized from a book depot and destroyed by protesters. On 23 June, leaders of twelve different Muslim organizations sent separate memorandums to the chief minister, V. S. Achuthanandan, promising future agitations if the textbook was not withdrawn by 5 July.[48] Since it was not withdrawn, Muslim organizations called for a major march to Thiruvananthapuram's secretariat on 21 July.[49] The protests turned tragic when the headmaster of the Valilappuzha Aided Mappila Lower Primary School, James Augustine, was killed; Augustine had become caught in the middle of a protest led by the Muslim Youth League as he attempted to attend a teacher cluster meeting in Malappuram. Although the KPCC expressed sadness over Augustine's death, the party immediately informed the press that the protest would continue.[50] The opposition also alleged that Education Minister Baby had entered the autopsy room and influenced the coroner's ruling on the cause of Augustine's death, changing it from "natural death" to "murder." These allegations resulted in long debates within the Kerala Legislative Assembly and in calls for judicial probes.[51]

But the communal front was arguably led by the Syrian Christians. Organizing again in defense of their minority rights under Article 30(1), Christian managements claimed that the textbook interfered with their constitutional right to morally educate children. Syro-Malabar Cardinal Varkey Vithayathil issued a circular letter in late June contending that the Communist-led government was trying to propagate a denial of religion in schools.[52] Archbishop Powathil issued a similar circular letter, stating, "Education is one such means for atheistic governments to relinquish God and religion from the minds of youth. The Church cannot but interfere in the poisoning propaganda of the governmental authorities."[53] Over thirty-five bishops met and decided that 30 June would be the official day of protest against the textbook. For the protest day, seminars were organized in Catholic churches, and marches and meetings were held at the parish level. On 28 July 2008, the Syro-Malabar Catholic archdiocese of Changanacheri held a massive rally where more than twenty-five thousand of the faithful gathered to demand the withdrawal of the textbook. I attended this rally and spoke to many protesters about morality and religion in textbooks. A nun had this to say: "This is our [Christian] right, that's why we are protesting. The constitution gives us this right to say what we want to do in our schools. The current government is trying to tell schoolchildren that there is no God. There is no Church. If you tell small children that there is no God, it's like brainwashing, isn't it? Then their belief in God will be compromised. We will not tolerate this brainwashing, and so we are protesting that this textbook has to go. We will not stop protesting until this textbook is gone."[54]

Protesters also chanted during the rally:

Children of India, Christian Children,
hear our voice as we say:
We who created the educational institutions
have a history of spreading the
tradition of independence

. . . .

If you try to bring us Communist ideology
in educational institutions with public money,
we will make sure that you fail

. . . .

Swords will be provided to the hands carrying writing pens

. . . .

You will never succeed at increasing membership in your party
    by poisoning tender brains.[55]

The Latin Catholic Church joined forces with the Syro-Malabar Catholic Church and announced a seminar for priests of their dioceses and teachers employed in Latin Catholic Schools. The seminar itself was led by Father Paul Thelakkat, spokesman for the Syro-Malabar Church.

Because of the fury over the alleged antireligious content, the state government set up an expert committee to examine the textbook, headed by the historian K. N. Panikkar. Communal leaders refused to send representatives to the committee and instead supported a rival expert committee that had been commissioned by the KPCC and was chaired by another historian, M. G. S. Narayanan. The government committee ended up caving in to much of the communal pressure and suggested revisions to the entire chapter. The title of the story, "Mathamillatha Jeevan," was changed to "Viswasu Swathantriyam" ("Freedom of Belief"). The names in the story were replaced by "boy" and "parents," which completely erased the religious- and caste-blind position the story had intended to promote; this change also removed the interfaith marriage from the story and thus the double meaning of the story's title ("Jeeven, the Boy without Religion" or "A Life without Religion"). In addition, the excerpts from Nehru's will requesting that no religious ritual be performed for his funeral were taken out and replaced with a speech he had made on secularism.

The rival KPCC committee found numerous problems with the textbook and recommended that the first three chapters of the book be entirely deleted. However, by this time most private institutions had banned teaching the textbook anyway. The Kerala Catholic Bishops Council released its own workbook for teachers, which included content on faith in God and the need to be religious.[56] The KSU also released a textbook to the general public and to the state government for schools to use as an alternative to the seventh-standard textbook.[57]

The 2008 protest was extremely successful, especially in the changes proposed by the state government's own expert committee. Interestingly, the success of this communal protest followed a minority rights protest in 2007 over unaided minority self-financing colleges, a protest that was arguably ineffective in comparison. On 8 July 2007, a full year before the textbook controversy, Archbishop Andrus Thazhath had spoken at a Minority Rights Protection Convention, stating that if the Communist-led ministry continued to try to regulate self-financing colleges, then the Catholic Church would not hesitate to enact another *vimochana samaram*.[58] But this 2007 protest did not resonate as a second *vimochana samaram* as the textbook controversy did in 2008. The 2007 protest did not unite communal groups, nor was it completely successful in convincing the Christian faithful that their minority rights needed to be defended.

THE FIRST "SECOND *VIMOCHANA SAMARAM*": MINORITY-RUN SELF-FINANCING COLLEGES

How does it happen that one call for minority rights can succeed in uniting people across group boundaries, whereas another such call achieves only lukewarm results? To understand the difference, it is useful to examine the intricacies surrounding the first "second *vimochana samaram*": the 2007 protest for minority rights in self-financing professional colleges.

In 2001, the Kerala government enacted provisions to allow for the establishment of "self-financed" colleges, or colleges that operate without state aid. They were initially met with appreciation from the population because, over the decades, there had been a large increase in the number of students seeking professional degrees, and a shortage of seats in government and affiliated colleges. Students had, for many years, been migrating to other states for college instruction and to have a higher-quality education as Kerala colleges struggled with infrastructure problems, lack of funds, poor administration, inadequate libraries and labs, and shortages of qualified and dedicated teachers.[59] Many politicians, both from the Congress Party and the Communist Party, supported self-financing colleges especially because this presented a way for Kerala to become more of a player in the internet technology (IT) sector by producing qualified engineers and IT

professionals. In comparison to other communities, Christian managements had more funds as well as experience in the private school industry,
and thus many of these unaided self-financing colleges in Kerala are
managed by minorities. In 2007, thirty-five of the forty-nine engineering
colleges, six of the nine medical colleges, and the majority of colleges offering degrees in dentistry, pharmacy, and nursing were under minority management.[60] By 2012, there were more than three hundred private colleges of
arts and sciences (aided as well as unaided), while the number of government colleges was only forty.[61]

While applauded at first, self-financing colleges soon provoked ire from
the population because of alleged corruption in admissions. The Christian
managements in Kerala had originally verbally agreed to a 50/50 seat-
sharing system with the state government, whereby 50 percent of admitted
students would be from a government quota list, with the other 50 percent
determined by the management. The government seats have a lower admissions fee, to accommodate students from disadvantaged communities, and
so they are often referred to as "free seats." The management seats, by contrast, tend to have higher fees to offset the cost of running the schools.
Christian managements reneged on this verbal agreement after two Supreme
Court cases, *T. M. A. Pai Foundation v. State of Karnataka* (2002) and *PA
Imamdar v. State of Maharashtra* (2005). The *Pai* case looked at 50/50 seat
sharing and determined that, in many cases, affluent students from disadvantaged communities had funds to go to higher-end private schools and
receive "tuition," or tutoring. As a result, these students from the creamy
layer were getting higher marks on exams and filling the free seats while
students from the poorer sections of society were paying higher fees to
attend college through the management quotas. But for unaided minority
schools, the *Pai* bench ruled that under Article 30(1), unaided minority
schools had the freedom to determine their own admissions structures, as
long as they were not profiting from admissions, and as long as the merit of
students was taken into account. The *Imamdar* case furthered the *Pai* ruling,
finding that, for unaided minority institutions, a quota system for seats
should be only voluntary and that it could not be mandated by the government. The bench also ruled that the admissions structure needed to be
transparent. After these cases, the number of schools in Kerala requesting
minority status increased significantly, as the "minority unaided self-
financing" label was seen as a way to give managements more autonomy in
determining fee structures and in admissions.[62]

The *Pai* bench also discussed individual donations to schools, called "capitation fees," which were often rumored to be the deciding factor in student admissions. Christian managements in Kerala have claimed that, with 50/50 seat sharing, capitation fees may once have been necessary in order to offset the costs of school management. But now, with schools having their own admissions standards, donations to schools only aided in providing fee concessions to disadvantaged students. In a circular letter to the faithful, Archbishop Perumthottam stated, "Our educational institutions are not working in terms of profit. To provide for students from lower-income backgrounds, we have to justifiably raise funds. For that, we have to receive help from alumni and well-wishers. Money should not be a criterion for admission and appointment. There should not be any activities in our institutions which affect the good name of the Church. Catholic institutions should be alert about corruption and should always stand against corruption."[63] However, there was no way of knowing if capitation fees were still in effect, as the line between a donation to a school and a capitation fee is not clear.

In 2006, the Communist-led coalition government brought The Kerala Professional Colleges or Institutions (Prohibition of Capitation Fee, Regulation of Admission, Fixation of Non-Exploitative Fee and Other Measures to Ensure Equity and Excellence in Professional Education) Act (2006) to the Kerala Assembly.[64] The act had provisions for a more egalitarian admissions process, including a single-window system of admissions whereby students were to be admitted on the basis of their rank as determined by a uniform criterion. It also attempted to make sure that only oppressed minorities could benefit from Article 30(1). To this end, clause 8 of the act specifically tried to redefine "minority" by having it match three conditions: (1) the population of said minority had to be less than 50 percent of the total population of Kerala; (2) the number of professional colleges run by minorities should be proportionally less than the number of professional colleges run by the nonminority in the state; and (3) the number of minority students belonging to the community of the minority school undergoing professional education in all professional colleges in the state should be proportionally less than the number of nonminority students in all professional colleges in Kerala. So, in essence, "minority" was defined by population, by numbers of institutions, and by numbers of students in those institutions. If, in all three categories, the numbers added up to less than the nonminority, then the school would qualify for the "minority" label.

This would ensure that minority institutions would benefit only disadvantaged minorities, and not minorities who might have any sort of caste or class privilege. Education Minister Baby explained it to me as follows:

> We gave a new scientific definition to what makes a minority education institution. Minority is something, and minority education institution is something else. . . . So studies prove, as against Hindus, more Christians are getting admission. So in the field of education, Christians may not be considered as a suffering lot. This is the point. Why are there minority protection clauses in the constitution? Minority protection is not to gain over majority. If they are suffering in comparison to the majority, there should be a protection. If they are not suffering, there is no special protection need to be given. Women would require some protection if they are not getting adequate representation. For example, now perhaps there is a good argument coming: will there be any protection for men in assemblies? No, why? They are already well represented! There is no requirement. Only because women are not getting sufficient representation in legislation, a protective clause is being sought after. So similarly, for minority students also if they are sufficiently represented in medical and engineering colleges, there is no special minority medical college or minority engineering college for these students or for any community. So this is our very sound scientific argument.[65]

In January 2007, the Kerala High Court struck down the Communist bill, finding that the state's provisions were unconstitutional under Article 30(1).[66] But the protest for "minority rights" continued. When the Communist-led coalition government appealed the court's decision, the Church inaugurated the Minority Rights Protection Convention in July 2007. It was at this convention that Archibishop Andrus Thazhat first warned that the Christian community was ready to stage a second *vimochana samaram*. On 12 August 2007, the Syro-Malabar Catholic Church held a large protest against regulating self-financing colleges in Kottayam City. The protest became violent, and several cameramen and journalists were injured when a mob began throwing rocks. This particular rally received widespread media coverage. Bishops wrote numerous pastoral letters, including this joint circular letter in late August 2007:

> We are sorry to write again about the educational sector in Kerala. This is not a political move against the state. We are the caretakers of the Church,

which respects the democratic system and stands for democratic values. But when the people who are in power show anti-people approaches and intolerance to court judgements, we don't have any other option but to respond. . . . Minority rights are not a contemporary need for socio-economic development. Minority rights are for the protection of the religious culture of minorities. This right is to establish and administer educational institutions to enhance our Christian culture in a secular culture that is not anti-religious.[67]

Church leaders went to the central government and met with the president, the prime minister, and the minister of human resources development to voice their opposition to the bill and the bill's encroachment on their constitutional rights.[68]

Despite the media attention on self-financing colleges, and despite the use of pastoral letters by bishops to incite a second *vimochana samaram*, the self-financing protest did not galvanize Christians to the same degree that the textbook controversy would galvanize them a year later. This is not to say that the mobilization against the Communist legislation wasn't big— thousands of Christian faithful attended the 12 August 2007 rally. But the Christian community itself was sharply and publicly divided on the issue. The Kerala Latin Catholic Association came out against the pastoral letters issued by the Syro-Malabar Catholic bishops, saying that the clergy had "appropriated minority rights to themselves for their own benefit."[69] The Syrian Christian Jacobite Church didn't support the agitation, with Father Varghese Kallappara stating, "The issues between the government and the minority institutions should be settled through mediation and talks."[70] Many Syro-Malabar Catholics saw this not as a minority rights issue but as a way to protect profits in the self-financing college industry. Mathai spoke to me at length about his dissatisfaction with Christian managements, the Communist-led government, and the "second generation" of priests: "The [Christian management's] motives are for money. And the government wants three schools to every one Christian school, because that is the ratio of the population. After getting those schools, the government is making money off this from appointments and fees. But what [the government] is telling is also only partial truth, not full truth. Right now, the second generation of priests [is also] telling . . . part[ial] truth. The full truth is money."[71]

The populace was not about to see the self-financing issue as one that could unite peoples as successfully as the original *vimochana samaram*, either. Although the Syrian Christians were politically powerful, "the idea of a second liberation struggle [failed] to enthuse even the hardcore among the faithful."[72] Indeed, many of my research participants discussed the self-financing issue as entirely different from the first *vimochana samaram*:

> Cheriyan: There was unity back then. Between Muslims, Hindus, Ezhavas. Then we were strong.
>
> Sonja Thomas: Now is there no unity?
>
> Cheriyan: No! There is just fighting between us. Then, we had more of a desire to develop the state. Now, it's an "all for oneself" attitude. Then, it was for our Christian community. And we would work with Muslims and Hindus, the Nair Service Society . . . now, in the education sector, with what the managements are showing . . . my God! The Christian-managed schools have *so much* corruption. You have to pay to get in. It's become an industry.
>
> ST: In the past was education like this?
>
> Cheriyan: In the past, it was about giving education to the entire Kerala community. Now, it is about taking money. That's what the priests want control over. In my opinion, we need more control from the government.
>
> ST: Are self-financing colleges a minority right?
>
> Cheriyan: The priests say that, but what the Communist government is saying is actually right. To get an education now, you need money. Donation. Capitation. You aren't able to give a donation, too bad— no education.
>
> ST: Would a *vimochana samaram* for minority rights be possible today?
>
> Cheriyan: Oh no. If you tried to do a real *vimochana samaram* today for self-financing colleges [*laughing*], they'd lock you up. You'd be mad to think this is anything about minority rights. It's about money.[73]

Neither the Nair Service Society nor the Muslim community was on board with this push for a second *vimochana samaram*. The general secretary of the Sri Narayana Dharma Paripalana Yogam, the Ezhava caste group, stated, "This is not 1959. We will not allow Christians to cash in on our sentiments."[74] "Mathamillatha Jeevan" and the textbook controversy, by contrast, did unite across class, caste, and religious differences, whereas the 2007 demonstrations only seemed to exacerbate those differences. Clearly, there was something different in how minority rights were framed in the textbook controversy.

MIXED MARRIAGES AND CHILDREN WITHOUT A RELIGION

In the debates over the textbook that included the story "Mathamillatha Jeevan," minority rights and alleged antireligious sentiment were brought to the forefront of the protests. Yet there was an elephant in the room when it came to what was so antireligious about the textbook: the mixed marriage of Jeevan's parents. What are the cultural meanings of mixed marriages, of the status of children in a mixed marriage, and of how the outrage over the mixed marriage depicted in the story united peoples across group boundaries far more successfully than the protest over self-financing colleges? What is the marriage in the story "Mathamillatha Jeevan" really about?

On the surface, the names "Lakshmi Devi" and "Anwar Rasheed" depict only an interfaith marriage. However, for Malayalees, the combination invokes *both* an interfaith and an intercaste marriage. In Kerala, a history of tenancy and agricultural labor, as opposed to landownership, links the Mappila Muslim community in particular ways to a lower-caste and lower-class identity. Islam first arrived in Kerala when Arab traders began to settle in the area in the eighth century. These traders intermarried with women, presumably from the lower castes.[75] Over the centuries, this mercantile class grew and was concentrated in urban areas on the coasts. Prior to the arrival of the Portuguese in Kerala, Muslim missionaries also began to come to the region, and mosques were founded. Stephen Dale argues that because the Arab Muslims in Kerala were concentrated in urban areas, and because these areas would have been considered sites of pollution by upper-caste Hindus, the converts to Islam in this period must have come from the lower castes.[76] The Portuguese engaged in numerous battles for trading supremacy with the mercantile Muslim class in Kerala. Slowly, the upper-crust Muslims who were primarily Arab traders began to leave the area while the majority of converted Muslims became landless agricultural laborers. While some members of the Muslim population continued to be part of the mercantile class and were landowners, by 1871 the majority of Muslims in Malabar were tenants.[77] The eighteenth and nineteenth centuries saw a number of lower-caste conversions from Hinduism to Islam, first under Tipu Sultan's regime and then under the Madras presidency, when conversion became an economic incentive for lower-caste Hindus. Under the British landlord-tenant system, the Mappila Muslims were paid more money than lower-caste Hindus, and many Chemmar Hindus converted to Islam at this time.[78] The Muslim community in Kerala continues to function on a caste basis, with endogamous marriages and hierarchal arrangements based on ancestry and occupation.[79] While there is class and caste stratification among Muslim groups in Kerala today, they qualify homogeneously as other backward classes (OBCs).[80] This history is such that the interfaith marriage in "Mathamillatha Jeevan" can also be read as an intercaste marriage. Indeed, the title "Mathamillatha Jeevan" was translated into English as "Jeevan, the Casteless."[81]

"Mixed marriage" is the term most commonly used in Kerala to describe both interfaith and intercaste marriages. Arguably, there are differences between intercaste and interfaith marriages because caste and religion are not commutable social categories. An interfaith marriage is not always an intercaste marriage, as one can marry within the same caste and not within the same religion, just as one can marry within the same religion and not the same caste. For instance, a Syrian Christian can marry a Hindu from the Nayar caste, thus marrying across religions but staying (relatively) within the same caste. Or a Syro-Malabar Catholic can marry a Latin Catholic, marrying across castes but staying within the same religion. However, the community outrage associated with both hypothetical marriages would be the same. Indeed, Prem Chowdhry has found that in North India, the community response to intercaste and interfaith marriages is the same even though the community mostly discusses intercaste marriages.[82] Because the societal reaction to interfaith and intercaste marriages is similar, and because an interfaith marriage can also be an intercaste marriage, the term "mixed marriage" becomes appropriate as a description of the marriage in "Mathamillatha Jeevan."

Unlike endogamous marriages, which are governed by religious personal law in India, mixed marriages take place under the Special Marriage Act of 1954. Children of couples married under this act are governed by the Indian Succession Act unless they are Hindu, Buddhist, Sikh, or Jain, which brings them under the purview of the Hindu Succession Act. Although many people offhandedly reference an increasing number of mixed marriages as young people become more tech-savvy or are influenced by Western media and notions of romantic love, there is a noticeable lack of statistical data on the subject.[83] There is, however, a large number of examples of communities coming together to respond to mixed marriages, often with violence against the couple involved.

The communitarian response to mixed marriages has to do with the importance of the endogamous marriage to a caste's or a religious group's status. As discussed earlier, endogamy is crucial to the functioning of brahmanical patriarchy because marriage literally reproduces caste and religious divisions through procreation. This role of the arranged marriage in reproducing hierarchies makes marriage itself a tool that strengthens both the status of groups and the divisions between groups. A marriage is therefore viewed as a union between two families within a caste and/or religion and not as a union between two individuals.[84] In this system of exchange, women act as the source of community honor.[85] A woman with "oppositional agency" who engages in "autonomous reproduction" through a mixed marriage is treated as a threat to the entire community.[86] This threat is most often met with violence against the woman involved and is disproportionately leveled at the party whose status is considered lower.[87] Violence serves both as a punishment for the individual woman and as a deterrent to other women in the community.[88] India is rife with stories of caste *panchayats* and/or kin issuing violence as punishment for mixed marriages, sometimes even extending the punishment to the sisters of an eloping man or woman, in the form of gang rape.[89] The most extreme but all too common form of violence is the "honor killing" of a woman at the hands of her close kin. The forced suicide or murder of an eloping woman is seen to restore familial and community honor.[90]

The state itself is often complicit in and even sanctions the community response to a mixed marriage. Both Chowdhry and Parveez Mody have found that the state criminalizes love, especially by making marriages under the Special Marriage Act very difficult. Under the act, a couple must notify the state of the intention to marry and submit to a mandatory notice period of thirty days before the marriage can take place.[91] This makes it easier for the police, and for the kin of the parties involved, to find and return the eloping couple. Notice of the planned marriage is also posted in court for all to see, and this, Mody argues, stigmatizes couples.[92] Both parties must submit proof of age and residence in addition to the names of witnesses and their addresses. All these restrictions make obtaining a legally recognized mixed marriage extremely difficult.

The state's intervention into and prevention of mixed marriages is met, on the other side, with indifference toward prosecuting any sort of violence leveled at eloping couples by caste *panchayats* or by kin.[93] There have been cases in which the family members involved in an honor killing were even exempted from police investigation.[94] In its last two reports on India, the United Nations' Committee on the Elimination of Discrimination Against Women came out quite clearly against the provisions in the Special Marriage Act, and in 2014 the committee called for the removal of procedural barriers to civil unions.[95] Yet the removal of the procedural barriers may do little to change the system, since the procedures that prevent mixed marriages merely reflect wider societal support for arranged marriage and its pivotal role in the reproduction of caste and religious divisions.

Many studies of endogamous marriage have focused on North India and ignored South India because of the assumption that all of South India practices Dravidian kinship, as characterized by the prevalence of cross-cousin marriage and marriage within a village as opposed to village exogamy.[96] (A cross-cousin marriage is assumed to keep a woman in contact with her natal family and thus to give her a better support system.) For example, in her examination of dowry murders, Veena Oldenburg focuses on the Punjab and on North India since South India seems "less prone to the pathological strain" of dowry because of cross-cousin marriage.[97] Similarly, Chowdhry's study of elopement focuses on North India because of the presumed differences between North Indian village exogamy and South Indian Dravidian kinship.[98] However, such assumptions about cross-cousin marriage grossly mischaracterize marriage in South India, and specifically in Kerala. The historian Thomas Trautmann has complicated the idea of a concrete north/south division of kinship systems, revealing that some Indo-Aryan language speakers have practiced Dravidian kinship.[99] The idea that cross-cousin marriage keeps a woman in contact with her natal family and thus shields her from violence fails to account for the way in which patriarchal forms of control extend into the natal family as well. As Clark-Decès shows in her study of marriage in Tamil Nadu, "It is not accurate to characterize South Indian kinship by means of clear-cut axes (mother's side, father's side) and crystallized ideas (sibling and gender hierarchy, and so on). Because the 'right' marriages are associated with privilege and plain power, their field of action includes dynamics such as compulsion (let's marry more children together), repetition (let's marry again), imitation (let's marry like them), competition (let's beat them to it), exclusion (let's not marry them), resentment (why did they not marry us?), and so on."[100]

In these assumptions concerning cross-cousin marriage in South India, aspects of privilege and plain power have been glossed over. Further, many of the influential studies have focused specifically on Tamil Nadu. As mentioned in chapter 2, in connection with linguistic studies, the regional hegemony of scholarship in South Asian studies leads to the over-representation of Tamil Nadu in studies on South India, which are then extrapolated as representative of all South Indian regions. In Kerala, preferential kin marriages have been disappearing within communities, and cross-cousin marriages are often considered part of "Old Kerala," a place far removed from the modern Kerala of Kerala's development model. This profoundly affects how marriages are imagined and practiced in postcolonial Kerala. And, finally, the Syrian Christians are a community in South India that did not practice Dravidian kinship. In fact, village exogamy and marriage outside the family are the defining features of endogamous marriage for Syrian Christians.

Many examples of opposition to mixed marriage in Kerala resemble the way in which Chowdhry discusses local opposition to intercaste marriages in Haryana. For example, in 2006, a Hindu priest, Melsanthi Viswamithran Namboodiri, was fired from Lord Siva Temple in Venniyur and allegedly beaten by temple authorities for marrying an Ezhava woman.[101] In 2017, the Kerala High Court annulled the marriage between a twenty-four-year-old Hindu woman and a twenty-seven-year-old Muslim man in a high profile "love jihad" case. The marriage was annulled on the basis of a petition filed by the woman's father, who alleged that she had been forcefully converted to Islam. The court referred to the woman only by the name "Akhila" (her Hindu name) as opposed to her name after conversion, "Hadiya." In spite of Hadiya's age and her assertion that her conversion had not been forceful, the Kerala High Court found that "a girl aged 24 years is weak and vulnerable [and] capable of being exploited in many ways" and returned her to her father.[102] Hadiya's husband, Jahan, has appealed the decision, and the Supreme Court ruled that she was not brainwashed (although they continued to hold hearings on Jahan's alleged association with the Popular Front of India, a militant Islamic group).[103]

Within the Syrian Christian community specifically, there is very clear opposition to mixed marriage. Prema Kurien notes that during her field research in Kerala she was told of two Syrian Christian women who had married outside their communities, with "disastrous consequences"; according to Kurien, "community members used these two cases to deter youngsters who might otherwise have entertained the thought of marrying non-Syrian Christians."[104] During field research, I too was often told stories of women marrying outside the religion or caste and suffering personal hardships as a result. While interviewing three elderly Syrian Christian women who wore the *chatta* and *thuni*, I was told of a mixed marriage between a Syro-Malabar Catholic man and a Latin Christian woman in the village. Soon after their marriage, the husband died in a motorcycle accident. Even though her in-laws began to mistreat her, the young woman continued to live in her husband's family house, in keeping with the Syrian Christian patrilineal custom. The elderly Syrian Christian women I spoke with had no sympathy for the Latin Christian woman. "This is the danger of marrying outside the caste. Things like this can happen to you," I was warned.[105] Because of her love marriage with a Hindu man, a Syro-Malabar Catholic woman I interviewed was excommunicated from her family, which quite severely affected her mental health.[106] A Syro-Malabar Catholic family recounted a story to me of a family member who had fallen in love with a lower-caste Hindu man. When her half-brother found out, he publicly beat her. Afterward, the woman was forced into a convent in order to "save the family honor."[107] And another Syro-Malabar Catholic woman I interviewed, a woman who had married outside the community, was not allowed to contact her sister, let alone enter her sister's husband's house. Even my own mixed marriage was discussed in a negative light. During field research, I was told by a Syro-Malabar priest that the physical abuse I had endured at the hands of my (now former) husband was a direct result of my love marriage with a Hindu man.[108]

Kerala does have many spaces in which caste and religious interaction do occur, especially among young people, and, as I have argued, within certain class- and caste-based political movements. However, these spaces have not led to an increase in or an acceptance of mixed marriages. For example, Anna Lindberg has discussed how upper-caste Hindus began to join unions alongside other castes in the 1940s and 1950s, in an era when the Communist Party became more prominent and caste regulations were breaking down.[109] But, as Lindberg further notes, the caste cooperation of workers usually did not factor into intermarriage between communities.[110] Similarly, Caroline Osella and Filippo Osella's anthropological work on masculinity has shown that physical contact and sharing among young men of different castes in Kerala subvert existing social hierarchies.[111] However, these authors also explain that the intermixing of castes in all-male spaces ends upon marriage; the cross-community friendships disappear, and men take on caste and gender hierarchies.[112] Even Kerala's famed political Left has been silent on mixed marriages. Devika reminds us of Sahodaran K. Ayyappan, a caste reformer in Kerala who advocated for intercaste dining and for social acceptance of mixed marriages; Devika points out that in all of Kerala's leftist policies, social welfare schemes, and land reforms, the Left has never been able to actually do the political work of Ayyappan's teachings.[113] Rather than Kerala being the exception (as it is often viewed), I would argue that these responses to mixed marriage and the vitriol leveled at women with "oppositional agency" are, unfortunately, as entirely present in Kerala society as in North India.[114]

For Syro-Malabar Catholics specifically, marriages are regulated not only by the state and the community but also by religious dictates. To marry a (lower-caste) Protestant Christian, a canonical form is needed. But if a Syro-Malabar Catholic marries a (within-caste) Jakoba, no dispensation is needed.[115] The Syro-Malabar Church has not devised a liturgical celebration for mixed marriages, simply because they are seen to be rare.[116] However, the Latin Catholic Church in India does have a particular celebration for mixed marriages. In this configuration, the Syro-Malabar Church ritually understands only an endogamous union as legitimate—and, simultaneously, the absence of a sanctioned celebration for a mixed marriage in the Syro-Malabar Church rigidifies an upper-caste boundary in relation to Latin Catholics, who are "allowed" to have mixed marriages by virtue of having a particular celebration. It is the Syro-Malabar side of the equation that makes it difficult to marry outside the caste, even when it is within the Catholic faith and/or Christian religion.[117]

The Syro-Malabar Catholic hierarchy has lately taken quite a vocal and public stand against mixed marriages, encouraging women to have more Christian children and discouraging Catholics from love matches. The Kerala Catholic Bishops Council declared 2007 the Year of the Family, and campaigns were initiated to encourage women to have more (Syrian Christian) children. At a prayer group I attended in August 2007, the parish priest spoke nostalgically of the days when women had, on average, seven or eight children, with all members of the household working together to make the family strong.[118] At a family reunion I attended four months later, the invited speaker lectured for over an hour, condemning Syrian Christian women for using birth control and citing big families as the key to happiness.[119] The KCBC released a statement against single-window (rank-based) admissions in 2008 and, in the same breath, encouraged women to have more children and bring them up morally.[120] The KCBC even promised new programs aimed at encouraging parents to have more children. By 2011, the Church was offering incentives for the fifth child including free education, free health care, and bonds that would mature when the fifth child came of age.[121] In December 2013, Syro-Malabar Cardinal George Alencherry wrote a pastoral letter strongly warning the faithful against entering into "non-sacramental" mixed marriages.[122] The pastoral letter also warned Syro-Malabar Catholics that children of mixed marriages would grow up lacking a sound Christian example and that, because of their parents' differing belief systems, their own belief that they can be saved by Jesus Christ would be destroyed.[123] He concluded the letter by encouraging Christian couples to have more (Syrian Christian) children.[124] A month later, the KCBC issued a pastoral letter warning parents that selfies and applications like WhatsApp could entice young people into "unholy relations"[125] and into terrorism: "Extremism and religious fundamentalism are growing in our state. There is an increase in the trend of youths and children being trapped in love affairs and taking them into terrorism and other danger zones. Hence, children should be taught to grow in Catholic faith."[126]

In June 2015, Bishop Mathew Anikuzhikkattil specifically targeted Syro-Malabar Catholic girls. He warned that because Christian girls were growing up without values and without guidance in the faith, they were being enticed into relationships by Muslims and lower-caste Hindus. The bishop accused the Ezhava caste group, the Sri Narayana Dharma Paripalana Yogam, and Muslims of abducting Christian girls in a "love jihad."[127] It is notable that the bishop's statements were specifically aimed at marriages to Hindus (but only lower-caste Hindus) and to Muslims of any caste background. Here again, it is the caste and religious status of the Syrian Christians that is protected through endogamous marriage, which engenders the hierarchy it also protects.

Uma Chakravarti argues that the principles of marriage are inseparable from the principles of hierarchy.[128] Rituals around the exchange of women abound because the purity of marriage practices yields the hierarchies themselves.[129] Elsewhere I have discussed how rituals concerning marriage and childbirth in the Syrian Christian community are rigidly guarded and preserved as "tradition," while others, like the use of Aramaic or use of the *chatta* and *thuni*, have been abandoned.[130] Here, I want to reexamine these rituals in the Syrian Christian community, not only to illustrate how the principles of marriage are inseparable from the principles of hierarchy but also to explore how those principles ensure that the hierarchy is maintained into the next generation and embodied in the children of endogamous unions.[131]

To marry within the caste and religion, all Syro-Malabar Catholic children must attend rigorous religious education training, from the lower grades of primary school to at least the tenth standard. The name of this instruction is *vedapaadam*, literally "the lessons of the *vedas*." This name ties the Syro-Malabar Catholic community to upper-caste Hinduism, and specifically to brahmanical patriarchy, because in Kerala's caste-stratified, temple-oriented, precolonial past, only Brahmin males were allowed to learn from the *vedas*. Religious education is no joke in the community. Children attend *vedapaadam* on Saturdays as well as Sundays, with priests and nuns in the parish ensuring strict discipline at all times. In fact, at one parish I attended, the priest often resorted to corporal punishment if children were late for *vedapaadam*.

The tying of the Syrian Christian *minnu* is considered the most important ritual of the Syrian Christian marriage ceremony. The *minnu* differs from a Hindu *thali* in its shape; the Hindu *thali* is in the shape of a leaf, while the Syrian Christian *minnu* is smaller, resembles a teardrop, and has seven raised dots in the form of a cross. Lower-caste Christians use the same *thali* as Hindus, but with an engraved cross on its face. The *minnu* therefore represents the symbiotic relation Syrian Christianity has with upper-caste Hinduism while it also distinguishes the community as a unique group of Christians. The tying of the *minnu* is followed by the veiling of the *manthrakodi*. The *manthrakodi* is a sari gifted to the bride from the groom's family. The priest blesses the *manthrakodi* while the groom drapes it over the bride's head. The thread used to tie the *minnu* is taken from the *manthrakodi*. After marriage, the bride enters her husband's house with a lighted lamp, stepping over the threshold with the right foot, again according to Hindu custom.

Other rituals that are fiercely held on to as "tradition" are practices that center on pregnancy and childbirth, rituals that Susan Visvanathan has described as having ritual substances of the Hindu community.[132] I discussed some of these rituals in chapter 3 because many of them are linked to fair skin. For example, the newborn is rubbed with turmeric and given a mixture of gold and honey. This ritual is supposed to ensure that the child will have fair skin.

Naming rituals especially carry on the tradition of patrilineal inheritance in the Syrian Christian community, linking the Syrian Christians to the patrilineal Namboodiri Brahmins of Kerala. A Syrian Christian is known first by the house name, then by the father's name, and then by the given name. For example, my father's name is T. M. Thomas: Theempalangad (house name), Mathew (father's name), Thomas (his name). The eldest son of the eldest son is given the paternal grandfather's name, and many families have alternating names for their eldest sons. In my father's Theempalangad family tree, the name of the eldest son will be either "Thomas Mathew" or "Mathew Thomas." Many Syrian Christian families who emigrate to the United States take the father's name as the surname, as was the case with my family and my surname, "Thomas." Hence it is common for many second-generation Syrian Christian Indian Americans to have last names like "Thomas," "Alex," "Philip," or "Antony," a custom that

TABLE 5.1. Women's Names from the Aramaic/Greek

Women's Names	Translations
Akkamma	Rebecca
Achamma, Suszamma, Sosa, Susamma	Susan
Aleyamma, Elia, Elsiekutty	Elizabeth
Orotha, Kocharotha	Rose
Mariamma	Mary
Rahel	Rachel
Saramma	Sara
Threshamma, Thresia	Teresa

again reveals the centrality of patrilineal inheritance to the community, as the father's name is given the most importance.[133] Boys' names as well as girls' names are mostly biblical and Aramaic or Greek in origin; tables 5.1 and 5.2 display (noncomprehensive) lists of Syrian Christian biblical names and their English equivalents.

Even as Hindu or nonreligious names were becoming popular in the late twentieth century, many families continued to baptize their children with traditional Aramaic or Greek names, and to use Hindu or nonreligious names only as pet names. Today, Aramaic or Greek names are back in vogue for Syrian Christians. This naming tradition denotes not only paternal lineage but also synergy with the past as Syrian Christian names are unique to the Eastern Christian roots of the community.

I have discussed these rituals in depth because they are exalted as "traditions," but without any interrogation into what those traditions signify. The rituals that have become traditions are specifically patrilineal, Aryan, upper-caste Hindu, and Eastern Christian in nature. They are rituals that reproduce caste, race, and religious hierarchies. The sanctity of the whole system, of course, rests on endogamous marriage and the literal reproduction of caste, race, and religious divisions. There is, by contrast, no tradition of mixed marriage, and thus there are no rituals ensuring that children of mixed marriages are brought up within any tradition at all. This, then, is why the mixed marriage in "Mathamillatha Jeevan" was seen as antireligious.

The mixed marriage in "Mathamillatha Jeevan" was not overtly discussed by protesters or in the media. In fact, there was a definite removal of the mixed marriage from discussions around the story's alleged antireligious sentiment, even as the mixed marriage of the story was clearly the linchpin on which the entire protest depended. Srimati Basu discusses how

TABLE 5.2. Men's Names from the Aramaic/Greek

Men's Names	Translations
Ausep, Ipe	Joseph
Chacko	Jacob
Chandy, Chandapillai	Alexander
Devasia	Sebastian
Eapen, Estha, Panyose	Stephen
Itty	Isaac
Cherian, Scaria	Zachariah
Lukose	Luke
Markos	Mark
Mathai, Mathan	Matthew
Oomen, Thomma, Thomachan	Thomas
Paulose	Paul
Pothan, Philipose, Peely	Philip
Varghese, Gevarghese, Varkey	George
Yohanan, Ninan	John
Koshy	Joshua
Kurian, Kuriakose	Cyril
Avarachan	Abraham

silences, linguistic intricacies, and slippages occur in family courts adjudicating marriage, especially when it comes to taboo and intimate topics.[134] This is also the case with respect to the lack of public discourse on the marriage in "Mathamillatha Jeevan," which involves what is certainly a taboo and intimate topic: conjugal relations between a Muslim man and a Hindu woman that resulted in a child. On a bus ride from a village church to the 28 July 2008 rally against the textbook, I asked a group of over twenty protesters about the mixed marriage. There were instant denials and vocal shouts against the very idea that mixed marriage had anything to do with the protest. According to one rallygoer, "Mixed marriage is not where the problem is coming from—the protest is not about the marriage, it's about the Communist ideology"; and, in the background, another participant just as knowingly contradicted that opinion: "Actually, mixed marriage *is* a problem."[135]

In the KPCC expert committee's recommendations concerning the textbook, it was argued briefly that the interfaith marriage was indeed a cause for concern: "Teaching the students of seventh standard about mixed marriage is very inappropriate. Many communities have had painful experiences with mixed marriages—experiences that have caused rifts in communities. We do not need to teach seventh grade students about this. It may be appropriate for students who have reached maturity. There is fundamental mistake to minimize its consequence."[136] The KPCC committee's comment on mixed marriage ends there. It is somehow taken for granted that the reader will understand how and why mixed marriages are "painful" and cause "rifts in communities." The committee's head, M. G. S. Narayanan, wrote an article for the Syro-Malabar Catholic publication *Kudumbajyothis* and warned about teaching "trivial things," such as mixed marriage; religious ideology, he argued, is supposed to be given to children by their parents from an early age, and a deep sense of faith comes from the family; only if one is brought up this way, he claimed, can one honor one's faith and make a judgment about religion in general.[137] Embedded in Narayanan's argument is the assumption that one is usually born into a single religious ideology because of an arranged marriage. Mixed marriage can be discussed only as the inappropriate "other" of endogamous marriage.

The taboo nature of mixed marriage is always heightened when children are involved, as was the case with the textbook controversy in Kerala. According to Chowdhry, villagers in Hariyana only sometimes mentioned the children of intercaste marriages, although with "discomfort" that was "noticeable," and she was informed that the children of such marriages would "suffer from . . . ambiguous caste and kinship identity."[138] The discomfort arises because there is no concept of a mixed child of a mixed marriage. With a mixed child, there is only the concept of choosing a religion later in life, which, as Mody explains, was "anathema to the vast majority" in India even when civil marriages were first proposed, in 1868.[139] When one is born into a religious and caste-stratified system, one is always already interpolated as a particular subject. This is why rituals of marriage and childbirth are fiercely held on to as "tradition" and have not disappeared even though other traditions have. Without this sort of interpolation, gendered codes of being cannot be enacted, let alone recognized. These gendered codes shape "correct" behavior, not only for Syrian Christian women but also for men, especially if we think of entitlement to property, the role of head of household, and "trusteeship" over a woman's *stridhanam*. These normalized roles then shape all sorts of other ways of being. Outside those gendered codes, how can we understand patrilineal inheritance, social entitlement, land reforms, or women's rights? This is why Devika states that "those born into the faith are easier to control than those who choose to enter it."[140] To be "born into" means being subject to mandatory compliance with the hierarchical principles that an endogamous union both engenders and ensures, whereas to "choose to enter" signifies that there has been a reworking of the hierarchy itself.

The product of a mixed marriage therefore becomes subject to ontological anomie.[141] By that, I mean subject to an existence lacking in agreed-upon moral standards. The child of a mixed marriage who has the ability to "choose" a faith later in life is a child who is assumed to be without morality. This definition of morality operates only through the principles of the hierarchies of group difference. This is why, in India, there can be no concept of a mixed-caste or mixed-religion child. A life of ontological anomie is not an existence that can be aspired to in any way.

The textbook controversy in Kerala engendered a second *vimochana samaram*, but the self-financing protest did not, exactly because of ontological anomie. During the textbook controversy in Kerala, the volatility of moral content in textbooks was appended to a volatile idea: the idea of a life without religion, a "mathamillatha Jeevan." The "secular" message of the story stepped on the toes of what Devika has called the "near-total monopoly" the Church has over what is considered spiritual and moral.[142] At the crux of this morality is endogamous marriage. It becomes the unspoken referent in the ability to live a moral life. Since textbook content is so thoroughly shaped by ideas of morality that are informed by religion, the very idea of ontological anomie called for a minority rights movement that would be supported across caste, class, and religious boundaries. "Jeevan, the boy without religion" is the same as a person living an immoral "life without religion." And a life without religion is so completely disruptive to the established hegemonic relations that it cannot even be depicted in a fictitious story in a children's textbook.

South Asian feminist scholarship has had a rich history of engaging with the law and religion.[143] Nivedita Menon argues that Indian feminists have usually turned toward the state and advocated for legal intervention, especially where it concerns the family (personal laws) and sexuality.[144] But the mere fact that a law exists doesn't mean that social change has occurred. The Special Marriage Act may be one of the best examples of this: the state makes provisions for civil unions, but the family, law enforcement, and the courts make it difficult to obtain a mixed marriage, a situation that leads to the criminalization of love. Laws can also be modified and can actually come to work against those they were originally intended to protect. The Special Marriage Act itself was modified in 1976 so that Hindus who married under the act would still be governed by Hindu personal laws. This, as Flavia Agnes explains, ensured male coparcenary rights and protected the property interests of Hindu males entering into mixed marriages.[145]

Women are, of course, not a united group of people, and laws may affect women of various groups differently. Rajeswari Sunder Rajan discusses the "gendering of citizenship" and how the state constructs women as different from men, with laws geared specifically to women, but simultaneously differentiates between women of different religions, occupations (housewife versus prostitute), and castes.[146] Therefore, Indian feminism needs to be more than just representing other voices in the women's movement. As Anupamo Rao reminds us, "The question of how *representative* Indian feminism has been evokes both senses of the term representation: as a set of political claims from within the discourse of parliamentary democracy, as well as the impossible demand for the 'authentic' reproduction of presence. Exposing the limits of feminism's capacity to represent women as somehow unmarked or disembodied from their caste or religious identity stands to throw feminism (and its conceptions of gender identity) into crisis."[147] I take Rao's argument here to be a productive one. That is, throwing feminism and its conceptions of gender identity into crisis is a necessary good that can allow South Asian feminisms to rethink feminist activism across group boundaries in postsecular times.

As the women's movement undergoes a "belated awakening"[148] on mixed marriages, it is important not only to examine the violence leveled at women with "oppositional agency" but also to address the lack of conceptual space for what is "mixed," in both public and private spaces. This is not just an issue of the law, then, or of finding a location for the actualization of women's rights. Because mixed marriage sits at the apex of caste and religious hierarchies in its capacity to stabilize a socially accepted definition of morality, it is an analysis of *morality* that can intervene in this void, this space of the "mixed," and more clearly articulate the possibilities for efficacious rights-based activism against casteist heteropatriarchies.

Conclusion

Postsecular Feminisms and the Charismatic Movement

IN 2013, I PARTICIPATED IN A CHARISMATIC RETREAT IN WASH-ington, New Jersey, organized and attended largely by Syrian Christians in the United States. During a sermon at this retreat, a priest recounted the following story about a woman and her abusive alcoholic husband:

> On the day they married, the husband told the wife that he didn't drink. But he lied. He got drunk on that first night of the marriage and every night after. So from the very first day of her marriage, the woman prayed for her husband to change.
>
> She came to her priest asking what she could do to change her husband. The priest replied, "You never have thanked God for the husband you have. You only ask for a different husband. You should thank the Lord for giving you a husband."
>
> The next day, the woman called her priest, saying, "This isn't working. While he was beating me, I thanked God for my husband, and he beat me more."
>
> Days passed, and the woman did not visit her priest or call.
>
> Then, one day, she came to the priest with her husband. The husband told the priest, "I never felt loved, from the first day of my marriage on. So I drove my sorrow into alcohol. Now I realize that my wife appreciates me."[1]

The priest then went on to explain how we all need to be thankful for what God gives us instead of praying for something else. After a call and response of "Hallelujah" and "Praise the Lord," Bible passages were read.

The Charismatic movement is a religious movement that has become popular not only among Indian Christians but among Christians through-out the Global South.[2] Charismatic Christianity in the Global South is discussed within scholarship on Global Pentecostalism. Pentecostalism and Charismatic Christianity are united in similar forms of worship charac-terized by attention to the Holy Spirit, testimonials, sermons, dynamic devotional songs, calls and responses, and speaking in tongues. The term "Charismatic" is especially, but not exclusively, used to describe this type worship within Catholicism.

In South Asia, the Charismatic movement has attracted millions of people from across all faiths and castes. Charismatic prayer groups and intensive multiday retreats have sprung up all over the state of Kerala. The Charismatic retreat center in Potta, India, for instance, boasts having acquired over ten million participants since its founding, in 1977.[3] The Kerala Catholic Charismatic Renewal Services, created in 2004 to promote the re-evangelization of baptized Syro-Malabar Catholics and the evangelization of non-Christians, has established over ninety Charismatic centers all over Kerala.[4] The Charismatic Movement has proved to be so popular that many nonresident Indian Christians have established these retreat centers in the United States. In 2010 alone, retreats were conducted in (to name a few locations) Washington, New Jersey; Seattle; Annandale, Minnesota; Detroit; Nutley, New Jersey; Dallas; Santa Ana, California; Washington, DC; and Boston.

Charismatic worship has allowed Syrian Christian women to take part in public life and take up leadership roles in a way never before possible. Syrian Christian women act as retreat organizers and councilors, and they give testimonials themselves. The secretary of the Kerala Catholic Charismatic Renewal Services, Father Jose Anchanikal, explained to me, "Without women, these retreats would not be possible."[5] Women tend to far outnumber men at retreats. At one Charismatic Bible study I attended in Kerala in 2012, there were three times as many women as men. At the retreat I attended in Washington, New Jersey, there were twice as many women as men. Katrinamma, a Syrian Christian retired teacher in Kerala, explained to me:

> You'll mostly find women at the retreats. Men don't have the time. Women, after they make breakfast and send the kids off to school, can go to Charismatic study. At the retreat, you will find people who will explain things to you. Marriage issues, family and children issues, how we got to this point in life, about women's jobs, and other things that cause women tension. I just went to a four-day retreat with my friend. She called me up, and on Sunday we went, together with her sister and sister-in-law. Now we have the opportunity to go, and it's good for women to go. We can make our tensions go away by understanding our faith.[6]

As Katrinamma explained, the Charismatic movement focuses on testimonies and sermons that speak to women's issues. Similar to the *vimochana samaram* of 1959, the Charismatic movement stresses women's roles as wives and mothers and thus falls within the boundaries of acceptable female public participation. By attending with other women, Katrinamma can access the public sphere within the bounds of respectable womanhood (see chapter 2), as defined through sex-segregated spaces.

The Charismatic movement can be an escape from the pressures Kerala women face, from alcoholism in families to boredom at home. According to Kochamma, who was very involved in the movement, it may be men who drink alcohol, but women are on the receiving end of alcohol abuse. Kochamma explained to me that a woman with an alcoholic husband can escape the situation by attending a weeklong retreat. And in the course of time, multiple Charismatic retreats can build strength for a woman, which will, in turn, help in initiating new family dynamics.[7] Susamma also spoke with me about the way in which the Charismatic movement offers women an escape from the pressures of family life:

> From the few examples that I have seen in my life, I think mostly it is an escape, you know, from the pains of life. I myself can't just go off to a tea party. All the neighbors are going to be talking, and you feel terribly guilty doing that for yourself, whereas there is no stigma with the Church. I can go to a church and spend my afternoon there all by myself. I can meditate. And there won't be any guilt associated with it, the guilt imposed by the family, the "Where were you?" kind of thing. Women don't get that if they go off to church. So I think of it as a way of getting out of the house. You can't just take off, even if you are bored and doing nothing at home. So that's what I think a lot of women do in the Charismatic movement. It's an escape.[8]

As Susamma explained, the Charismatic movement offers an outlet for public participation that isn't stigmatized or judged. We may read the participation of Syrian Christian women in the Charismatic movement as something that gives women an escape from the narrow confines of domesticity, gives them tools for coping with social and family issues, and provides them a path toward leadership in the Church. In other words, participation in the Charismatic movement can be quite empowering for Syrian Christian women.

However, there are elements of the Charismatic movement that seem to limit women's capacity to act and that relegate women to traditional roles. The sermon offered at the retreat I attended in 2013 is an example of this. How are we to understand women's participation in the Charismatic movement as liberating or even empowering in the context of this story that lauds wifely obeisance within an abusive marriage? Why would women participate in a religious movement if it works against their interests?

The postsecular turn in feminism has begun to reframe the conversation on women's agency and religious movements. Postsecular feminisms critique the ways in which white Western feminisms often begin from a particular reading of agency that assumes both the secularity of feminism and women's oppositional consciousness as preconditions for political subjectivity. Examining women's participation in the piety movement in Egypt, Saba Mahmood has pointed out that such a reading of agency prevents feminists from seeing the agency of women who may be indifferent to opposing social norms.[9] Mahmood has instead asked, "How do we conceive of individual freedom in a context where the distinction between the subject's own desires and socially prescribed performances cannot be easily presumed, and where submission to certain forms of (external) authority is a condition for achieving the subject's potentiality?"[10] Mahmood's work urges us to think through embodied capacities of acting/action and subjectivities that may not be encompassed within feminism's conventional understanding of political action and actors.

Rosi Braidotti has also questioned the links between feminism and secularism in Europe. Braidotti explains, "The postsecular turn challenges European feminism because it makes manifest the notion that agency, or political subjectivity, can actually be conveyed through and supported by religious piety, and may even involve significant amounts of spirituality."[11] Braidotti points out that European feminisms operate from the assumption that agency is produced through countersubjectivities. Braidotti argues that the conditions for political and ethical agency may not be oppositional or tied to the present, as European feminists would have it. Rather, the conditions for political and ethical agency may be affirmative and geared toward futures.

The "post" of postsecularism denotes a break from the past and sits within ongoing scholarship that has critiqued the links between secularism and modern progress. Postcolonial critiques of secularism have examined how the modern nation-state is predicated on a model of secularism that has a base in Western Protestant Christianity; how European imperialism relied on a particular notion of the West as secular and the non-West as religious; and how the nationalisms of many postcolonial nations necessarily engaged with Western secularism while simultaneously crafting their own nation-specific versions of secularism in newly formed constitutions, laws, and policies.[12] In short, the Western model of secularism may not be the best or the most progressive. As Braidotti further argues, Western Christian secularism and the modernization process didn't necessary lead to the emancipation of women in the West.[13]

There is no doubt that there has been a backlash against state-sponsored secularism in postcolonial India. In Kerala specifically, the exaltation of religion over secularism often occurs in the field of education, where private Christian education with moral or catechism classes is held up as morally superior to state-sponsored secular education. As discussed in chapters 4 and 5, when these educational institutions are regulated in any way by the government, religion can be mobilized across denominations and religious groups' boundaries. In the very mobilization of religion and a superior morality, women within the community are used as sites to legitimate the ascendancy of certain patriarchal religious practices that are then glorified as "tradition." Postsecular feminisms provide new ways of understanding multiple modernities and can help illuminate how "tradition" may be embraced by women or even be the condition for accessing freedom.

South Asian feminisms in particular have discussed women's participation in right-wing Hindu nationalist movements.[14] Paola Bacchetta has shown that Hindutva ideology glorifies the role of the Hindu wife and mother while it simultaneously sexualizes Muslim women.[15] In turn, the Hindu man becomes the benevolent savior of Muslim women and protector of Hindu women, recuperating a masculinity that was supposedly effeminized by Muslim invaders in India's medieval past.[16] Hindu women may find in these roles a sense of community unavailable to them or different from what a feminist (read as secular) community could offer.[17] Much of this feminist scholarship on the Hindu Right questions the conventional feminist view that tends to see women primarily as passive victims of religious fundamentalisms rather than as participants in right-wing movements and, more frighteningly, as perpetrators of communal violence themselves.

Following South Asian feminist work on the Hindu Right, I would argue that we need to think critically about how we make sense of women's participation in movements for minority rights and about who gets to be represented by the label "minority women." Nandini Deo has argued that "the affective and religious rewards of participation are difficult to study but do more to hold together activist networks than shared ideological fervor."[18] In this book, I have argued that it is difficult to study the affective rewards of participation in religious movements precisely because when we do, there is no easy definition of "religion"—or, for that matter, of "religious women"— within a given movement. As discussed in chapter 2, religious clothing in Kerala was never simply religious but intersected with race, caste, class, and gender hierarchies in ways that were only seemingly overcome by secular modernity. These hierarchies continue to work in veiled ways, regulating female mobility and leading to the continued "othering" of Dalit women, working-class women, and raced women. Ethical embodiment was determined not just by the donning of religious clothing but by the social norms of a religious community, consolidated through existing hierarchies, which themselves were based in a long history of the subordination of Dalit, lower-class, and Dravidian peoples.

The difficulty in studying women's participation in religious movements may be that our frames of reference for an intersectional understanding of religion and religious movements are wanting. As discussed in chapter 3, this is especially the case with work on race and religion in South Asian studies. Religion-based mythhistories and reliance on pseudoscience explain and justify racialized discrimination and racial hierarchies on an everyday basis. However, within academic scholarship, we are relegated to single vectors of analysis on racialized discrimination in India, which separate linguistics from caste, class from female sexual morality, and color from religion. What are our frames of reference, then, for understanding pious or spiritual women within a religious movement?

There is often a sliding between the religious and the spiritual in post-secular feminisms that needs unpacking. Braidotti, in her often quoted essay, traces "various schools of spirituality and alternative spiritual practices," referencing the ways in which feminists have discussed the spiritual dimension of "non male-centered spiritual and religious practices."[19] But is the spiritual the same as religious? (Or, as Gregor McClennan asks in a critique of Braidotti's work, is the secular never spiritual?)[20] One may describe oneself as "spiritual" but not necessarily "religious" in an effort to distinguish between the two.[21] As Amy Hollywood has argued, practicing ritual or abiding by doctrine can make a person seem less spiritual because dogma invokes a sort of rigidity and submission to authority as opposed to the freedom inherent in one's individual experience of a spiritual connection to God.[22] Indeed, the appeal of the Charismatic movement for many

Syrian Christians is that it marks a break with organized religion and the rituals of Syrian Christianity.[23] The "spiritual" in this case is set up as separate from and superior to the "religious." Examining the postsecular turn in literary studies, Tracy Fessenden explains how the postsecular impulse tends to see spirituality as the "good religion" set in opposition to a "bad religion" that is constraining, backward and undemocratic; for Fessenden, "'spirituality' too easily functions in scholarship as shorthand for good religion—good insofar as it is spiritual, spiritual insofar as it is good—all the while seeming to float free of its own normative power."[24] Fessenden recommends that we understand the postsecular turn without naturalizing a good religion/bad religion schema.[25]

To return to the Charismatic movement, there is evident danger in operationalizing the spiritual as good religion, which can then "float free of its own normative power." As mentioned earlier, in much of the literature on the Charismatic movement, Pentecostal Christianity and Charismatic Christianity are seen as one and the same because the spiritual dimensions of worship are identical.[26] But for many of my research participants, Pentecostalism is associated with Dalit Christians.[27] As Alphonsa told me, Syro-Malabar Christians and upper-caste Hindus do not attend Pentecostal services because a Pentecostal service is seen as a space for lower-caste Hindus.[28] Littyamma, a Syro-Malabar Catholic woman who regularly attends Charismatic prayer groups, told me that when Pentecostal Christians come to her door with pamphlets, she speaks roughly to them because she is "against their brainwashing and how they preach hatred of the Virgin Mother, Mary."[29] Littyamma also spoke about how her Syro-Malabar parish priest warned congregants about Pentecostal Christianity; as a result, Littyamma had no desire even to enter a Pentecostal service, regardless of whether the form of worship was similar.[30]

There are very clear ways in which peoples are policed within this spiritual worship, ways that reaffirm hierarchies even though all castes and all religions are welcome at a given Charismatic service. The Syro-Malabar Catholic hierarchy in Kerala has very strongly dissuaded upper-caste Catholics from attending Charismatic spiritual worship services not endorsed by the Church, and from reading nonapproved religious literature. The hierarchy has also instructed priests to "correct those who have fallen into these new sects" by visiting Syro-Malabar Catholic houses, and by giving direction to all congregants at Syro-Malabar masses. At a Charismatic mass I attended in India, a Syro-Malabar Catholic priest announced that if any person in the congregation had not been baptized in the Church, or if a

Syro-Malabar Catholic in the congregation had married outside the caste/religion, he or she was not welcome to take communion. Thus, even though Latin Christians were welcome to attend the service, the clear caste divides between Christians regulated by endogamous marriages reified the differences between people participating in this Charismatic mass. Shalom TV, a Christian channel that broadcasts many Charismatic programs aimed specifically at the Syrian Christian community, is entirely separate from Powervision, the Pentecostal channel in Kerala. As in the *vimochana samaram*, what we see in the Charismatic movement is not a united "women" in a united "religious movement" being similarly "spiritual" but a reification of differences between women, reformulated in a new era of religious movements.

As discussed in chapter 4, there has never been a clear definition of "Christians" in Kerala, or in the Indian nation-state. "Minority" has never been defined in the Indian constitution. In debates and political protests over minority schools, what emerges is a dominant minority paradigm whereby the interests of the privileged few stand in for the homogenized whole. Similarly, to see Christians united in the Charismatic movement because of spirituality alone is to risk masking the inherent divisions among Christian minorities and the inequalities that these divisions work to sustain, despite the participants' shared spirituality in Charismatic Christianity and Pentecostal Christianity.

One of the most fascinating elements of the postsecular turn, and one worthy of further exploration, is the relation between ritualized behavior and self-formation.[31] P. Sonal Mohan's work on prayer and subaltern space among the slave castes of Kerala examines how prayer itself was not merely confined to the spiritual dimension of life but produced excess meanings and opened up spiritual and social dimensions of salvation.[32] Command of prayer could give members of the slave castes leadership roles in the community or even be used as a weapon against landlords as slaves defied landlords by continuing to frequent missionary schools and to take refuge in prayer.[33] Analyzing prayer in the context of the piety movement, Mahmood critiques how the discipline of anthropology tends to sees ritual as socially prescribed and distinct from pragmatic activity, noting that for women in the piety movement, ritualized behavior and prayer actually exist along a continuum of practices that shape the pious self.[34] Similarly, in the Charismatic movement, group prayer has become an element of what it is to craft the pious self. Susamma explained to me how prayer became such an integral part of Charismatic spiritual renewal for her:

There's very minimal food at a retreat, and you wake up at six o'clock, and you go to church, and it goes all the way till ten o'clock. So it's just prayer and prayer and prayer, and songs, and healings, and just—in the end, it changes you. Well, it does—a lot! There are thousands of people attending from all over the state, and from all over the country, too. It's quite a huge group. You know it's in the air—there is something. As [Jesus says in] the Bible, "Where two or three are gathered in my name, there I am in the midst of them." So you can find that energy. There is a spiritual energy. There is an energy that prayer brings about, and constant prayer also, which changes you.[35]

For Susamma, the ritualized behavior of prayer is the condition for her being able to access spiritual energy.

While prayer may be a type of ritual that is reiterated to craft the pious self, other rituals may not be formative in the same way. As discussed in chapter 5, certain rituals, such as naming practices, have become ever more popular among Syrian Christians. Television series depicting Syrian Christian rituals and practices of the past—including *Kadamattathu Kathanar, St. Thomas Sleha, St. Antony,* and *Madhava* —have become extremely popular in Kerala. Many of these programs focus on extraordinary miracles performed on behalf of pious, prayerful individuals. Syrian Christian women are portrayed in these serials in the traditional *chatta* and *thuni* and with *kunniku* indicating some sort of taken-for-granted acceptance of the links between rituals of the past and piety. But, as shown in chapters 1 and 5, naming rituals invoke the Eastern roots of Syrian Christians and distinguish them from lower-caste converts with Western Christian traditions. Similarly, as shown in chapter 2, the wearing of the *chatta* and *thuni* may have been less about crafting piety than about uniting upper-caste Hindus and Christians and distinguishing upper-caste Christians from lower-caste Christians. Rituals within the Syrian Christian community may survive not because they constitute a pious self but because they center on female sexuality and childbirth and dictate what a moral life—a life with religion—should look like. As discussed in chapter 5, a life with religion is intimately tied to and regulated by the ritualization of female sexuality through endogamous marriages. What the continued adherence to these types of rituals says about agency and self-formation requires further study.

This book has offered a feminist analysis of how minority rights can provide a platform to address social inequalities in postcolonial India. However, since belonging to a minority group demands homogenization, vulnerable communities may be separated from each other, and a dominant minority culture may thus be allowed to ascend over and against subaltern communities. Collapsing the concepts of numerical subordination and political vulnerability can actually obscure the struggles of the most marginalized minorities in postcolonial India. Dominant minority culture also overlays and interacts with a "dominant woman" paradigm. From clothing to racialized discrimination to protests for minority rights, the question is not only whether women benefit from the struggle for minority rights but also which women are in a position to benefit and what sort of benefit it is. As women's studies undergoes a widening of feminisms, taking on aspects of women's participation in religious movements and grappling with postsecular feminisms, those of us in South Asian studies also have to be committed to an intersectional widening of what constitutes a minority. Taken together, the insight gained can help in understanding how feminist solidarity across religions, castes, races, and classes and among minority populations is yet possible.

Notes

Introduction

1   Claramma, interview by author, 14 December 2007. Interviews have been translated from Malayalam into English. I have used pseudonyms for my research participants.

2   Census of India, "Religion," accessed 27 November 2017, http://censusindia.gov.in /Census_And_You/religion.aspx; Zachariah, "Religious Denominations of Kerala," 9; Zachariah, *The Syrian Christians of Kerala*, 10.

3   Subramanian, *Shorelines*, 24–25.

4   See for example, Bauman and Young, *Constructing Indian Christianities*; Viswanathan, *Outside the Fold*; S. Sarkar, "Christian Conversions, Hindutva, and Secularism," 356–68.

5   See Lila Abu-Lughod, "The Romance of Resistance," 41–42.

6   Syrian Christians are also called St. Thomas Christians or Nazranis.

7   Zachariah, *The Syrian Christians of Kerala*, 28.

8   India is the fourth largest exporter of natural rubber in the world, and 92 percent of total natural rubber production comes from Kerala; see Mathews, "Foreign Trade in Natural Rubber." One of India's oldest banks was founded in Thrissur, Kerala, by Syrian Christians and is called the Syrian Catholic Bank. In the 1930s, the two Christian-owned banks, Travancore National Bank and Quilon Bank, were ranked first in India in terms of number of branches, and third (after the Central Bank of India and the Bank of India) in terms of volume of business; see Devika and Varghese, "To Survive or to Flourish?," 21, 2010. In the chapters to come, I especially discuss the community's investment in private education.

9   Thottathil, *India's Organic Farming Revolution*, 127, documents how Syrian Christians in Malabar became a community integral to organic farming in the northern parts of the state and explains that they migrated to Malabar from the Travancore region because they were denied land ownership and government jobs, although they still had small amounts of capital with which they purchased cheap land in jungle areas of Malabar's Wayanad district.

10 Mathew, *Communal Road to a Secular Kerala*, 59. See also F. Osella and C. Osella, *Social Mobility in Kerala*, 39, for a discussion of how other communities in Kerala, including the Ezhuva community, admire the Syrian Christians for their ability to "turn one rupee into two."

11 Sreekumar, *Scripting Lives*, 12.

12   Ibid.

13   Agnes and Ghosh, "Introduction," xii.

14   S. Roy, "Introduction," 7–8.

15   See Rao, *Gender and Caste*; Gupta, *The Gender of Caste*; articles in Shankar and Gupta, "Caste and Life Narratives"; articles in "Review of Women's Studies"; Chakravarti, *Gendering Caste through a Feminist Lens*; Brueck, *Writing Resistance*; Rao, *The Caste Question*.

16   Gupta, *The Gender of Caste*, 5–6.

17   Rao, *The Caste Question*, 234. See also Brueck, *Writing Resistance*, which examines the broad range inherent in the writings of Dalit authors; whereas the dominant scholarship on Dalit literature tends to focus on autobiographies, resistance, and the differences between Dalit and conventional (non-Dalit) Indian literature, Brueck examines the "aesthetics, politics and varied discourses of identity" in Dalit literature (7).

18   Rao, "Introduction," 5.

19   Chakravarti, *Gendering Caste through a Feminist Lens*, 26.

20   For example, Agnes, "From *Shah Bano* to *Kausar Bano*," 51, draws on Crenshaw's work to argue for a nuanced understanding of the dynamics between majority and minority populations: "Covenants of equality and equal protection may unfold in diagonally opposite trajectories for the mainstream and the marginalized. We cannot even see these trajectories, let alone chart the best way forward, unless we bring questions of gender and community into not just simultaneous but *intersectional* focus. Otherwise our analysis will be fragmented and inadequate to the task of addressing the concerns of minority women in India" (emphasis in original). Gupta, *The Gender of Caste*, 6, notes the similarities between Black feminists who argue that "all the women are white [and] all the blacks are men" and South Asian feminists who critique the paradigm "all the women are upper-caste [and] all the Dalits are men." Chakravarti, in *Gendering Caste through a Feminist Lens*, discusses the intersections of casteism and patriarchy, using the term "brahmanical patriarchy" in a way that is similar to the way in which Black feminists in the United States have used the term "racist patriarchy." Others, such as Natrajan and Greenough, "Introduction," 25, drawing inspiration from critical race theory in the United States, argue for a critical caste theory.

21   Roth, "Entangled Inequalities as Intersectionalities," 20.

22   Purkayastha, "Intersectionality in a Transnational World," 60.

23   Crenshaw, "Demarginalizing the Intersection of Race and Sex." See also Crenshaw, "Mapping the Margins"; Collins and Bilge, *Intersectionality*; May, *Pursuing Intersectionality, Unsettling Dominant Imaginaries*.

24   See Chakravarti, *Gendering Caste through a Feminist Lens*; Chowdhry, *Contentious Marriages, Eloping Couples*.

25   Chowdhry, *Contentious Marriages*, 15.

26   Chakravarti, *Gendering Caste through a Feminist Lens*, 2.

27   U. Narayan, "Essence of Culture and a Sense of History," 97.

28   Thomas, "Researching Minorities and Subalterns." In my discussion of Christians as a limit figure, I follow Megan Moodie's ethnographic work on the Dhanka in Rajasthan. Moodie explains that in South Asian studies, "despite repeated references to

the Adivasi woman [as] a limit figure, there are few studies that engage directly with Adivasi women's lives today or in earlier historical moments, particularly as agentive political actors"; see Moodie, *We Were Adivasis*, 7.

29 Lukose, *Liberalization's Children*, 170.

30 Asad, *Formations of the Secular*, 174; P. Kumar, *Limiting Secularism*, 15, 28.

31 Needham and Rajan, "Introduction," 10.

32 Chhachhi, "Identity Politics, Secularism, and Women," 81–82, further argues that the retention of the personal law system allowed the Indian state to continue to regulate the family.

33 Shah Bano, a Muslim woman, was divorced by her husband and denied maintenance. After a seven-year court battle, she was finally granted maintenance under section 125 of India's criminal code. Muslim groups claimed that the ruling infringed on Muslim personal law. The 1986 Muslim Women's Bill passed soon after this backlash and ended up exempting Muslim women from the secular protections of section 125. Many feminists saw the passage of this bill as a step backward in women's rights. But Indian feminists' research on the impact of the Shah Bano case also revealed how feminist calls for a uniform civil code, once supported by many feminists as a secular alternative to religious personal laws, actually mirrored the discourse of the Hindu Right, which constructed Muslim women as victims of a patriarchal religion, and the Muslim community as unpatriotic for holding on to religious personal laws; see N. Menon, "State, Community, and the Uniform Civil Code in India." The 1916 Travancore Christian Succession Act gave Kerala Christian women the right to inherit only one-quarter of the share of the familial property or 5,000 rupees, whichever was less; if a Christian woman received a dowry, she had no claim to the quarter share or to the 5,000 rupees. In 1986, the Supreme Court overturned the Travancore Christian Succession Act because it violated women's right to equality before the law. For Kerala Christians, the 1925 Indian Succession Act became the secular alternative to the 1916 Christian Succession Act. Syrian Christian women now have equal rights to property, but taking a case to court is seen as going against the community's tradition of dowry and as challenging conventional gender roles within the family. Syrian Christian women who exercise their property rights may face a backlash as well as ostracism from their families and their religious community. See Thomas, "Education as Empowerment?," 83–86.

34 Rao, *The Caste Question*, 3.

35 See P. Chatterjee, "Religious Minorities and the Secular State"; N. Menon, "State/Gender/Community"; Madan, "Freedom of Religion"; Bhargava, "India's Secular Constitution"; Nandy, "The Politics of Secularism and the Recovery of Religious Toleration"; Bhargava, *Secularism and Its Critics*; Needham and Rajan, *The Crisis of Secularism in India*.

36 Needham and Rajan, "Introduction," 6.

37 Ibid. Asad, *Formations of the Secular*, 13–14, argues that it is important to interrogate how the modern becomes a hegemonic political goal for postcolonial states, and to question how and why nonmodern peoples are made to "assess their adequacy" through their relation to constructions of the secular and religious.

38 See Articles 15, 16, and 25–30.

39   In *T. M. A. Pai Foundation v. State of Karnataka* (2002), the bench found that since linguistic minorities were listed alongside religious minorities in the constitution, and since the Indian states were divided on linguistic lines, "religious minority" should be determined numerically at the state level.

40   For exceptions, see K. Kumar, *Prejudice and Pride*; Jain, "Minority Rights in Education"; and R. Sen, *Articles of Faith*.

41   On Muslims as India's "national minority," see P. Kumar, 31.

42   R. Sen, *Articles of Faith*, 95.

43   Jain, "Minority Rights in Education," 2435.

44   The Supreme Court ruled in *P. A. Inamdar v. State of Maharashtra*, 6 S.C.C. 537 (2005), that "the real purpose of Article 30 is to prevent discrimination against members of the minority community and to place them on an equal footing with non-minority. Reverse discrimination was not the intention of Article 30."

45   Jain, "Minority Rights in Education," 2431–32, sees a "continuous struggle" in the courts concerning the status of sects and whether they qualify as minority religions under Article 30(1).

46   Thomas, "Education as Empowerment?"

47   For a synopsis, see Devika and Varghese, "To Survive or to Flourish?," 104–5, 2011.

48   Varshney, *Ethnic Conflict and Civic Life*, 166.

49   Nandy, "Time Travel to a Possible Self," 322.

50   In February 2014, Syrian Christian church leaders met with Narendra Modi before he became prime minister. One aspect of the meeting was Syrian Christians' opposition to the Gadgil Commission report on the conservation of the Western Ghat Mountains. The Syrian Christian leaders claimed that conservation efforts would affect farming on spice and tea plantations. On 14 December 2015, Modi met with the leaders of the Syrian Christian faiths in Thrissur, Kerala, on his first visit to the state as prime minister. He discussed the earlier meeting as well as the friendship between Syrian Christians and the BJP. Syro-Malabar Cardinal George Alencherry urged Modi to give special attention to rubber tree farmers, since the price of rubber had by then dropped drastically.

51   Halliburton, *Mudpacks and Prozac*, 26.

52   During the period of colonial rule in India, the state now known as Kerala was divided into the regions of Thiruvithaamkoor (Travancore), Kochi (Cochin), and Malabar. Cochin and Travancore operated as princely states under British colonial rule, whereas Malabar came under the British East India Company in 1801–02 and later was under the direct rule of the Madras presidency.

53   Caldwell, *Oh Terrifying Mother*, 202.

54   Mingwei Huang, "Vulnerable Observers: Notes on Fieldwork and Rape," *Chronicle of Higher Education*, 12 October 2016.

55   Thomas, "Cowboys and Indians."

56   For a discussion of second-generation Indian Americans and religion in urban areas of the United States, see Joshi, *New Roots in America's Sacred Ground*, 6.

Chapter 1: Syrian Christians and "God's Own Country"

1   Gundert, *Keralolpatti*, 31.

2   Ibid., 31–32.

3   Malabar Marriage Commission, *Report of the Malabar Marriage Commission*, 14.

4   Jeffrey, *The Decline of Nair Dominance*, 11.

5   Veluthat, *The Early Medieval in South India*, 139.

6   Ibid., 131.

7   T. Menon, "Translator's Introduction," 16.

8   Gangadharan, *Evolution of Kerala History and Culture*, 185.

9   Veluthat, "The Nambudiri Community," 122.

10 Jeffrey, *Decline of Nair Dominance*, 25.

11 "Bitter and resentful, some broke down completely and were dismissed as mad or hysterical"; see Krishnankutty, "Introduction," xiv.

12 S. Menon, *A Survey of Kerala History*, 275.

13 Matrilineal inheritance was also a feature of some Muslim communities; it was not a uniform practice throughout Kerala, but by the nineteenth century almost 50 percent of the state of Kerala practiced matrilineal inheritance. See Arunima, *There Comes Papa*.

14 The British interpreted the matrilineal system as backward, since anthropologists held that most "civilized" societies had moved from matrilineal to patrilineal inheritance. Further, British missionaries saw the system as promoting visiting husbands and polyandry. According to the British understanding of Nayar inheritance customs, the eldest male member of the joint family was considered to be the head (the *karanavan*). In this reading, younger members of the Nayar complex, the *tharavadu*, were tenants. Disputes coming from younger male members of Nayar families led to a flurry of court cases in the late nineteenth and early twentieth centuries, and to legislation aimed at curbing the exploitative actions of *karanavans*. A series of laws initiated by young men and women of the Nayar caste reformed the matrilineal system of inheritance. In 1912, polyandry was declared illegal. The 1925 Nair Act gave any member of a *tharavadu* the right to demand a share of family assets. There were 120,000 partitions in the next five years; see Jeffrey, *Politics, Women and Well-Being*, 45. This redefining of marriage and the matrilineal system served to facilitate the move toward capitalism and the individualization of property; see Arunima, *There Comes Papa*, 134.

15 Kurien, *Kaleidoscopic Ethnicity*, 45.

16 Mohan, *Modernity of Slavery*, 156.

17 S. Menon, *A Survey of Kerala History*, 390–91.

18 Vijayakumar, "The Influence of Caste in Kerala Politics," 259.

19 Dempsey, *Kerala Christian Sainthood*, 6; Kurien, *Kaleidoscopic Ethnicity*, 57; Jeffrey, *Decline of Nair Dominance*, 17.

20 Vijayakumar, "Influence of Caste in Kerala Politics," 259.

21 Narayanan, *Cultural Symbiosis in Kerala*, 90–94.

22 Lindberg, "The Historical Roots of Dowries in Contemporary Kerala," 30.

23 Anikuzhikattil, "Reconciliation," 372.

24 Mannooranparampil, "General Considerations on the Liturgical and Sacramental Theology," 195.

25 Kurian, *The Caste Class Formation*, 15; Mohan, *Modernity of Slavery*, 59.

26 Chakravarti, *Gendering Caste through a Feminist Lens*, 18 (emphasis in original).

27 Podipara, "Hindu in Culture, Christian in Religion, Oriental in Worship," 107.

28 An exception is Dempsey, *Kerala Christian Sainthood*, 5; Dempsey makes it a point to include the different denominations in her analysis of "localized manifestations of religion." Zachariah, "Religious Denominations of Kerala," explains the demographic and socioeconomic differences between religious groups in Kerala.

29 This tendency was compounded by the Supreme Court's ruling in *T. M. A. Pai Foundation v. State of Karnataka* (2002). The court found that because the Indian constitution discusses linguistic minorities in tandem with religious minorities, and because the Indian states are divided along linguistic lines, the question of what constitutes a religious minority should be determined numerically at the state level.

30 Kerala Public Service Commission, "List of Other Backward Classes in Kerala State," accessed November 2017, www.keralapsc.gov.in/index.php?option=com_content&id=338&Itemid=198.

31 Visvanathan, "Legends of St. Thomas of Kerala," 29.

32 Much of the evidence that may have existed was destroyed in an inquisition in Goa in the late sixteenth century; see Visvanathan, *The Christians of Kerala*, 16.

33 There are some scholarly works that attempt to examine the origin story of Syrian Christians and speculate about their early traditions. See, for example, Mundaden, *Indian Christians*; Puthur, ed, *The Life and Nature of the St. Thomas Christian Church in the Pre-Diamper Period*; Puthur, ed, *St. Thomas Christians and Nambudiris*.

34 Swiderski, "Northists and Southists"; Philips, "Gendering Colour," 257. Other histories place the arrival of Thomas Cana at 745 CE. See Zacharia, "Introduction," 12; see also K. C. Zachariah, *The Syrian Christians of Kerala*, 51.

35 See Philips, "Gendering Colour," 257; S. Bayly, *Saints, Goddesses and Kings*, 246; Brown, *The Indian Christians of St. Thomas*, 175.

36 See K. C. Zachariah, *The Syrian Christians of Kerala* 51; Swiderski, "Northists and Southists," 76–77.

37 K. C. Zachariah, *The Syrian Christians of Kerala*, 52.

38 Subramanian, *Shorelines*, 41–42.

39 K. C. Zachariah, *The Syrian Christians of Kerala*, 59.

40 K. C. Zachariah, "Religious Denominations of Kerala," 10.

41 Ibid.

42 A British court ruling gave the Jakoba Church property to the Bava faction, and this settlement has been a sticking point between the factions ever since.

43 K. C. Zachariah, *The Syrian Christians of Kerala*, 145.

44 K. C. Zachariah, "Religious Denominations of Kerala," 29.

45 *Sui juris* status gives the Syro-Malabar Church autonomy as a rite of Catholicism separate from the Latin rite but still within the Roman Catholic faith. The Eastern churches (as opposed to the Western or Latin-rite churches) are all considered part of the one holy Catholic Apostolic Church. They follow the Eastern Code of Canons. The Eastern rites comprise many different churches, including but not limited to the Syro-Malabar Catholic Church, the Maronite Catholic Church, the Chaldean Catholic Church, and the Coptic Catholic Church.

46 For an exception, see Dempsey, *Kerala Christian Sainthood*.

47 See, for example, Kollamparampil and Perumthottam, *Bride at the Feet of the Bridegroom*; Payyappilly, *Mixed Marriage in the Code of Canons of the Eastern Churches*

and the Particular Law of the Syro-Malabar Church; Kannookadan, *The Mission The-ology of the Syro-Malabar Church*; Vithayathil, *The Origin and Progress of the Syro-Malabar Hierarchy.*

48   They are concentrated in the state's central districts (north Travancore) of Ernakulam, Alappurzha, Kottayam, Pathanamthitta, and Idduki; see K. C. Zachariah, *The Syrian Christians of Kerala*, 10–11.

49   Between the 1990s and 2017, the mushrooming of independent Pentecostal churches may prove to be an exception. Many Syrian Christian youth have been attracted to the nonritualistic nature of independent Pentecostal churches. The Syro-Malabar Church has embraced more Charismatic forms of worship with the proliferation of Charismatic retreats and prayer groups throughout the state. However, it cannot be said that there is wholesale and widespread enthusiasm for the Charismatic move-ment; see Thomas, "The Tying of the Ceremonial Wedding Thread."

50   Jeffrey, *Politics, Women, and Well-Being*, 97.

51   Ibid., 31.

52   Desai, "Indirect British Rule, State Formation, and Welfarism in Kerala," 473.

53   Ibid. This was not wholesale acceptance, however. Dalits and lower-caste Hindus had to fight for the right to attend government schools, were discriminated against by the Travancore government when they sought to build their own schools, and were seg-regated from upper castes in government schools; see Padmanabhan, "Learning to Learn," 106–7.

54   Tharakan, "Socio-economic Factors in Educational Development," 1924.

55   Jeffrey, *Politics, Women, and Well-Being*, 3.

56   D. M. Menon, *Caste, Nationalism, and Communism in South India*, 147.

57   G. Arunima, "Imagining Communities—Differently," 74.

58   Arunima, *There Comes Papa.*

59   Mathew, *Communal Road to a Secular Kerala*, 59–60.

60   Jeffrey, *Politics, Women, and Well-Being*, 39.

61   D. M. Menon, *Caste, Nationalism, and Communism in South India*, 23n58.

62   Devika and Varghese, "To Survive or to Flourish?," 111. See also F. Osella and C. Osella, *Social Mobility in Kerala.*

63   There are, however, Christians who are card-carrying communists. And there is reason to believe that Syrian Christians are increasingly joining the Communist Party of India, Marxist, or CPI(M). In fact, the CPI(M)'s 2007 conference was held in the Christian stronghold of the Kottayam district because the party was aiming to strengthen its Christian membership. A representative of the CPI(M) coalition government stated that 20 percent of CPI(M) members are minorities, and of those minorities, there are more Christians than Muslims in the party; see "Twenty Per-cent of CPM Members Minorities: LDF Convener," *New Indian Express*, 13 February 2008.

64   See, for example, A. Sen and Drèze, *India*; Nussbaum, "Women's Education."

65   Susuman, Lougue, and Battala, "Female Literacy, Fertility Decline and Life Expec-tancy in Kerala, India," 39.

66   See Drèze and Murthi, "Fertility, Education, and Development."

67   Halliburton, "Suicide"; Chua, *In Pursuit of the Good Life*, 45.

68 Thomas, "Education as Empowerment?"; Rammohan, "Caste, Public Action, and the Kerala Model"; Padmanabhan, "Learning to Learn"; Nampoothiri, "Confronting Social Exclusion."

69 Kabir, "On the Periphery," 88–89.

70 Raman, "The Kerala Model," 4.

71 Sreekumar, *Scripting Lives.*

72 Chua, *In Pursuit of the Good Life,* 8.

73 Arunima, *There Comes Papa*; Devika, *Engendering Individuals*; Sreekumar, *Scripting Lives*; Mukhopadhyay, *The Enigma of the Kerala Woman.*

74 Devika and Thampi, *New Lamps for Old,* xx.

75 National Crime Records Bureau, *Crime in India 2012,* 23, https://www.scribd.com/document/231245080/Compendium-2012. The NCRB defines the crime rate as the number of crimes per 100,000 people. Violent crimes include murder, dowry deaths, rape, robbery, riots, and arson.

76 Deeptimaan Tiwary, "Kerala Is Country's Most Crime-Prone State, NCRB Statistics Show," *The Times of India,* 24 June 2012, http://timesofindia.indiatimes.com/india/Kerala-is-countrys-most-crime-prone-state-NCRB-statistics-show/articleshow/14364473.cms. According to the NCRB, crimes against women include rape, kidnapping, dowry deaths, torture, assault with intent to outrage modesty, insult to the modesty of women, and the importation of girls from a foreign country.

77 "Alarming Rise in Crime against Women," *New Indian Express,* 9 March 2008; "90 percent Women Feel Unsafe on Kerala Roads: Study," *Kerala Women* (blog), 24 May 2013, www.keralawomen.gov.in/index.php/headlines/265-90-women-feel-unsafe-on-kerala-roads-study.

78 Mukhopadhyay, *The Enigma of the Kerala Woman*; Sreekumar, *Scripting Lives*; Devika, *Engendering Individuals*; Bhaskaran, "Informed by Gender?"

79 Thomas, "Education as Empowerment?"; Lukose, *Liberalization's Children,* 104.

80 Kodoth and Eapen, "Looking Beyond Gender Parity," 3278.

Chapter 2: Clothes Reading

1 Devika, *Engendering Individuals,* 29–30.

2 I define clothing as that which covers and adorns the body, both as an extension of the body and as a part of bodily comportment. I include ornamentation in this definition of clothing. Tarlo, *Clothing Matters,* 1, differentiates clothing from costume in India, arguing that the term "costume" invokes a static understanding of culture, encapsulated in the notion that the costume of a people is often viewed as a museum artifact, and that costume separates clothes from the people who wear them. I follow Tarlo's formulation, focusing on clothing over costume, especially in order to talk about the embodied significations of group belonging inherent in certain clothing "choices."

3 Ibid., 16.

4 Ibid., 17.

5 See Arthur, "Introduction"; Graybirl and Arthur, "The Social Control of Women's Bodies in Two Mennonite Communities."

6 There is evidence that the Syrian Christians wore clothing that was distinct from other communal groups before the nineteenth century. The Synod of Diamper men-

tions the clothing practices of the Syrian Christians, and the similarity of their clothing to Nayar clothing; see Zacharia, *The Acts and Decrees of the Synod of Diamper,
1599*. This chapter, however, focuses on women's communal clothing in the early
modern period of Kerala to present day.

7 There is a wealth of untapped sources on the material practice of dress, especially for
the Syrian Christians. As an affluent community, the Syrian Christians had the means
to photograph women's dressing practices on an everyday level through vernacular
photography, or amateur photos taken of women at family events. While Hindu and
Muslim women in Kerala have completely abandoned their communal clothing, a large
number of elderly Syrian Christian women continue to wear the *chatta* and *thuni*. It is
not clear why these Syrian Christian women wore the communal garments for a longer
period of time than Hindu or Muslim women. I would argue that the idea of Christians
being more tradition-bound than other communities and the patriarchal nature of the
Church may have contributed to this. At any rate, there exists a significant oral historical record of the material practice of dress within the Syrian Christian community.

8 Mary Kutty, interview by author, 15 December 2007.

9 Threshamma, interview by author, 27 July 2007.

10 Philips, "Gendering Colour," 258, discusses color and the Syrian Christians, noting
the connection between white clothes and high-caste status, and between high-caste
status and both morality and fair skin.

11 Cohn, *Colonialism and Its Forms of Knowledge*, 130; C. A. Bayly, "The Origins of
Swadeshi (Home Industry)," 296; Tarlo, *Clothing Matters*, 28–9.

12 Tarlo, *Clothing Matters*, 28.

13 Ibid., 29.

14 Philomenamma, interview by author, 12 December 2007.

15 The *motheeshu* was worn by Syro-Malabar Catholic women and the *vaaleeku* by
Jakoba Syrian Christians (Lissyamma, interview by author, 6 January 2008; Mari-
amma, interview by author, 27 February 2008; Kochorotha, interview by author, 17
December 2007).

16 Podipara, "Hindu in Culture, Christian in Religion, Oriental in Worship," 107.

17 In Travancore, before Indian Independence and adoption of the rupee, the chrakram
was a unit of currency.

18 Chinamma, interview by author, 15 January 2008.

19 Achamma, interview by author, 19 December 2007.

20 Antherjanam, "In the Moonlight," 13.

21 Mariamma, interview by author, 22 February 2008. Women were allowed to go to
church, but they were barred from learning Aramaic and from church leadership.
This meant that Mariamma and other women in the house or village could attend
mass but not understand the service. Many women prayed the rosary in their minds
over and over during the Aramaic mass. However, Mariamma and other women I
spoke with were extremely pious and led evening prayers within their families. It may
be that their limited mobility regarding religious services provided women with a
sort of capacity to act.

22 Welter, "The Cult of True Womanhood," 152.

23 Mariamma, interview by author, 22 February 2008.

24   Krishnankutty, "Introduction," xiv.

25   Renjini, *Nayar Women Today*, 19, 34.

26   Bauman, "Redeeming Indian 'Christian' Womanhood?," 12.

27   The Mappila Muslim women of Kerala wore a dark blue *mundu*, a long stitched blouse, a black head scarf, and gold earrings along the helix of their ears; see Kurien, *Kaleidoscopic Ethnicity*, 77. Unfortunately, space does not permit me to discuss the relation between Muslim and Christian dress; more research on the history of Muslim dress is necessary. For a discussion of Muslim women's sartorial choices today, see C. Osella and F. Osella, "Muslim Style in South India."

28   S. Bayly, *Saints, Goddesses, and Kings*, 296.

29   Mohan, *Modernity of Slavery*, 177.

30   Kurian, *The Caste Class Formation*, 13.

31   Gangadharan, *Evolution of Kerala History and Culture*, 293.

32   Malabar Marriage Commission, *Report of the Malabar Marriage Commission*, 10.

33   Yesudas, *A People's Revolt in Travancore*, 15.

34   Devika, *Engendering Individuals*, 260.

35   Punishments for caste infractions could include the death penalty, trampling by elephant, being blown from the mouth of a cannon, hanging spread-eagled for over three days, and mutilation; see S. Menon, *A Survey of Kerala History*, 391.

36   See Cohn, *Colonialism and Its Forms of Knowledge*; Devika, *Engendering Individuals*; Kent, *Converting Women*; Yesudas, *A People's Revolt in Travancore*; Joy Gnanadason, *A Forgotten History*; Hardgrave, *Essays in the Political Sociology of South India*; Awaya, "Becoming a 'Female Citizen' in Colonial Kerala"; Sheeju, "The Shanar Revolts, 1822–99."

37   Hardgrave, *Essays in the Political Sociology of South India*, 73.

38   Kent, *Converting Women*, 205.

39   Stoler, *Race and the Education of Desire*, 7.

40   Tarlo, *Clothing Matters*, 4.

41   Cohn, *Colonialism and Its Forms of Knowledge*, 134.

42   Yesudas, *A People's Revolt in Travancore*, 73.

43   Ibid., 118.

44   Cohn, *Colonialism and Its Forms of Knowledge*, 141.

45   T. Rao, "Proclamation Issued by the Dewan of Travancore, December 27, 1858," 170.

46   Rev. F. Baylis, "Letter from Rev. F. Baylis to the Resident, January 10, 1859," 182.

47   Mohan, *Modernity of Slavery*, 39, 134

48   Podipara, *The Latin Rite Christians of Malabar*, 60.

49   Ibid.

50   See Arunima, *There Comes Papa*.

51   Banerjee and Miller, *The Sari*, 196.

52   Lynton, *The Sari*, 11.

53   Selim, interview by author, 22 February 2008.

54   C. Osella and F. Osella, "Muslim Style in South India," 234.

55   Rouse, *Shifting Body Politics*, 99. The *salwar kamize* is commonly called the *churidar* in South India. The *salwar* is not exclusively an Islamic/Pakistani form of dress. It is also widely used by Sikh women in North India.

56 Threshamma and Thangamma, interview by author, 22 January 2008.

57 Threshamma, interview by author 27 July 2007.

58 Penamma, interview by author, 11 January 2008.

59 Chua, *In Pursuit of the Good Life*, 35.

60 P. Chatterjee, "Secularism and Tolerance," 353.

61 Acevedo, "Secularism in the Indian Context," 147.

62 Ibid., 146, 157.

63 Bhargava, "India's Secular Constitution," 117.

64 Upadhyaya, "The Politics of Indian Secularism," 815; Baxi, "The Constitutional Discourse on Secularism," 231.

65 R. Sen, *Articles of Faith*, xxix–xxxi, shows that the Supreme Court has homogenized and rationalized religion (especially Hinduism), thus narrowing the scope of religious freedom and actually strengthening Hindu nationalism by privileging a certain sense of "national unity" that resonates with the Hindu nationalist view of secularism.

66 Jain, "Minority Rights in Education," 2436.

67 Agnes, "Women's Movement within a Secular Framework," 1126.

68 N. Menon, "State/Gender/Community," PE-5.

69 Kocharotha, interview by author, 17 December 2007.

70 The *kaili* comes in a variety of colors and often has a checkered pattern. The *kaili* is also worn by Syrian Christian women at home but would never be worn in public by middle-class women.

71 Anna, interview by author, 5 April 2008.

72 Subramanian, *Shorelines*, 101.

73 John, "Dalit Women's Socio-economic Status," 183. Dalit women also reported being discriminated against on the basis of their skin color, a topic discussed in chapter 3.

74 N. Menon, "Living with Secularism," 134, 135.

75 See V. Kannabiran and K. Kannabiran, "Caste and Gender"; Tharu, "The Impossible Subject"; Rao, "Understanding *Sirasgaon.*"

76 Kimmel, "Masculinity as Homophobia"; Kimmel, *Guyland.*

77 Kimmel, "Masculinity as Homophobia," 68.

78 C. Osella and F. Osella, "Friendship and Flirting," 192.

79 Kodoth, "Gender, Caste, and Matchmaking in Kerala," 280–81.

80 Sreekumar, *Scripting Lives*, 170.

81 Jayasree, "Searching for Justice for Body and Self in a Coercive Environment," 60.

82 Devi, "Education, Employment, and Job Preference of Women in Kerala," 42.

83 Eapen, "Women and Work Mobility," 21.

84 John, "Dalit Women's Socio-economic Status,"183.

85 Venkitakrishnan and Kurien, "Rape Victims in Kerala," 87.

86 Brueck, "At the Intersection of Gender and Caste," 227.

87 Jessica Pudussery, "The Dying Art of the Sari," *Time*, 25 June 2009.

88 C. Osella and F. Osella, "Muslim Style in South India," 239.

89 "Temple's Decision Upheld," *The Hindu*, 28 November 2007, www.thehindu.com /todays-paper/tp-national/tp-newdelhi/temples-decison-upheld/article1956922.ece.

90 Ibid.

91 Quoted in K. A. Shaji, "Old Folds and a Wrap-Around," *Tehelka* 4, no. 50 (2007).

92   Leelamma, interview by author, 13 December 2007.

93   Kocharotha, Elsiekutty, and Annakutty, interview by author, 17 December 2007.

94   V. Ratheesh, letter to author, 17 December 2007.

95   Lukose, *Liberalization's Children*, 78.

96   For a discussion of racism against Northeast Indians, see McDuie-Ra, " 'Is India Racist?'" G. Reddy, "'We Are Indian Now,'" discusses the caste and racial discrimination against the Siddis, Ethiopian Indians who have lived in Hyderabad for generations.

97   "Tarun Vijay Apologises for Controversial Comments on South Indians," *Mathrubhumi*, 7 April 2017, http://english.mathrubhumi.com/news/india/tarun-vijay-apologises-for-controversial-comments-on-south-indians-1.1854257.

98   McDuie-Ra, *Debating Race in Contemporary India*, 2.

Chapter 3: Aryans and Dravidians

1   Savatri, interview by author, 8 September 2007.

2   There is new and emerging work on this subject. For example, Natrajan, *The Culturalization of Caste in India*, 5, examines how castes have "'branded' themselves as ethnicities in order to market their existence in a world where cultural identity is not 'utility function' and where ethnicity as a political claim is frequently conflated with ethnicity as cultural substance." In his analysis, Natrajan examines how the culturalization of caste is embedded in the changing nature of the developmental state, India's neoliberal economy and class inequalities affecting the *kumhar* potters (and *Kumhar* as a caste group) in Chhattisgarh.

3   Crenshaw, "Demarginalizing the Intersection of Race and Sex," 322.

4   An exception to this is Northeast India, which, as Duncan McDuie-Ra has argued, is discussed almost exclusively in terms of race; see McDuie-Ra, "'Is India Racist?'" Scholarship on Sri Lanka has long discussed "ethnicity," but within the history of ethnic conflict between the Tamilians and Sinhalese which may gloss over caste, class, and religious differences and lead to its own overdetermined frames.

5   See Trautmann, *The Aryan Debate*; Natrajan and Greenough, *Against Stigma*.

6   See Slate, *Colored Cosmopolitanism*; Saldhana, *Psychedelic White*.

7   Visweswaran, *Un/common Cultures*, 11.

8   Bate, *Tamil Oratory and the Dravidian Aesthetic*.

9   Natrajan and Greenough, "Introduction," 18–25; Lopez, "The Social Construction of Race," 28–37.

10   Tartakov, "Why Compare Dalits and African Americans?," 106–24.

11   Chakravarti, *Gendering Caste through a Feminist Lens*, 34–6; Lorde, "The Master's Tools Will Never Dismantle the Master's House," 110.

12   See Anirvan Chatterjee, "Beyond Gandhi and King: The Secret History of South Asian and African American Solidarity," accessed 30 November 2017, http://blackdesisecrethistory.org. These transnational connections were extremely complex. Slate, *Colored Cosmopolitanism*, 3–4, argues that although there were many ambiguities in how South Asians and African Americans drew on analogies of oppression, many social activists promoted social change in their countries by connecting the nation-specific struggles of anti-imperialism and segregation. In examining these connections, Slate

argues that the nation cannot be left behind, especially because the ability to create links depended on how activists understood oppression in their respective nations.

13   D. Reddy, "The Ethnicity of Caste," 569.

14   See Johnson, *The Myth of Ham in Nineteenth-Century American Christianity*; for a discussion of race in early Christianity, see Buell, *Why This New Race*.

15   Pandey, *A History of Prejudice*.

16   Peter Lalor, "India Makes Monkey of Racism Row," *The Australian*, 18 October 2007, www.theaustralian.com.au/archive/news/india-makes-monkey-of-racism-row/story -e6frg7mo-1111114667413. A few months later in January 2008, cricket player Harbhajan Singh of India was suspended for calling Andrew Symonds a monkey. After a hearing and immense public outcry in India, Singh's suspension was lifted.

17   Thapar, *The Aryan*, 9.

18   Parpola, "The Horse and the Language of the Indus Civilization," 235. In addition, the Harrappan Seals of the Indus Valley depict many different animals, but not horses.

19   Cohn, *Colonialism and Its Forms of Knowledge*, 71.

20   B. B. Lal, "It Is Time to Rethink," 146.

21   Gurukkal, *Social Formations of Early South India*, 262.

22   Hellman-Rajanayagam, "Is There a Tamil 'Race'?," 132.

23   Thapar, *The Aryan*, 33, 67.

24   Trautmann, "Introduction," in *The Aryan Debate*, xxv.

25   Philips, "Gendering Colour," 256.

26   Ratnagar, "The End of the Harappan Civilization."

27   Thapar, *The Aryan*, 33, 67..

28   Ibid., 31.

29   Robb, *The Concept of Race in South Asia*.

30   Stoler, *Race and the Education of Desire*, 7–9.

31   S. Bayly, "Caste and 'Race' in the Colonial Ethnography of India," 168.

32   In chapter 5, I discuss NCERT textbooks and revisions in depth. Currently, there is evidence to suggest that similar sorts of revisions are happening on a state levels in India; see Raksha Kumar, "Hindu Right Rewriting Indian Textbooks," *Aljazzera*, 4 November 2014, www.aljazeera.com/indepth/features/2014/11/hindu-right-ideology -indian-textbooks-gujarat-20141147028501733.html.

33   Bhan, "'Aryan Valley' and the Politics of Race and Religion in Kashmir."

34   See S. Sarkar, "Christian Conversions, Hindutva, and Secularism," 360; Viswanathan, "Literacy and Conversion in the Discourse of Hindu Nationalism," 341.

35   Thapar, *The Aryan*, 38.

36   Mohan, *Modernity of Slavery*, 289.

37   Sukhadeo Thorat, "Caste, Race, and United Nations' Perspective on Discrimination," 154.

38   Ibid.

39   Ibid., 144–45.

40   Ibid., 146.

41   Ibid., 147.

42   A year later, ICERD revisited caste, "strongly reaffirming" that descent-based discrimination includes caste.

43   See Gurukkal, "St. Thomas Christians and Nambudiri Brahmins," 109; George Men-
     achery, "Social Life and Customs of the St. Thomas Christians in the Pre-Diamper
     Period," 197; Gangadharan, *Evolution of Kerala History and Culture*, 92.

44   Narayanan, "Nambudiris," 87–92.

45   Fuller and Narasimhan, *Tamil Brahmins*, 225.

46   During the period of British colonialism, Namboodiri Brahmins were only 0.5 per-
     cent of the population in Kerala, while foreign Brahmins in Kerala constituted 1.2
     percent of the population; see Namboodiri, "Caste and Social Change in Colonial
     Kerala," 430–31.

47   Lopez, "The Social Construction of Race," 27.

48   Natrajan and Greenough, "Introduction," 20.

49   Mathai, interview by author, 11 December 2007.

50   Markos, interview by author, 3 December 2007.

51   Sarakutty, interview by author, 3 December 2007.

52   Ayyar, *Anthropology of the Syrian Christians*, 50, 242.

53   Fuller, "Kerala Christians and the Caste System," 62.

54   Philip, comment on "Subsequent Divisions and the Nasrani People," 13 February
     2007, www.nasrani.net/2007/02/13/kerala-syrian-christian-the-tomb-of-the-apostle
     -persian-church-syond-of-diamper-coonan-cross-oath-divisions.

55   "Join the 'Syrian Christians' Group Project," FamilyTreeDNA.com, accessed 9
     December 2017, www.familytreedna.com/group-join.aspx?code=A22299&Group=
     SyrianChristians.

56   F. Osella and C. Osella, "Articulation of Physical and Social Bodies in Kerala," 43.

57   Lucy, interview by author, 10 May 2008.

58   Lindberg, *Modernization and Effeminization in India*, 55–82.

59   K. L. A. Iyer, *The Dravidians*, 8.

60   See, for example, the Kavailai Veettil family history, accessed 30 November 2017,
     http://kavilaiveettilzachariahfamily.org/myfamily.php.

61   Sheeba George's work on Syrian Christian nurses and migration has argued that
     nursing was looked down upon by many in the community, and only Syrian Chris-
     tian families that struggled financially would send their daughters to nursing school.
     Only later, when many women started migrating to Europe and the United States,
     was nursing seen as a respectable profession. See George, *When Women Come First*.

62   Devi, "Education, Employment, and Job Preference of Women in Kerala," 76.

63   Coir is a stiff fibrous material that comes from the coconut's outer husk.

64   Eapen, "Women and Work Mobility," 21.

65   Ibid. See also Devi, "Education, Employment, and Job Preference of Women in Kerala,"
     81; Mitra and Singh, "Human Capital Attainment and Female Labor Force Participa-
     tion," 794.

66   Orotha, interview by author, 23 April 2008.

67   Glenn, "Yearning for Lightness," 282.

68   Advertisement for Fair & Lovely, accessed 6 January 2016, www.youtube.com/watch
     ?v=nWls3U7ZZ1E.

69   Lindberg, "The Historical Roots of Dowries in Contemporary Kerala," 33–34;
     Thomas, "Education as Empowerment?"

70   Philips, "Gendering Colour," 260.

71   Ibid., 262–63.

72   Gangadharan, *Evolution of Kerala History and Culture*, 197.

73   Visvanathan, *The Christians of Kerala*, 119.

74   Varghese, interview by author, 28 December 2007.

75   George, interview by author, 17 December 2007; Elia, interview by author, 9 January 2013; Susan, interview by author, 14 August 2015.

76   Rahel, interview by author, field notes, 29 April 2008.

77   A. Roy, *The God of Small Things*, 70.

78   Ibid., 168.

79   George Iype, "Obscenity Case Slammed against Arundhati Roy," Rediff, 7 August 1997, www.rediff.com/news/aug/07arun.htm.

80   A. Roy, *The God of Small Things*, 74.

81   Ibid., 73.

Chapter 4: Who Are the Minorities?

1   T. Pillai, *Kerala Legislative Assembly Proceedings*, 25 November 1958, 147.

2   Cardinal Varkey J. Vithayathil, remarks on the fiftieth anniversary of the liberation strike, 31 May 2009; Jeffrey, *Politics, Women, and Well-Being*, 79.

3   The amendment to the KEB suspended the implementation of clause 11. Amendments were also made to the Agrarian Relations Act, which was also a focus of the protest.

4   The CIA's involvement was mentioned in Moynihan, *A Dangerous Place*, 41: "We had twice, but only twice, interfered in Indian politics to the extent of providing money to a political party. Both times this was done in the face of a prospective Communist victory in a state election, once in Kerala and once in West Bengal, where Calcutta is located. Both times the money was given to the Congress Party, which asked for it." See also Isaac, *Vimochana Samarathinte Kaanapurangal*; T, "Dismissal of the First Communist Ministry in Kerala, and Extraneous Agencies."

5   See Leiten, *The First Communist Ministry in Kerala*; Leiten, "Education, Ideology, and Politics in Kerala"; Jeffrey, "Jawaharlal Nehru and the Smoking Gun"; P. Pillai, *The Red Interlude in Kerala*; H. Austin, *The Anatomy of the Kerala Coup*; Fic, *Kerala, Yenan of India*. Exceptions to all these studies can be found in Devika, "Negotiating Women's Social Space"; Devika and Sukumar, "Making Space for Feminist Social Critique in Contemporary Kerala"; and Devika and Thampi, *New Lamps for Old*. The latter three texts are not specifically on the first Communist ministry, but all three briefly mention women's participation in the 1959 protest, and the subsequent precluding of their participation in politics soon after.

6   Devika, *Engendering Individuals*, 297.

7   Ibid., 299.

8   T. M. A. Pai Foundation v. State of Karnataka, 2002, http://indiankanoon.org/doc/512761.

9   Jeffrey, *Politics, Women, and Well-Being*, 153.

10   "State of Literacy," accessed 4 June 2012, http://censusindia.gov.in/2011-prov-results/data_files/india/Final_PPT_2011_chapter6.pdf, 101.

11   Tharakan, "Socio-economic Factors in Educational Development," 1918.

12   Padmanabhan, "Learning to Learn," 105.

13   Mohan, *Modernity of Slavery*, 125.

14   Ibid., 134.

15   Padmanabhan, "Learning to Learn," 106.

16   Thomas," Education as Empowerment?"; Nampoothiri, "Confronting Social Exclusion."

17   Jeffrey, *Politics, Women, and Well-Being*, 155.

18   "Church and Communist Party Friction," *Malayala Manorama*, 17 September 1957; Jeffrey, *Politics, Women, and Well-Being*, 155.

19   Leiten, *The First Communist Ministry*, 35.

20   Ibid., 38.

21   Jeffrey, *Politics, Women, and Well-Being*, 151.

22   Leiten, *The First Communist Ministry*, 33.

23   Ibid., 33.

24   Ausep, interview by author, 31 December 2007.

25   R. K. Bhar, M. P. Rodrigues, P. K. Nambiar, and T. R. Balakrishna Ayyar, "Conference on Kerala Education Bill, 1957," Education 1956–68, RG 627, vol. 1, Kerala State Archives, Thiruvananthapuram.

26   *Deshabhimani*, August 1957, www.firstministry.kerala.gov.in/frame.php?img=2_aug_57_cartoon.gif&pg_id=4.

27   Quoted in Thekkedam, "The Catholics and the New Education Policy of the Travancore Government," 128.

28   In the P. A. Imamdar case, the bench listed these cases and the Kerala Education Bill as the four cases most often quoted with respect to litigation on education.

29   The other was the 1958 Kerala Agrarian Relations Act.

30   "Assembly Concludes Consideration," *The Hindu*, 24 May 1959.

31   Select Committee on the Kerala Education Bill, 1957, *Report of the Select Committee on the Kerala Education Bill, 1957, and the Bill as Reported by the Select Committee*, 15–35.

32   Govind Ballabh Pant, "17 June 1957 Correspondence," Education 1956–68, RG 627, vol. 1, Kerala State Archives, Thiruvananthapuram.

33   E. M. S. Namboodiripad, "17 June 1957 Correspondence," Education 1956–68, RG 627, vol. 1, Kerala State Archives, Thiruvananthapuram.

34   See, for example, "PT Chacko's Speech at Legislature," *Malayala Manorama*, 31 August 1957; "Education Bill: Government Wants to Recover Revenue from Managements," *Malayala Manorama*, 1 September 1957; "Poverty and Communist Cells," *Malayala Manorama*, 8 September 1957. Even today, both the Congress Party and the Communist Party in Kerala consider P. T. Chacko to be a renowned politician. A statue of Chacko now stands in Kottayam City, and on 1 August 2009, the fiftieth anniversary of his death, politicians throughout Kerala gathered in Thiruvananthapuram to commemorate his life.

35   Mathew Kavukatt and Sabastian Vallopilly, "Writ Petition no. 78 of 1958," Education 1956–68, RG 627, vol. 1, Kerala State Archives, Thiruvananthapuram.

36   "Protest Telegrams," Education 1956–68, RG 627, vol. 1, Kerala State Archives, Thiruvananthapuram.

37 M. C. Setelavad, "MC Setelavad's Statement," Education 1956–68, RG 627, vol. 1, Kerala State Archives, Thiruvananthapuram.

38 Ibid.

39 Mathew Kavukatt, quoted in "Catholics' Protest," *The Hindu*, 23 May 1959.

40 Kavukatt and Vallopilly, "Writ Petition No. 78 of 1958," 13.

41 Lindberg, "The Historical Roots of Dowries in Contemporary Kerala," 31.

42 Aishabai, *Kerala Legislative Assembly Proceedings*, 1 March 1958, 306–7.

43 Lindberg, "The Historical Roots of Dowries in Contemporary Kerala," 40.

44 Baba, *Kerala Legislative Assembly Proceedings*, 1 March 1958, 306.

45 Poulose, *Kerala Legislative Assembly Proceedings*, 1 March 1958, 302.

46 V. R. K. Iyer, *Kerala Legislative Assembly Proceedings*, 30 June 1958, 74.

47 Thomas, "Education as Empowerment?"

48 *Report of the Christian Community*, 10, 19.

49 Ibid., 27.

50 Ibid., 23.

51 Philips, "Stridhanam, 260.

52 Poulose, *Kerala Legislative Assembly Proceedings*, 1 March 1958, 302–3.

53 G. Austin, "Religion, Personal Law, and Identity," 23. Austin discusses how Muslim personal law became something fiercely defended by Muslims in postcolonial India because of the fear that a uniform civil code would lead to Hindus legislating Islam, and to the loss of the "last line of defense" (21) against Hindu majoritiarian politics.

54 For more on the Mary Roy case, see Thomas, "Education as Empowerment?"; see also Philips, "Stridhanam."

55 Philips, "Stridhanam," 255.

56 Thomas, "Education as Empowerment?"

57 For Kerala specifically, see Thomas, "Education as Empowerment?"; see also Philips, "Stridhanam." For India, see S. Basu, *She Comes to Take Her Rights*.

58 Philips, "Stridhanam," 256.

59 The bill was unsuccessful; see S. Vellapally and M. Vellapally, "Repeal of the Travancore Christian Succession Act."

60 Thomman, *Kerala Legislative Assembly Proceedings*, 30 June 1958, 63.

61 M. C. Abraham, *Kerala Legislative Assembly Proceedings*, 1 March 1958, 306.

62 T. Pillai, *Kerala Legislative Assembly Proceedings*, 1 March 1958, 319–20.

63 Ibid., 33–35.

64 V. R. K. Iyer, *Kerala Legislative Assembly Proceedings*, 1 March 1958, 328.

65 Kavukatt, "Pastoral Letter No. 44," 164.

66 *Report of the Christian Community*, 4. In addition, 934 males were interviewed, and only 31 females.

67 The Muslim League supported Christian opposition to the KEB as Muslim school managements too invoked their constitutional rights under Article 30(1). C. H. Mohammed Koya, representing the Indian Union Muslim League, wrote a dissenting note in the select committee's report on the KEB in 1958.

68 Government of Kerala, *Opposition Preparations for Violent Overthrow of the Government*, 7.

69 "Schools Will Close: Catholic Conference Decision," *Malayala Manorama*, 6 May 1959; "CSI Schools Will Close," *Malayala Manorama*, 13 May 1959; "Schools Will Close, Marthomas Passed Decision," *Malayala Manorama*, 14 May 1959; "Schools Will Close: All Private Schools Will Be Closed," *Malayala Manorama*, 15 May 1959; "Malankara Christians: June 14th Will Be the Day of Education, Schools Will Close, Children Will Not Be Sent to School," *Malayala Manorama*, 5 June 1959.

70 Yohinan, interview by author, 11 September 2007.

71 Paulose, interview by author, 3 December 2007.

72 "Today, Epic Vimochana Samaram: All Schools Will Be Closed," *Malayala Manorama*, 12 June 1959.

73 Government of India, Planning Commission, *Second Five-Year Plan*, 37.

74 Government of Kerala, *Kerala Economic Review, 1958–59*, 14.

75 Ibid.

76 E. M. S. Namboodiripad, quoted in "Communists in Kerala," *The Hindu*, 13 May 1959.

77 Annamma, interview by author, 15 December 2007.

78 Quoted in H. Austin, *The Anatomy of the Kerala Coup*, 55.

79 Ausep, interview by author, 31 December 2007.

80 Vithayathil, remarks on fiftieth anniversary of liberation strike.

81 "In Kerala, an Unprecedented *Samaram*, Women Involved," *Malayala Manorama*, 5 July 1959.

82 Scaria, interview by author, 14 May 2008.

83 "Kerala Women's Spark," *Malayala Manorama*, 28 July 1959.

84 Devika, *Engendering Individuals*, 101.

85 Devika, "Domesticating Malayalees," 8.

86 "Women's Samaram Presided Over by Chinamma," *Malayala Manorama*, 17 June 1959.

87 "Women Declare 'Our Children Will Know We Are Courageous,'" *Malayala Manorama*, 26 June 1959.

88 Father Saju Koren, "Heroic Women of Ankamali Court Arrest with Babies in Arms," *Vimochana Samaram 1959* (blog), accessed 2 December 2017, http://vimochanasamaram.blogspot.com.

89 Chakravarti, *Gendering Caste through a Feminist Lens*, 69.

90 Devika and Thampi, *New Lamps for Old*, xx.

91 Leiten, *The First Communist Ministry*, 140. In his memoir, Father Vadakkan claimed that he had nothing to do with the Christophers, and that he regretted his participation in the *vimochana samaram*; see Vadakkan, *A Priest's Encounter with Revolution*.

92 Government of Kerala, *Kerala Government's Reply to the KPCC Memorandum*.

93 Ibid.

94 Ibid.

95 Kurien, interview by author, 17 December 2007.

96 Leiten, *The First Communist Ministry*, 143.

97 Baby, "Communist Rule in Kerala," 226.

98 "2,949 Arrested," *Malayala Manorama*, 5 July 1959.

99 Rosamma, interview by author, 5 December 2007.

100 Yohinan, interview by author, 11 September 2007.

101 Achamma, interview by author, 19 December 2007.

102 Maruthur, "Sexual Figures of Kerala."

103 Ibid., 23.

104 Ibid., 26.

105 Ibid., 30–31; Mukhopadhyay, "Gender Disparity in Kerala," 176.

106 Mukhopadhyay, "Gender Disparity in Kerala," 176.

107 "If Hired Police Take Action, Then Women Should Show the Broom," *Malayala Manorama*, 12 June 1959.

108 T. Pillai, *Kerala Legislative Assembly Proceedings*, 25 November 1958, 147.

Chapter 5: A Life without Religion

1   "Learn from 1957, Mani Tells LDF," *The Hindu*, 1 July 2008, www.thehindu.com/todays-paper/tp-national/tp-kerala/Learn-from-1957-Mani-tells-LDF/article15251985.ece.

2   Gouridasan C. Nair, "Tolerance Under Attack," *The Hindu*, 26 June 2008.

3   Undeniably, debates over religion and textbook content happen not just in South Asia but also in many different national and religious contexts. The teaching of evolution in the United States is a great example of this type of debate.

4   Quoted in Kavukatt, "Pastoral Letter no. 48," 185.

5   K. Kumar, "Origins of India's 'Textbook Culture.'"

6   Thapar, "The History Debate and School Textbooks in India," 87.

7   See Smith, "The 'Golden Age' and National Renewal." Hindu nationalist revisionist histories, as I will discuss, also use this up-down-up trope of historical recovery.

8   P. Chatterjee, "History and the Domain of the Popular."

9   Thapar, "The History Debate and School Textbooks in India," 88; P. Chatterjee, "History and the Domain of the Popular."

10   Thapar, "The History Debate and School Textbooks in India," 88.

11   Guichard, *The Construction of History and Nationalism in India*, 47.

12   Ibid., 49–50.

13   K. Kumar, "Peace with the Past."

14   P. Chatterjee, "History and the Domain of the Popular."

15   When we speak of literacy in Kerala, we are discussing literacy in the Malayalam language. Although it would seem that the Malayalam language would unite all speakers, the print culture has actually encouraged communities to continue to differentiate themselves from each other. See Arunima, "Imagining Communities—Differently."

16   See Puthur, *St. Thomas Christians and Nambudiris*. For instance, in that volume, Narayanan, "Nambudiris: Migrations and Early Settlements in Kerala," 87, questions the way in which communalism shapes historical scholarship in Kerala, and lists the St. Thomas story alongside the mythic Parashuram narrative; the text is followed by a note from the volume editor: "This seems to be a sweeping generalization. There is an intrinsic difference between the legend of Parasurama and the tradition of the mission of St. Thomas in India. Almost all good historians today consider the Parusu Rama legend as myth. This is not the case with the tradition of St. Thomas. . . . The St. Thomas Christians have cherished this tradition from very early times and this consciousness

is a mark of their identity." Who, then, is the audience for this text? And do such histories allow for any questioning of a timeline that goes against one supported by the Syro-Malabar Catholic historians?

17   Bhattacharya, "Teaching History in Schools," 100.

18   Post-Emergency is the period following Emergency, when Indira Gandhi suspended civil liberties in 1975–77. The Janata Party is thought to have won because of Emergency.

19   V. Lal, *The History of History*, 107.

20   Guichard, *The Construction of History and Nationalism in India*, 55.

21   Ibid., 57–58.

22   See Kurien, "Who Speaks for Indian Americans?"; Visweswaran et al., "The Hindutva View of History"; Bose, "Hindutva Abroad."

23   See Raksha Kumar, "Hindu Right Rewriting Indian Textbooks," *Aljazzera*, 4 November 2014, www.aljazeera.com/indepth/features/2014/11/hindu-right-ideology-indian -textbooks-gujarat-20141147028501733.html.

24   Ibid.

25   Jennifer Medina, "Debate Erupts in California Over Curriculum on India's History," *New York Times*, 4 May 2016, www.nytimes.com/2016/05/06/us/debate-erupts-over -californias-india-history-curriculum.html.

26   Rohit Chopra, "Viewpoint: Why Hindu Groups Are Against California Textbook Change," *BBC News*, 27 May 2016, www.bbc.com/news/world-asia-india-36376110.

27   Mukherjee and Mukherjee, "Communalisation of Education, the History Textbook Controversy."

28   V. Lal, *The History of History*, 79.

29   Guichard, *The Construction of History and Nationalism in India*, 5.

30   Ibid., 134–48; V. Lal, *The History of History*, 18.

31   Bhattacharya, "Teaching History in Schools," 109.

32   Habib, "How to Evade Real Issues and Make Room for Obscurantism," 7.

33   Thapar, "National Curriculum Framework and the Social Sciences," 56.

34   See "Debating Education," special issue, *Social Scientist* 33, no. 9/10 (2005).

35   M. A. Baby, interview by author, 12 June 2008.

36   After the smoke cleared from the textbook controversy, regret was expressed at the lack of women's participation in writing and approving the textbook. As stated in the government report on the textbook, "All textbooks need to ensure gender sensitivity. More concrete narratives and case studies need to be incorporated in the text to address issues regarding unequal gender relations in society. A serious effort must be made to involve more women in the preparation of curriculum syllabi and textbooks"; see High Power Expert Committee on Textbook Review, *Report of the High Power Expert Committee on Textbook Review*, p. 20, committee chaired by K. N. Panikkar, submitted to the minister of education, Kerala, 10 June 2008, https://web .archive.org/web/20090617035732/http://www.education.kerala.gov.in/FINAL%20 REPORTnew.pdf.

37   The Vaikam Satyagraha was a movement to allow Dalits the right to travel on roads to the Vaikam temple. The Gururvayur Satyagraha was a movement to allow for the temple entry of all castes.

38 Sunny, "Communalisation of Education," 23.

39 "Kerala Textbook Says Don't Believe in God," *The Daily Pioneer*, 21 June 2008.

40 "Textbook Row Unjustified, Say Academics," *New Indian Express*, 26 June 2008.

41 The secular/communal duality is discussed in K. Kumar, *Prejudice and Pride.*

42 "Education Bandh," *The Hindu*, 8 August 2008. In a *hartal*, the call goes out for all businesses, schools, and modes of transportation to be shut down. The Kerala High Court differentiates between a *hartal* and a *bandh*: a *bandh* usually takes place with little public notice, is called for and enforced by political parties, and involves business closures, whereas a *hartal* is supposed to follow, more or less, the format of a general strike and should be declared two days in advance. The high court has forbidden *bandhs*. In actuality, however, there seems to be very little difference between a *bandh* and a *hartal* in Kerala. The group calling for a *hartal* on a particular day will take to the streets and forcibly shut down any establishment or mode of transportation that is open or running and will often resort to violence—throwing stones at shop windows, overturning buses, or beating proprietors who attempt to keep their businesses open. The state of Kerala is notorious for such strikes, a fact that perhaps stems from the success of the *vimochana samaram* in 1959.

43 "UDF Decries Government's Attitude Towards Fast," *The Hindu*, 15 July 2008.

44 "KSU Disrupts Cluster Meetings," *The Hindu*, 22 June 2008.

45 "No Talks on Textbooks: NSS, Church," *The Hindu*, 24 June 2008.

46 Ibid.

47 "Street Fights Throw Life Out of Gear, Feeder Organizations of CPI(M), BJP Clash Twice in Front of Secretariat," *The Hindu*, 27 June 2008.

48 "Muslim Bodies Seek Recall of Textbook," *The Hindu*, 24 June 2008.

49 "Muslim Outfits to Continue Stir," *New Indian Express*, 10 July 2008.

50 "DPI Seeks Report," *New Indian Express*, 20 July 2008.

51 "Uproar Over Teacher's Death: Government Rejects Plea for Judicial Inquiry," *The Hindu*, 22 July 2008.

52 "Textbook Row: Church to Observe 'Protest Day,'" *The Hindu*, 27 June 2008.

53 Perumthottam, "Circular Letter, July 2008."

54 Sister Elsie, interview by author, 28 July 2008.

55 This chant and others were handed out to protesters by rally organizers in a document titled "Revoke Controversial Education Plan: Protest March, Public Meeting."

56 "KCBC to Bring Out Workbook," *New Indian Express*, 11 August 2008.

57 The KSU textbook, like the government textbook, had passages on the Breast Cloth Movement, the Vaikam Satyagraha, the Guruvayur Satyagraha, and Vakkom Moulavi as well as passages from the Bible and the Mahabharata. It also included an interesting story about a little girl, Umakulasul, who got separated from her mother at a festival. The story uses terms like *ommachee* (mother), and *duniyava* (world), traditional in the Muslim community of Kerala, to indicate that Umakulasul and her mother are Muslims. After Umakulasul gets lost, a kind man finds her crying, says he'll help her, picks her up, and walks to the temple counter, where her name is announced over the microphone. When her mother comes to the temple counter, the man turns his head, hiding his tears of joy. The mother asks the man his name, and he responds by saying, "Balakrishnan" (a Hindu man's name). This exchange is

followed by the sound, over the speakers, of Muslims being called to evening prayers. Time and space do not permit me to dwell on the story, but I do find it striking that this story of religious tolerance in the KSU textbook is considered noncontroversial, by contrast with "Mathamillatha Jeevan." I find it especially interesting because this KSU "noncontroversial" story involves a Hindu man saving a Muslim girl. For me, this is indicative of an often politicized communal rescue paradigm wherein the Hindu male is the savior of a Muslim girl—a paradigm that defines Muslim women solely by their victimization, and Hindu men by their benevolence.

58 Archbishop Powathil later stated that Thazhath did not call for a second *vimochana samaram*; see R. Krishnakumar, "Matter of Survival for Us," *Frontline* 24, no. 15 (2007), www.frontline.in/static/html/fl2415/stories/20070810504203400.htm.

59 Panikkar, "Quest for Quality in Higher Education."

60 R. Krishnakumar, "Battle Cry," *Frontline* 24, no. 15 (2007), www.frontline.in/static/html/fl2415/stories/20070810504103200.htm.

61 Panikkar, "Quest for Quality in Higher Education."

62 When the Right to Education (RTE) Act was written, only a few years later, arrangements were made to exempt from its provisions any schools that qualified as "minority" schools under Article 30(1)of the constitution. The act makes free and compulsory education for children under the age of fourteen a constitutional right, but it also mandates a quota of 25 percent for disadvantaged students and has provisions for increased pay for teachers. After passage of the act, there was a large increase in the number of schools in Kerala seeking minority status; see Preetu Venugopalan Nair, "Schools Desperate for Minority Tag to Avoid RTE," *The Times of India*, 17 December 2012, http://timesofindia.indiatimes.com/city/kochi/Schools-desperate-for-minority-tag-to-avoid-RTE/articleshow/17644467.cms.

63 Perumthottam, "Circular Letter, July 2007."

64 This was the bill's actual title. The bill followed the UDF's Kerala Self Financing Colleges (Prohibition of Capitation Fees and Procedure for Admission and Fixation of Fees) Act, which also sought to regulate self-financing colleges in the state.

65 M. A. Baby, interview by author, 12 April 2008.

66 Since then, there have been other changes to higher education in Kerala. These include increased government funding for higher education, the formation of the Higher Education Council, the introduction of India's choice-based credit system, and the implementation of interuniversity centers in Kerala. Panikkar, "Quest for Quality in Higher Education," describes private management's opposition to these reforms: "Many of these initiatives have been defeated by private interests who have dominated the field by treating higher education as an arena for commercial ventures. The bill for controlling private agencies in professional education was blocked by them. Their attitude of non-cooperation has made the much acclaimed system of college clusters non-functional. Their participation in [the choice-based credit system] is at best lukewarm. On the whole, private managements are trying to undo the progressive policy of higher education which the state has implemented after wide-ranging discussion with stakeholders."

67 Archdiocese of Changanacherry, "Joint Circular Letter, 26 August 2007," 7–12.

68   R. Krishnakumar, "Act of Promise," *Frontline* 23, no. 14 (2006), www.frontline.in
      /static/html/fl2314/stories/2006072800371060o.htm.

69   Quoted in Krishnakumar, "Battle Cry."

70   "Jacobite Church Not with Agitation," *New Indian Express*, 7 August 2007.

71   Mathai, interview by author, 11 December 2007.

72   K. A. Shaji, "Classic Battle in Left Bastion: Church vs. State," *Vox Populi Vox Dei*
      (blog), 28 July 2007, https://kashaji.blogspot.com/2007/07.

73   Cheriyan, interview by author, 19 December 2007.

74   Shaji, "Classic Battle in Left Bastion."

75   Dale, "Trade, Conversion and the Growth of the Islamic Community of Kerala, South
      India," 163.

76   Ibid.

77   Lakshmi, *The Malabar Muslims*, 29.

78   Ibid., 10–11. These divisions between Hindu landlords and Muslim tenants led to the
      Mappila rebellion in 1921 and, later, to tenancy reforms in the Malabar government.

79   Mathur, "Social Stratification among the Muslims of Kerala," 133.

80   D'Souza, "Status Among the Moplahs on the South-West Coast of India," 45–46,
      locates five different classes/castes of Muslims in Kerala today: (1) the Thangals, high
      in status because they reportedly descended from the Prophet's daughter Fatima; (2)
      the Arabis, who descended from unions between Arab traders and native women; (3)
      the Mappila Malabaris, consisting of the largest group of Muslims, but lower in status
      than the Thangals and Arabis; (4) the Pusalars, consisting of the second largest group
      of Muslims, and descendants of converted Mukkavan Hindus (the fishing caste) in
      the eighteenth and nineteenth centuries; and (5) the Ossans, lowest in status, and
      converted from the barber castes, also in the eighteenth and nineteenth centuries.

81   Nair, "Tolerance Under Attack."

82   Chowdhry, *Contentious Marriages, Eloping Couples*, 16.

83   Ibid., 250.

84   Mody, "Love and the Law," 226.

85   Chowdhry, *Contentious Marriages, Eloping Couples*, 17.

86   On "oppositional agency," see Chakravarti, *Gendering Caste through a Feminist Lens*,
      159; on "autonomous reproduction ," see Chowdhry, *Contentious Marriages, Eloping
      Couples*, 1.

87   Ibid., 6.

88   Ibid., 11.

89   In May 2015, for example, a village caste *panchayat* in Uttar Pradesh ruled that
      because a Dalit boy had eloped with an upper-caste girl, his two sisters would be
      raped, their faces would be blackened, and then they would be paraded naked around
      the village. The Supreme Court intervened, but the family remains fearful of retribu-
      tion. See "Campaign Success: Protection Given to Indian Sisters Due to Be Raped as
      Punishment for Their Brother's 'Crime,'" Amnesty International UK, 18 September
      2015, www.amnesty.org.uk/india-dalit-sisters-protection-raped-punishment-brothers
      -crime.

90   Chakravarti, *Gendering Caste through a Feminist Lens*, 159.

91   The 1954 Special Marriage Act was based on an earlier colonial bill and actually lengthened the amount of time a couple needed to wait before getting married, from two weeks to thirty days; see Mody, "Love and the Law," 234.

92   Ibid., 247.

93   Chowdhry, *Contentious Marriages, Eloping Couples*, 202.

94   Ibid., 197.

95   Committee on the Elimination of Discrimination Against Women, "Concluding Observations on the Combined Fourth and Fifth Periodic Reports of India."

96   There is a large body of work on kinship in India; Dravidian kinship often separates North Indian practices from South Indian. For examples, see Rivers, "The Marriage of Cousins in India"; Karve, *Kinship Organization in India*; and Dumont, "The Dravidian Kinship Terminology as an Expression of Marriage."

97   Oldenburg, *Dowry Murder*, 8–9.

98   Chowdhry, *Contentious Marriages, Eloping Couples*.

99   Trautmann, *Dravidian Kinship*.

100 Clark-Decès, *The Right Spouse*, 168.

101 "Inter-Caste Marriage: Priest Loses Job," *The Hindu* , 12 August 2006, http://www .thehindu.com/todays-paper/tp-national/tp-kerala/intercaste-marriage-priest-loses -job/article3089168.ece.

102 "For the Record: 'It Is Absolutely Unsafe to Let (24-Year-Old) Be Free to Do as She Likes,'" *New Indian Express*, 31 May 2017, http://indianexpress.com/article/india/for -the-record-it-is-absolutely-unsafe-to-let-24-year-old-be-free-to-do-as-she-likes -4681708.

103 Rahul Bhatia, "The Year of Love Jihad in India," *New Yorker*, 31 December 2017.

104 Kurien, *Kaleidoscopic Ethnicity*, 23–24.

105 Kocharotha, Anna Kutty, and Elsi Kutty, interview by author, 17 December 2007.

106 Rosie, interview by author, 26 September 2007.

107 Scaria, interview by author, 12 January 2013.

108 Field notes, Kanjirapally, January 2013.

109 Lindberg, *Modernization and Effeminization in India*, 70.

110 Ibid., 73.

111 C. Osella and F. Osella, "Friendship and Flirting," 190–91.

112 Ibid., 201.

113 Devika, "Memory's Fatal Lure," 14.

114 It appears that Kerala does not have as many honor killings as North India. More research on this, however, is needed.

115 Payyappilly, *Mixed Marriage in the Code of Canons of the Eastern Churches and the Particular Law of the Syro-Malabar Church*, 73, 188.

116 Ibid., 174.

117 In a similar vein, Kent, "Civilisation and Conjugality," 157, has discussed how nineteenth-century Christian converts from both upper-caste and lower-caste communities shied away from divorce and remarriage in an effort to distance themselves from lower-caste Hindu practices, "thus anchoring patriarchal social formations that stigmatized low-caste status."

118 Field notes, Manimala, August 2007.

119 Field notes, Nedunkunam, December 2007.

120 "Catholic Bishops Slam Single-Window," *The Hindu*, 12 June 2008.

121 "Catholic Church to India: Have More Kids!," *CBS News*, 11 October 2011, www.cbs news.com/news/catholic-church-to-india-have-more-kids.

122 "Cardinal George Alencherry Campaign against Inter-Caste Marriages," Media-oneTV Live, 18 December 2013, www.youtube.com/watch?v=oJSZli9Kzko.

123 Ibid.

124 Ibid.

125 Shaju Philip, "Kerala: Church Warns Parents to Guard Children Against 'Selfie,'" *New Indian Express*, 6 February 2015, http://indianexpress.com/article/india/india -others/kerala-church-warns-parents-to-guard-children-against-selfie.

126 Ibid.

127 The SNDP spoke out strongly against this. The KCBC then distanced itself from Bishop Anikuzhikkattil's statements and met with the SNDP secretary. However, Archbishop Joseph Powathil, an extremely powerful and influential figure in the Syro-Malabar Church, published an article in the newspaper *Deepika* condemning the KCBC's actions and coming out in support of Bishop Anikuzhikkattil's state-ments against mixed marriages; see "Who Is More Right: Kerala Catholic Bishops Divided?," Almayasabdam, 17 June 2015, http://almayasabdam.com/who-is-more -right-kerala-catholic-bishops-on-inter-caste-marriages.

128 Chakravarti, *Gendering Caste through a Feminist Lens*, 31.

129 Ibid. According to J. Abraham, "Contingent Caste Endogamy and Patriarchy," 171, the sexuality of high-ranking Thiyya (Ezhava) men was also regulated in colonial Malabar because of anxiety about the potential mingling of these men with mixed-blood women born of liaisons between British men and Thiyya women, but this regu-lation did not come close to the types of sanctions that women in mixed unions faced.

130 Thomas, "The Tying of the Ceremonial Wedding Thread."

131 Dempsey, "Cross Currents in Kerala Christianity," 407, describes how life-cycle rituals (marriage, birth, death), the purifying touch that is still practiced in some churches and temples, and processions that use decorative umbrellas and Hindu drumming are encouraged, whereas other rituals, such as menstruation taboos and astrology, are labeled "Hindu superstition." In this fascinating article, Dempsey argues that these caste-neutral "Hindu superstitions" may actually have their roots in Eastern Christian-ity. Although my focus here is specifically the life-cycle rituals that concern the ritual-ization of female sexuality, it is important to note that in Dempsey's reading, acceptable rituals have ties to upper-caste Hinduism. Indeed, the eighth-century Syrian Christian Copper Plates allowed Syrian Christians to mark their privileged status by using deco-rative umbrellas in festivals and gave them the same rights as upper-caste Hindus. And death rituals—such as the period of ritual pollution followed by a feast seven days after a death in the family, or the ritual that prevents households where a death in the family has occurred from celebrating *Pesaha*, or the Christian Passover meal unique to Syrian Christianity—mirror upper-caste Hindu rituals related to death and purity.

132 Visvanathan, *The Christians of Kerala*, 102.

133 Less importance is given to girls' names, and many family histories do not even record the names of female family members. Traditionally, however, the eldest daughter of the

family is given the paternal grandmother's name, and the suffix "-amma" or "-kutty" would be added as a term of endearment.

134 S. Basu, *The Trouble with Marriage*, 70.

135 Devasia and unidentified protester, interview by author, 28 July 2008.

136 Kerala Pradesh Congress Committee, *KPCC Select Committee Report*, in possession of the author from the KPCC district offices.

137 Narayanan, "Communists Are Trying to Catch Fish in Dirty Water," 7, 8.

138 Chowdhry, *Contentious Marriages, Eloping Couples*, 233.

139 Mody, "Love and the Law," 230.

140 Devika, "Memory's Fatal Lure," 16.

141 "Ontological anomie" is a concept that was introduced to me by Dr. Jennifer Musto in a virtual conversation between myself and other scholars with PhDs in women's studies.

142 Devika, "Memory's Fatal Lure," 15.

143 See N. Menon, *Recovering Subversion*; Agnes, *Law and Gender Inequality*; R. S. Rajan, *The Scandal of the State*; K. Kannabiran, *Women and Law*; S. Basu, *She Comes to Take Her Rights*.

144 N. Menon, *Recovering Subversion*, 12.

145 Agnes, "Women's Movement within a Secular Framework," 1125. The term "coparcenary rights" refers to the birthright of a Hindu male to become a partner in the ancestral property; under Hindu personal law, women did not have this right until 2005, when the Hindu Succession Act was amended.

146 R. S. Rajan, *The Scandal of the State*, 2.

147 Rao, "Introduction," 3.

148 Chowdhry, *Contentious Marriages, Eloping Couples*, 305.

Conclusion

1 Charismatic retreat, field notes, 22 June 2013.

2 See Hefner, *Global Pentecostalism in the 21st Century*.

3 "How the Potta-Divine Ministry Began," website of the Divine Retreat Center, Muringoor, accessed 30 November 2017, www.drcm.org/about-us/overview.

4 Fr. Jose Anchanikal, interview by author, 3 January 2013.

5 Ibid.

6 Katrinamma, interview by author, 7 January 2013.

7 Kochamma, interview by author, 9 January 2013.

8 Susamma, interview by author, 23 June 2013.

9 Mahmood, *The Politics of Piety*, 2.

10 Ibid., 31.

11 Braidotti, "In Spite of the Times," 2.

12 See Bhargava, *Secularism and Its Critics*; Needham and Rajan, *The Crisis of Secularism in India*; Asad, *Formations of the Secular*.

13 Braidotti, "In Spite of the Times," 9. Postcolonial and women of color scholars have also pointed out the complexities of agency and dissent. See Mohanty, Russo, and Torres,

Third World Women and The Politics of Feminism; Raheja and Gold, *Listen to the Heron's Words*; Abu-Lughod, *Do Muslim Women Need Saving?*

14 See the edited collections T. Sarkar and Butalia, *Women in the Hindu Right*; Jeffery and Basu, *Appropriating Gender.*

15 Bacchetta, "Hindu Nationalist Women as Ideologues." See also Sethi, "Avenging Angels and Nurturing Mothers."

16 Blom-Hansen, "Recuperating Masculinity."

17 A. Basu, "Hindu Women's Activism and the Questions It Raises"; K. D. Menon, *Everyday Nationalism.*

18 Deo, *Mobilizing Religion and Gender in India*, 32–33.

19 Braidotti, "In Spite of the Times," 7.

20 McClennan, "The Postsecular Turn," 10.

21 Hollywood, "Spiritual but Not Religious," 1.

22 Ibid.

23 K. P. M. Basheer, "Independent Churches Mushroom in the State," *The Hindu*, 17 June 2002; Thomas, "The Tying of the Ceremonial Wedding Thread."

24 Fessenden, "The Problem of the Postsecular," 165.

25 Ibid.

26 Berger, "Afterword," 253.

27 Thomas, "The Tying of the Ceremonial Wedding Thread," 106.

28 Alphonsa, interview by author, 10 January 2013.

29 Littyamma, interview by author, 20 January 2012.

30 Ibid.

31 As scholars have discussed, domestic rituals and folk practices can be linked to agency and freedom. K. Narayan, *Everyday Creativity*, shows how the crafting of songs about goddesses and female saints offers Kangara women a variety of benefits, including community building. In a similar vein, Dempsey, "Pilgrimage," discusses women's agency and pilgrimages.

32 Mohan, "Creation of Social Space through Prayers among Dalits in Kerala, India," 56.

33 Ibid., 48–49.

34 Mahmood, *The Politics of Piety*, 128.

35 Susamma, interview by author, 23 June 2013.

Bibliography

Abraham, Janaki. "Contingent Caste Endogamy and Patriarchy." In *Conjugality Unbound: Sexual Economies, State Regulation, and the Marital Form in India*, edited by Srimati Basu and Lucinda Ramberg, 161–89. New Delhi: Women Unlimited, 2015.

Abraham, M. C. *Kerala Legislative Assembly Proceedings*, 1 March 1958. Trivandrum: Government Press, 1959.

Abu-Lughod, Lila. *Do Muslim Women Need Saving?* Cambridge: Harvard University Press, 2013.

———. "The Romance of Resistance: Tracing Transformations of Power through Bedouin Women." *American Ethnologist* 17, no. 1 (1990): 41–55.

Agnes, Flavia. "From *Shah Bano* to *Kausar Bano*: Contextualizing the 'Muslim Woman' Within a Communalized Polity." In *South Asian Feminisms*, edited by Ania Loomba and Ritty A. Lukose, 33–53. Durham: Duke University Press, 2012.

———. *Law and Gender Inequality: The Politics of Women's Rights in India*. 2nd ed. New Delhi: Oxford University Press, 1999.

———. "Women's Movement within a Secular Framework: Redefining the Agenda." *Economic and Political Weekly* 29, no. 19 (1994): 1123–28.

Agnes, Flavia, and Shoba Venkatesh Ghosh. "Introduction." In *Negotiating Spaces: Legal Domains, Gender Concerns, and Community Constructs*, edited by Flavia Agnes and Shoba Venkatesh Ghosh, xi–xxvii. New Delhi: Oxford University Press, 2012.

Aishabai, K. O. *Kerala Legislative Assembly Proceedings*, 1 March 1958. Trivandrum: Government Press, 1959.

Anikuzhikattil, Mathew. "Reconciliation." In *Bride at the Feet of the Bridegroom: Studies in East Syrian Liturgical Law*, edited by A. G. Kollamparampil and J. Perumthottam, 349–75. Changanassery: HIRS, 1997.

Antherjanam, Lalithambika. "In the Moonlight." In *Cast Me Out If You Will: Stories and Memoir*, translated by Gita Krishnakutty, 12–17. New York: The Feminist Press at CUNY, 1998.

Archdiocese of Changanacherry. "Joint Circular Letter, 26 August 2007." Translated by P. Sreekumar. *Madhyastan* 80, no. 2 (2007), 7–12.

Arthur, Linda. "Introduction." In *Undressing Religion: Commitment and Conversion from a Cross-Cultural Perspective*, edited by Linda Arthur, 1–6. New York: Berg, 2000.

Arunima, G. "Imagining Communities—Differently: Print, Language and the (Public Sphere) in Colonial Kerala." *Indian Economic Social History Review* 43, no. 63 (2006): 63–76.

———. *There Comes Papa: Colonialism and the Transformation of Matriliny in Kerala, Malabar, c. 1850–1940.* New Delhi: Orient Longman, 2003.

Asad, Talal. *Formations of the Secular: Christianity, Islam, Modernity.* Stanford: Stanford University Press, 2003.

Austin, Granville. "Religion, Personal Law, and Identity." In *Religion and Personal Law in Secular India: A Call to Judgment,* edited by Gerald J. Larson, 15–23. Bloomington: Indiana University Press, 2001.

Austin, H. *The Anatomy of the Kerala Coup.* New Delhi: People's Publishing House, 1959.

Awaya, Toshie. "Becoming a 'Female Citizen' in Colonial Kerala." In *Gender and Modernity: Perspectives from Asia and the Pacific,* edited by Hayami Yoko, Tanabe Akio, and Tokita-Tanabe Yumiko, 41–60. Kyoto: Kyoto University Press, 2003.

Ayyar, L. K. Anantakrishna. *Anthropology of the Syrian Christians.* Ernakulam: Cochin Government Press, 1926.

Baba, T. O. *Kerala Legislative Assembly Proceedings,* 1 March 1958. Trivandrum: Government Press, 1959.

Baby, Ampat Koreth. "Communist Rule in Kerala." PhD diss., Indiana University, 1964.

Bacchetta, Paola. "Hindu Nationalist Women as Ideologues: The 'Sangh,' the 'Samiti,' and Their Differential Concepts of the Hindu Nation." In *Embodied Violence: Communalising Women's Sexuality in South Asia,* edited by Kumari Jayawardena and Malathi de Alwis, 126–67. London: Zed Books, 1996.

Banerjee, Mukulika, and Daniel Miller. *The Sari.* Oxford: Berg, 2003.

Basu, Amrita. "Hindu Women's Activism and the Questions It Raises." In *Appropriating Gender: Women's Activism and Politicized Religion in South Asia,* edited by Patricia Jeffery and Amrita Basu, 167–84. New York: Routledge, 1998.

Basu, Srimati. *She Comes to Take Her Rights: Indian Women, Property, and Propriety.* Albany: SUNY Press, 1999.

———. *The Trouble with Marriage: Feminists Confront Law and Violence in India.* Oakland: University of California Press, 2015.

Bate, Bernard. *Tamil Oratory and the Dravidian Aesthetic.* New York: Columbia University Press, 2009.

Bauman, Chad M. "Redeeming Indian 'Christian' Womanhood? Missionaries, Dalits, and Agency in Colonial India." *Journal of Feminist Studies in Religion* 24, no. 2 (2008): 5–27.

Bauman, Chad M., and Richard Fox Young. *Constructing Indian Christianities: Culture, Conversion and Caste.* New Delhi: Routledge, 2014.

Baxi, Upendra. "The Constitutional Discourse on Secularism." In *Reconstructing the Republic,* edited by Upendra Baxi, Alice Jacob, and Tarlok Singh, 211–33. New Delhi: Har-Anand, 1999.

Baylis, F. "Letter from Rev. F. Baylis to the Resident, January 10, 1859." In R. N. Yesudas, *A People's Revolt in Travancore: A Backward Class Movement for Social Freedom,* 181–83. Trivandrum: Kerala Historical Society, 1975.

Bayly, C. A. "The Origins of *Swadeshi* (Home Industry): Cloth and Indian Society, 1700–1930." In *The Social Life of Things: Commodities in Cultural Perspectives,* edited by Arjun Appadurai, 285–322. Cambridge: Cambridge University Press, 1986.

Bayly, Susan. "Caste and 'Race' in the Colonial Ethnography of India." In *The Concept of Race in South Asia*, edited by Peter Robb, 165–218. New Delhi: Oxford University Press, 1997.

———. *Saints, Goddesses, and Kings: Muslims and Christians in South Indian Society, 1700–1900*. Cambridge: Cambridge University Press, 2004.

Berger, Peter L. "Afterword." In *Global Pentecostalism in the 21st Century*, edited by Robert W. Hefner, 251–57. Bloomington: Indiana University Press, 2013.

Bhan, Mona. "'Aryan Valley' and the Politics of Race and Religion in Kashmir." Hot Spots, *Cultural Anthropology*, 24 March 2014. https://culanth.org/fieldsights/504-aryan-valley-and-the-politics-of-race-and-religion-in-kashmir.

Bhargava, Rajeev. "India's Secular Constitution." In *India's Living Constitution: Ideas, Practices, Controversies*, edited by Zoya Hasan, E. Sridharan, and R. Sudarshan, 105–33. London: Anthem Press, 2005.

———, ed. *Secularism and Its Critics*. New Delhi: Oxford University Press, 1998.

Bhaskaran, Seema. "Informed by Gender? Public Policy in Kerala." *Economic and Political Weekly* 46, no. 43 (2011): 75–84.

Bhattacharya, Neeladri. "Teaching History in Schools: The Politics of Textbooks in India." *History Workshop Journal* 67 (Spring 2009): 99–110.

Blom-Hansen, Thomas. "Recuperating Masculinity: Hindu Nationalism, Violence, and the Exorcism of the Muslim 'Other.'" *Critique of Anthropology* 16, no. 2 (1996): 137–72.

Bose, Purnima. "Hindutva Abroad: The California Textbook Controversy." *The Global South* 2, no. 1 (2008): 11–34.

Braidotti, Rosi. "In Spite of the Times: The Postsecular Turn in Feminism." *Theory, Culture & Society* 25, no. 6 (2008): 1–23.

Brown, Leslie. *The Indian Christians of St. Thomas*. Cambridge: Cambridge University Press, 1982.

Brueck, Laura. "At the Intersection of Gender and Caste: Rescripting Rape in Dalit Feminist Narratives." In *South Asian Feminisms*, edited by Ania Loomba and Ritty A. Lukose, 224–43. Durham: Duke University Press, 2012.

———. *Writing Resistance: The Rhetorical Imagination of Hindi Dalit Literature*. New York: Columbia University Press, 2014.

Buell, Denise Kimber. *Why This New Race: Ethnic Reasoning in Early Christianity*. New York: Columbia University Press, 2005.

Caldwell, Sarah. *Oh Terrifying Mother: Sexuality, Violence, and Worship of the Goddess Kali*. New Delhi: Oxford University Press, 1999.

Chakravarti, Uma. *Gendering Caste through a Feminist Lens*. Calcutta: Stree, 2006.

Chatterjee, Partha. "History and the Domain of the Popular." In "Rewriting History," special issue, *Seminar* 522 (February 2003). www.india-seminar.com/2003/522/522%20partha%20chatterjee.htm.

———. "Religious Minorities and the Secular State: Reflections on an Indian Impasse." *Public Culture* 8 (1995): 11–39.

———. "Secularism and Tolerance." In *Secularism and Its Critics*, edited by Rajeev Bhargava, 345–79. New Delhi: Oxford University Press, 1998.

Chhachhi, Amrita. "Identity Politics, Secularism, and Women: A South Asian Perspective." In *Forging Identities: Gender, Communities, and the State in India*, edited by Zoya Hasan, 74–95. New Delhi: Kali for Women, 1994.

Chowdhry, Prem. *Contentious Marriages, Eloping Couples: Gender, Caste, and Patriarchy in Northern India*. New Delhi: Oxford University Press, 2007.

Chua, Joceyln Lim. *In Pursuit of the Good Life: Aspiration and Suicide in Globalizing South India*. Berkeley: University of California Press, 2014.

Clark-Decès, Isabelle. *The Right Spouse: Preferential Marriages in Tamil Nadu*. Stanford: Stanford University Press, 2014.

Cohn, Bernard. *Colonialism and Its Forms of Knowledge: The British in India*. Princeton: Princeton University Press, 1996.

Collins, Patricia Hill, and Sirma Bilge. *Intersectionality*. Maldan: Polity Press, 2016.

Committee on the Elimination of Discrimination Against Women. "Concluding Observations on the Combined Fourth and Fifth Periodic Reports of India." Presented to the Convention on the Elimination of All Forms of Discrimination Against Women, United Nations, Human Rights, Office of the High Commissioner, 24 July 2014.

Crenshaw, Kimberlé. "Demarginalizing the Intersection of Race and Sex: A Black Feminist Critique of Antidiscrimination Doctrine, Feminist Theory and Antiracist Politics." *University of Chicago Legal Forum* 1 (1989): 139–67.

———. "Mapping the Margins: Intersectionality, Identity Politics, and Violence against Women of Color." *Stanford Law Review* 43, no. 6. (1991): 1241–99.

Dale, Stephen F. "Trade, Conversion and the Growth of the Islamic Community of Kerala, South India." *Studia Islamica* 71 (1990): 155–75.

Das Acevedo, Deepa. "Secularism in the Indian Context," *Law & Social Inquiry* 38, no. 1 (2013): 138–67.

Dempsey, Corinne. "Cross Currents in Kerala Christianity: Status and Taboo in the Indigenization Process." *Vidyajyoti: Journal of Theological Reflection* 69, no. 6 (2005): 404–14.

———. *Kerala Christian Sainthood: Collisions of Culture and Worldview in South India*. New York: Oxford University Press, 2001.

———. "Pilgrimage." In *The Encyclopedia of Women in World History*, 4 vols., edited by Bonnie G. Smith. New York: Oxford University Press, 2008.

Deo, Nandini. *Mobilizing Religion and Gender in India: The Role of Activism*. New York: Routledge, 2016.

Desai, Manali. "Indirect British Rule, State Formation, and Welfarism in Kerala." *Social Science History* 29, no. 3 (2005): 457–88.

Devi, Lakshmy. "Education, Employment, and Job Preference of Women in Kerala: A Micro-level Case Study." Working Paper Series no. 42, Centre for Development Studies, Thiruvananthapuram, Kerala, 2002.

Devika, J. "Domesticating Malayalees: Family Planning, the Nation, and Home Anxieties in Mid-20th Century Keralam." Working Paper Series no. 340, Centre for Development Studies, Thiruvananthapuram, Kerala, 2002.

———. *Engendering Individuals: The Language of Re-Forming in Early Twentieth Century Keralam*. New Delhi: Orient Longman, 2007.

———. "Memory's Fatal Lure: The Left, the Congress and 'Jeevan' in Kerala." *Economic & Political Weekly* 43, no. 30 (2008), 13–16.

———. "Negotiating Women's Social Space: Public Debates on Gender in Early Modern Kerala, India." *Inter-Asia Cultural Studies* 7, no. 1 (2006): 43–61.

Devika, J., and Mini Sukumar. "Making Space for Feminist Social Critique in Contemporary Kerala." *Economic and Political Weekly* 41, no. 42 (2006): 4469–75.

Devika, J., and Binitha V. Thampi. *New Lamps for Old: Gender Paradoxes of Political Decentralisation in Kerala*. New Delhi: Zubaan, 2012.

Devika, J., and V. J. Varghese. "To Survive or to Flourish? Minority Rights and Syrian Christian Community Assertions in Twentieth-century Travancore/Kerala." Working Paper Series no. 427, Centre for Development Studies, Thiruvananthapuram, Kerala, 2010.

———. "To Survive or to Flourish? Minority Rights and Syrian Christian Community Assertions in Twentieth-century Travancore/Kerala." *History and Sociology of South Asia* 5, no. 2 (2011): 103–28.

Drèze, Jean, and Mamta Murthi. "Fertility, Education, and Development: Evidence from India." *Population and Development Review* 27, no. 1 (2001): 33–63.

D'Souza, Victor S. "Status Among the Moplahs on the South-West Coast of India." In *Caste and Social Stratification Among Muslims in India*, edited by Imitaz Ahmad, 41–56. New Delhi: Manohar, 1978.

Dumont, Louis. "The Dravidian Kinship Terminology as an Expression of Marriage." *Man* 53 (1953): 34–39

Eapen, Mridul. "Women and Work Mobility: Some Disquieting Evidences from the Indian Data." Working Paper Series no. 358, Centre for Development Studies, Thiruvananthapuram, Kerala, 2004.

Fessenden, Tracey. "The Problem of the Postsecular." *American Literary History* 26, no. 1 (2014): 154–67.

Fic, Victor M. *Kerala, Yenan of India: Rise of Communist Power, 1937–1969*. Bombay: Nachiketa, 1979.

Fuller, C. J. "Kerala Christians and the Caste System." *Man* 11, no. 1 (1976): 53–70.

Fuller, C. J., and Haripriya Narasimhan. *Tamil Brahmins: The Making of a Middle Class*. Chicago: University of Chicago Press, 2014.

Gangadharan, T. K. *Evolution of Kerala History and Culture*. Calicut: Calicut University Central, 2003.

George, Sheeba. *When Women Come First: Gender and Class in Transnational Migration*. Berkeley: University of California Press, 2005.

Glenn, Evelyn Nakano. "Yearning for Lightness: Transnational Circuits in the Marketing and Consumption of Skin Lighteners." *Gender and Society* 20, no. 10 (2008): 281–302.

Gnanadason, Joy. *A Forgotten History: The Story of the Missionary Movement and the Liberation of People in South Travancore*. Madras: Gurukul Lutheran Theological College and Research Institute, 1994.

Government of India, Planning Commission. *Second Five-Year Plan*. Trivandrum: Government Press, 1958.

Government of Kerala. *Kerala Economic Review, 1958–59*. Trivandrum: State Planning Board, 1959.

———. *Kerala Government's Reply to the KPCC Memorandum*, annexure 7. Trivandrum: Department of Public Relations, Government of Kerala, 1959.

———. *Opposition Preparations for Violent Overthrow of the Government: Facts Placed*

Before the Prime Minister. Trivandrum: Department of Public Relations, Government of Kerala, 1959.

Graybirl, Beth, and Linda Arthur. "The Social Control of Women's Bodies in Two Mennonite Communities." In *Religion, Dress, and the Body*, edited by Linda Arthur, 9–30. New York: Berg, 1999.

Guichard, Sylvie. *The Construction of History and Nationalism in India: Textbooks, Controversies, and Politics*. New York: Routledge, 2010.

Gundert, Hermann. *Keralolpatti*. Translated by T. Madhava Menon. Thiruvananthapuram: International School of Dravidian Linguistics, 2003.

Gupta, Charu. *The Gender of Caste: Representing Dalits in Print*. Seattle: University of Washington Press, 2016.

Gurukkal, Rajan. *Social Formations of Early South India*. New Delhi: Oxford University Press, 2010.

———. "St. Thomas Christians and Nambudiri Brahmins: A Note." In *St. Thomas Christians and Nambudiris: Jews and Sangam Literature—A Historical Appraisal*, edited by Bosco Puthur, 108–16. Kochi: LRC, 2003.

Habib, Irfan. "How to Evade Real Issues and Make Room for Obscurantism." *Social Scientist* 33, no. 9/10 (2005): 3–12.

Halliburton, Murphy. *Mudpacks and Prozac: Experiencing Ayurvedic, Biomedical and Religious Healing*. Walnut Creek: Left Coast Press, 2009.

———. "Suicide: A Paradox of Development in Kerala." *Economic and Political Weekly* 33, no. 36/37 (1998): 2341–45.

Hardgrave, Robert L. *Essays in the Political Sociology of South India*. New Delhi: Usha Publishers, 1979.

Hefner, Robert W., ed. *Global Pentecostalism in the 21st Century*. Bloomington: Indiana University Press, 2013.

Hellman-Rajanayagam, Dagmar. "Is There a Tamil 'Race'?" In *The Concept of Race in South Asia*, edited by Peter Robb, 109–45. New Delhi: Oxford University Press, 1997.

Hollywood, Amy. "Spiritual but Not Religious: The Vital Interplay Between Submission and Freedom." *Harvard Divinity Bulletin* 38, nos. 1/2 (2010): 1–14.

Isaac, T. M. *Vimochana Samarathinte Kaanapurangal*. Thiruvananthapuram: Chintha, 2011.

Iyer, Krishna L. A. *The Dravidians*. Vol. 2 of *Social History of Kerala*. Madras: Book Centre, 1970.

Iyer, V. R. Krishna. *Kerala Legislative Assembly Proceedings*, 1 March 1958. Trivandrum: Government Press, 1959.

———. *Kerala Legislative Assembly Proceedings*, 30 June 1958. Trivandrum: Government Press, 1960.

Jain, Ranu. "Minority Rights in Education: Reflections on Article 30 of the Indian Constitution." *Economic and Political Weekly* 40, no. 24 (2005): 2430–37.

Jayasree, A. K. "Searching for Justice for Body and Self in a Coercive Environment: Sex Work in Kerala, India." *Reproductive Health Matters* 12, no. 23 (2004): 58–67.

Jeffery, Patricia, and Amrita Basu, eds. *Appropriating Gender: Women's Activism and Politicized Religion in South Asia*. New York: Routledge, 1998.

Jeffrey, Robin. *The Decline of Nair Dominance: Society and Politics in Travancore, 1847–1908.* London: Chatto & Windus/Sussex University Press, 1976.

———. "Jawaharlal Nehru and the Smoking Gun: Who Pulled the Trigger on Kerala's Communist Government in 1959?" *Journal of Commonwealth & Comparative Politics* 29, no. 1 (1991): 72–85.

———. *Politics, Women, and Well-Being: How Kerala Became "A Model."* New Delhi: Oxford University Press, 1992.

John, Achamma. "Dalit Women's Socio-economic Status: A Study." In *Confronting Violence against Women: Engendering Kerala's Development Experience,* edited by Vineetha Menon and K. N. Nair, 175–86. New Delhi: Daanish Books, 2008.

Johnson, Sylvester A. *The Myth of Ham in Nineteenth-Century American Christianity: Race, Heathens, and the People of God.* New York: Palgrave MacMillian, 2004.

Joshi, Khyati Y. *New Roots in America's Sacred Ground: Religion, Race, and Ethnicity in Indian America.* New Brunswick: Rutgers University Press, 2006.

Kabir, M. "On the Periphery: Muslims and the Kerala Model." In *Development, Democracy, and the State: Critiquing the Kerala Model of Development,* edited by K. Ravi Raman, 87–101. New York: Routledge, 2010.

Kannabiran, Kalpana, ed. *Women and Law: Critical Feminist Perspectives.* New Delhi: SAGE, 2014.

Kannabiran, Vasanth, and Kannabiran Kalpana. "Caste and Gender: Understanding Dynamics of Power and Violence." In *Gender and Caste,* edited by Anupama Rao, 249–60. New Delhi: Kali for Women, 2003.

Kannookadan, Pauly, ed. *The Mission Theology of the Syro-Malabar Church.* Kochi: Syro-Malabar Liturgical Research Centre, 2008.

Karve, Irawati. *Kinship Organization in India.* New York: Asia Publishing House, 1953.

Kavukatt, Mathew. "Pastoral Letter no. 44." In *Pastoral Letters of Arch Bishop Mar Mathew Kavukatt,* compiled by Father Jacob Kattor and Sister Jane Kottaram, C.M.C., 163–67. Changanacherry: Vice-Postulators, 2007.

———. "Pastoral Letter no. 48: Joint Pastoral Letter of the Indian Hierarchy." In *Pastoral Letters of Arch Bishop Mar Mathew Kavukatt,* compiled by Father Jacob Kattor and Sister Jane Kottaram, C.M.C., 183–85. Changanacherry: Vice-Postulators, 2007.

Kent, Eliza. "Civilisation and Conjugality: Indian Christian Marriage in Law and Literature." In *Conjugality Unbound: Sexual Economies, State Regulation, and the Marital Form in India,* edited by Srimati Basu and Lucinda Ramberg, 133–60. New Delhi: Women Unlimited, 2015.

———. *Converting Women: Gender and Protestant Christianity in Colonial South India.* Oxford: Oxford University Press, 2005.

Kimmel, Michael. *Guyland: The Perilous World Where Boys Become Men.* New York: HarperCollins, 2008.

———. "Masculinity as Homophobia: Fear, Shame, and Silence in the Construction of Gender Identity." In *Women, Culture, Society: A Reader,* edited by Barbara J. Balliet, 59–74. Dubuque: Kendall/Hunt, 2004.

Kodoth, Praveena. "Gender, Caste, and Matchmaking in Kerala: A Rationale for Dowry." *Development and Change* 30, no. 2 (2008): 263–83.

Kodoth, Praveena, and Mridul Eapen. "Looking Beyond Gender Parity: Gender Inequities of Some Dimensions of Well-Being in Kerala." *Economic & Political Weekly* 40, no. 30 (2005): 3278–86.

Kollamparampil, A. G., and J. Perumthottam, eds. *Bride at the Feet of the Bridegroom: Studies in East Syrian Liturgical Law.* Changanassery: HIRS, 1997.

Krishnankutty, Gita. "Introduction." In Lalithambika Antherjanam, *Cast Me Out If You Will: Stories and Memoir,* translated by Gita Krishnankutty, xiii–xxxi. New York: The Feminist Press at CUNY, 1998.

Kumar, Krishna. "Origins of India's 'Textbook Culture.'" *Comparative Education Review* 32, no. 4 (1988): 452–64.

———. "Peace with the Past." In "Rewriting History," special issue, *Seminar* 522 (February 2003). www.india-seminar.com/2003/522/522%20krishna%20kumar.htm.

———. *Prejudice and Pride: School Histories of the Freedom Struggle in India and Pakistan.* New Delhi: Penguin, 2001.

Kumar, Priya. *Limiting Secularism: The Ethics of Coexistence in Indian Literature and Film.* Minneapolis: University of Minnesota Press, 2008.

Kurian, Mathew V. *The Caste Class Formation: A Case Study of Kerala.* New Delhi: BR Publishing, 1986.

Kurien, Prema. *Kaleidoscopic Ethnicity: International Migration and the Reconstruction of Community Identities in India.* New Brunswick: Rutgers University Press, 2002.

———. "Who Speaks for Indian Americans? Religion, Ethnicity, and Political Formation." *American Quarterly* 59, no. 3 (2007): 759–83.

Lakshmi, L. R. S. *The Malabar Muslims: A Different Perspective.* New Delhi: Cambridge University Press, 2012.

Lal, B. B. "It Is Time to Rethink." In *The Aryan Debate,* edited by Thomas R. Trautmann, 145–56. New Delhi: Oxford University Press, 2005.

Lal, Vinay. *The History of History: Politics and Scholarship in Modern India.* New Delhi: Oxford University Press, 2003.

Leiten, Georges Kristoffel. "Education, Ideology, and Politics in Kerala." *Social Scientist* 6, no. 2 (1977): 3–21.

———. *The First Communist Ministry in Kerala: 1957–1959.* Calcutta: Bagchi, 1982.

Lindberg, Anna. "The Historical Roots of Dowries in Contemporary Kerala." *South Asia: Journal of South Asian Studies* 37, no. 1 (2014): 22–42.

———. *Modernization and Effeminization in India: Kerala Cashew Workers Since 1930.* Copenhagen: NIAS Press, 2005.

Lopez, Ian Haney. "The Social Construction of Race: Some Observations on Illusion, Fabrication, and Choice." *Harvard Civil Rights–Civil Liberties Law Review* 29, no. 1 (1994): 1–62.

Lorde, Audre. "The Master's Tools Will Never Dismantle the Master's House." In *Sister Outsider: Essays and Speeches by Audre Lorde,* 110–13. Trumansburg: Crossing Press, 1984.

Lukose, Ritty A. *Liberalization's Children: Gender, Youth, and Consumer Citizenship in Globalizing India.* Durham: Duke University Press, 2009.

Lynton, Linda. *The Sari: Styles, Patterns, History, Techniques.* London: Thames & Hudson, 1995.

Madan, T. N. "Freedom of Religion." *Economic and Political Weekly* 38, no. 11 (2003): 1034–41.

Mahmood, *The Politics of Piety: The Islamic Revival and the Feminist Subject*. Princeton: Princeton University Press, 2005.

Malabar Marriage Commission. *Report of the Malabar Marriage Commission, with Enclosures and Appendices*. Madras: Lawrence Asylum Press, 1891.

Mannooranparampil, Thomas. "General Considerations on the Liturgical and Sacramental Theology." In *Bride at the Feet of the Bridegroom: Studies in East Syrian Liturgical Law*, edited by A. G. Kollamparampil and J. Perumthottam, 81–214. Changanassery: HIRS, 1997.

Maruthur, Navaneetha Mokkil. "Sexual Figures of Kerala: Cultural Practices, Regionality, and the Politics of Sexuality." PhD diss., University of Michigan, 2010.

Mathew, George. *Communal Road to a Secular Kerala*. New Delhi: Concept, 1989.

Mathews, Tia. "Foreign Trade in Natural Rubber: A Case Study with Reference to Kerala." PhD diss., Mahatma Gandhi University, 2011.

Mathur, P. R. G. "Social Stratification among the Muslims of Kerala." In *Frontiers of Embedded Muslim Communities in India*, edited by Vinod K. Jairath, 113–35. New York: Routledge, 2011.

May, Vivian. *Pursuing Intersectionality, Unsettling Dominant Imaginaries*. New York: Routledge, 2015.

McDuie-Ra, Duncan. *Debating Race in Contemporary India*. New York: Palgrave MacMillan, 2015.

——. "'Is India Racist?': Murder, Migration and Mary Kom." *South Asia: Journal of South Asian Studies* 38, no. 2 (2015): 304–19.

McLennan, Gregor. "The Postsecular Turn." *Theory, Culture & Society*. 27, no. 4 (2010): 3–20.

Menachery, George. "Social Life and Customs of the St. Thomas Christians in the Pre-Diamper Period." In *The Life and Nature of the St. Thomas Christian Church in the Pre-Diamper Period*, edited by Bosco Puthur, 188–203. Kochi: LRC, 2000.

Menon, Dilip M. *Caste, Nationalism, and Communism in South India: Malabar, 1900–1948*. Cambridge: Cambridge University Press, 1994.

Menon, Kalyani Devaki. *Everyday Nationalism: Women of the Hindu Right in India*. Philadelphia: University of Pennsylvania Press, 2010.

Menon, Nivedita. "Living with Secularism." In *The Crisis of Secularism in India*, edited by Anuradha Dingwaney Needham and Rajeswari Sunder Rajan, 118–40. Ranikhet: Permanent Black Press, 2007.

——. *Recovering Subversion: Feminist Politics Beyond the Law*. Chicago: University of Illinois Press, 2004.

——. "State, Community, and the Uniform Civil Code in India." In *Beyond Rights Talk and Culture Talk: Comparative Essays on the Politics of Rights and Culture*, edited by Mahmood Mamdani, 75–96. New York: St. Martin's Press, 2000.

——. "State/Gender/Community: Citizenship in Contemporary India." *Economic and Political Weekly* 33, no. 5 (1998): PE3–10.

Menon, Sreedhara. *A Survey of Kerala History*. New Delhi: Sterling, 1979.

Menon, T. Madhava. "Translator's Introduction." In Hermann Gundert, *Keralolpatti*, translated by T. Madhava Menon. Thiruvananthapuram: International School of Dravidian Linguistics, 2003.

Mitra, Aparna, and Pooja Singh. "Human Capital Attainment and Female Labor Force Participation: The Kerala Puzzle." *Journal of Economic Issues* 40, no. 3 (2006): 779–98.

Mody, Perveez. "Love and the Law: Love-Marriage in Delhi." *Modern Asia Studies* 35, no. 1 (2002): 223–56.

Mohan, Sanal P. "Creation of Social Space through Prayers among Dalits in Kerala, India." *Journal of Religious and Political Practice* 2, no. 1 (2016): 40–57.

———. *Modernity of Slavery: Struggles against Caste Inequality in Colonial Kerala.* Oxford: Oxford University Press, 2015.

Mohanty, Chandra Talpade, Ann Russo, and Lourdes Torres, eds. *Third World Women and the Politics of Feminism.* Bloomington: Indiana University Press, 1991.

Moodie, Megan. *We Were Adivasis: Aspiration in an Indian Scheduled Tribe.* Chicago: University of Chicago Press, 2015.

Moynihan, Daniel Patrick. *A Dangerous Place.* Boston: Little, Brown, 1978.

Mukherjee, Mridula, and Aditya Mukherjee. "Communalisation of Education, the History Textbook Controversy: An Overview." In *Communalisation of Education: The History Textbooks Controversy*, edited by Delhi Historians' Group. New Delhi: Jawaharlal Nehru University, 2001.

Mukhopadhyay, Swapna, ed. *The Enigma of the Kerala Woman: A Failed Promise of Literacy.* New Delhi: Social Science Press, 2007.

———. "Gender Disparity in Kerala: Some Visual Images." In *The Enigma of the Kerala Woman: A Failed Promise of Literacy*, edited by Swapna Mukhopadhyay, 175–84. New Delhi: Social Science Press, 2007.

Mundaden, Mathias. *Indian Christians: Struggle to Reclaim Religious Autonomy.* Bangalore: Dharmaram, 1984.

Namboodiri, Damodaran. "Caste and Social Change in Colonial Kerala." In *The Second Millennium*, edited by P. J. Cherian, pt. 2, 426–55. Vol. 2 of *Perspectives on Kerala History*, edited by P. J. Cherian. Trivandrum: Kerala Gazetteers, 1999.

Nampoothiri, D. D. "Confronting Social Exclusion: A Critical Review of the CREST Experience." In *Beyond Inclusion: The Practice of Equal Access in Indian Higher Education*, edited by Satish Deshpande and Usha Zacharias, 252–88. New Delhi: Routledge, 2012.

Nandy, Ashis. "The Politics of Secularism and the Recovery of Religious Toleration." In *Secularism and Its Critics*, edited by Rajeev Bhargava, 321–44. New Delhi: Oxford University Press, 1998.

———. "Time Travel to a Possible Self: Searching for the Alternative Cosmopolitanism of Cochin." *Japanese Journal of Political Science* 1, no. 2 (2000): 295–327.

Narayan, Kirin. *Everyday Creativity: Singing Goddesses in the Himalayan Foothills.* Chicago: University of Chicago Press, 2016.

Narayan, Uma. "Essence of Culture and a Sense of History: A Feminist Critique of Cultural Essentialism." *Hypatia* 13, no. 2 (1998): 86–106.

Narayanan, M. G. S. "Communists Are Trying to Catch Fish in Dirty Water." *Kudumbajyothis* 27, no. 318 (2008): 6–9.

———. *Cultural Symbiosis in Kerala*. Trivandrum: Kerala Historical Society, 1972.

———. "Nambudiris: Migrations and Early Settlements in Kerala." In *St. Thomas Christians and Nambudiris: Jews and Sangam Literature—A Historical Appraisal*, edited by Bosco Puthur, 80–97. Kochi: LRC, 2003.

Natrajan, Balmurli. *The Culturalization of Caste in India: Identity and Inequality in a Multicultural Age*. New York: Routledge, 2012.

Natrajan, Balmurli, and Paul Greenough, eds. *Against Stigma: Studies in Caste, Race, and Justice since Durban*. Hyderabad: Orient Blackswan, 2009.

———. "Introduction." In *Against Stigma: Studies in Caste, Race, and Justice since— Durban*, edited by Balmurli Natrajan and Paul Greenough, 1–44. Hyderabad: Orient Blackswan, 2009.

Needham, Anuradha Dingwaney, and Rajeswari Sunder Rajan, eds. *The Crisis of Secularism in India*. Ranikhet: Permanent Black Press, 2007.

———."Introduction." In *The Crisis of Secularism in India*, edited by Anuradha Dingwaney Needham and Rajeswari Sunder Rajan, 1–44. Ranikhet: Permanent Black Press, 2007.

Nussbaum, Martha. "Women's Education: A Global Challenge." *Signs: Journal of Women in Culture and Society* 29, no. 2. (2003): 325–55.

Oldenburg, Veena Talwar. *Dowry Murder: The Imperial Origins of a Cultural Crime*. Oxford: Oxford University Press, 2002.

Osella, Caroline, and Filippo Osella. "Friendship and Flirting: Micro-Politics in Kerala, South India." *Journal of the Royal Anthropological Institute* 4, no. 2 (1998): 189–206.

———. "Muslim Style in South India." *Fashion Theory* 11, no. 2/3 (2007): 233–52.

Osella, Filippo, and Caroline Osella. "Articulation of Physical and Social Bodies in Kerala." *Contributions to Indian Sociology* 30, no. 1 (1996): 37–68.

———. *Social Mobility in Kerala: Modernity and Identity in Conflict*. London: Pluto Press, 2000.

Padmanabhan, Roshni. "Learning to Learn: Dalit Education in Kerala," in *Development, Democracy and the State: Critiquing the Kerala Model of Development*, edited by K. Ravi Raman, 102–17. New York: Routledge, 2010.

Pandey, Gyan. *A History of Prejudice: Race, Caste, and Difference in India and the United States*. New York: Oxford University Press, 2013.

Panikkar, K. N. "Quest for Quality in Higher Education." In "God's Own Country," special issue, *Seminar* 637 (September 2012). www.india-seminar.com/2012/637/637_k __panikkar.htm.

Parpola, Asko. "The Horse and the Language of the Indus Civilization," in *The Aryan Debate*, edited by Thomas R. Trautmann, 230–33. New Delhi: Oxford University Press, 2005.

Payyappilly, Sebastian. *Mixed Marriage in the Code of Canons of the Eastern Churches and the Particular Law of the Syro-Malabar Church*. Bangalore: Dharmaram, 2014.

Perumthottam, Joseph. "Circular Letter, July 2007." Translated by Sree Kumar and S. Prema. *Madhyastan* 80, no. 1 (2007): 5–9.

———. "Circular Letter, July 2008." Translated by Tommathew T. Thomas. *Madhyastan* 81, no. 1 (2008), 3–10.

Philips, Amali. "Gendering Colour: Identity, Femininity and Marriage in Kerala." *Anthropologica* 46, no. 2 (2004): 253–72.

———. "*Stridhanam*: Rethinking Dowry, Inheritance and Women's Resistance among the Syrian Christians of Kerala." *Anthropologica* 45, no. 2 (2003): 245–64.

Pillai, Padmanabha Kainikkara. *The Red Interlude in Kerala.* Trivandrum: Kerala Pradesh Congress, 1959.

Pillai, Thanu. *Kerala Legislative Assembly Proceedings*, 1 March 1958. Trivandrum: Government Press, 1959.

———. *Kerala Legislative Assembly Proceedings*, 25 November 1958. Trivandrum: Kerala Gazetteers, 1958.

Podipara, Placid. "Hindu in Culture, Christian in Religion, Oriental in Worship," in *The St. Thomas Christian Encyclopedia of India*, edited by George Menachery, vol. 2, 107. Madras: P.N.K. Press, 1973.

———. *The Latin Rite Christians of Malabar.* Kottayam: Denha, 1986.

Poulose, E. P. *Kerala Legislative Assembly Proceedings*, 1 March 1958. Trivandrum: Government Press, 1959.

Purkayastha, Bandana. "Intersectionality in a Transnational World." *Gender and Society* 26, no. 1 (2012): 55–66.

Raheja, Gloria Goodwin and Ann Grodzins Gold. *Listen to the Heron's Words: Reimagining Gender and Kinship in North India.* Berkeley: University of California Press, 1994.

Rajan, Rajeswari Sunder. *The Scandal of the State: Women, Law and Citizenship in Postcolonial India.* Ranikhet: Permanent Black Press, 2003.

Raman, K. Ravi. "The Kerala Model: Situating the Critique," in *Development, Democracy, and the State: Critiquing the Kerala Model of Development*, edited by K. Ravi Raman, 1–22. New York: Routledge 2010.

Rammohan, K. T. "Caste, Public Action, and the Kerala Model," in *Development, Democracy, and the State: Critiquing the Kerala Model of Development*, edited by K. Ravi Raman, 25–39. New York: Routledge, 2010.

Rao, Anupama. *The Caste Question: Dalits and the Politics of Modern India.* Berkeley: University of California Press, 2009.

———, ed. *Gender and Caste.* New Delhi: Kali for Women, 2003.

———. "Introduction: Caste, Gender, and Indian Feminism," in *Gender and Caste*, edited by Anupama Rao, 1–47. New Delhi: Kali for Women, 2003.

———. "Understanding *Sirasgaon*: Notes Towards Conceptualising the Role of Law, Caste and Gender in a Case of Atrocity." In *Gender and Caste*, edited by Anupama Rao, 276–309. New Delhi: Kali for Women, 2003.

Rao, T. Madhava. "Proclamation Issued by the Dewan of Travancore, December 27, 1858." In R. N. Yesudas, *A People's Revolt in Travancore: A Backward Class Movement for Social Freedom*, 166–70. Trivandrum: Kerala Historical Society, 1975.

Ratnagar, Shereen. "The End of the Harappan Civilization," in *The Aryan Debate*, edited by Thomas R. Trautmann, 131–44. New Delhi: Oxford University Press, 2005.

Reddy, Deepa S. "The Ethnicity of Caste." *Anthropological Quarterly* 78, no. 3 (2005): 543–84.

Reddy, Gayatri. "'We Are Indian Now': Siddis and the Un/Marking of Race in Contemporary Hyderabad." Paper presented at the 46th annual conference on South Asia, Madison, Wisconsin, 27 October 2017.

Renjini, D. *Nayar Women Today: Disintegration of Matrilineal System and the Status of Nayar Women in Kerala.* New Delhi: Classical Publishing Company, 2000.

Report of the Christian Community. Trivandrum: Government Press, 1912.

"Review of Women's Studies: Intersections of Gender and Caste." Special issue of *Economic and Political Weekly* 48, no. 18 (2013).

Rivers, W. H. R. "The Marriage of Cousins in India." *Journal of the Royal Asiatic Society* 39 (1907): 611–40.

Robb, Peter, ed. *The Concept of Race in South Asia.* New Delhi: Oxford University Press, 1997.

Roth, Julia. "Entangled Inequalities as Intersectionalities: Towards an Epistemic Sensibilization." Working paper no. 43, Research Network on Interdependent Inequalities in Latin America, Berlin, 2013. www.desigualdades.net/Resources/Working_Paper/43 _WP_Roth_Online.pdf.

Rouse, Shanaz. *Shifting Body Politics: Gender, Nation, State in Pakistan.* New Delhi: Women Unlimited, 2004.

Roy, Arundhati. *The God of Small Things.* New York: HarperCollins, 1997.

Roy, Srila. "Introduction: Paradoxes and Possibilities." In *New South Asian Feminisms,* edited by Srila Roy, 1–26. New Delhi: Zed Books, 2012.

Saldhana, Arun. *Psychedelic White: Goa Trance and the Viscosity of Race.* Minneapolis: University of Minnesota Press, 2007.

Sarkar, Sumit. "Christian Conversions, Hindutva, and Secularism," in *The Crisis of Secularism in India,* edited by Anuradha Dingwaney Needham and Rajeswari Sunder Rajan, 356–68. Ranikhet: Permanent Black Press, 2007.

Sarkar, Tanika, and Urvashi Butalia, eds. *Women in the Hindu Right: A Collection of Essays.* New Delhi: Kali for Women, 1995.

Select Committee on the Kerala Education Bill, 1957. *Report of the Select Committee on the Kerala Education Bill, 1957, and the Bill as Reported by the Select Committee.* Trivandrum: Government Press, 1957.

Sen, Amartya, and Jean Drèze. *India: Economic Development and Social Opportunity.* New York: Oxford University Press, 1995.

Sen, Ronojoy. *Articles of Faith: Religion, Secularism, and the Indian Supreme Court.* New Delhi: Oxford University Press, 2010.

Sethi, Manisha. "Avenging Angels and Nurturing Mothers: Women in Hindu Nationalism." *Economic and Political Weekly* 37, no. 16 (2002): 1545–52.

Shankar, S., and Charu Gupta, eds. "Caste and Life Narratives." Special issue, *Biography: An Interdisciplinary Quarterly* 40, no. 1 (2017).

Sheeju, N. V. "The Shanar Revolts, 1822–99: Towards a Figural Cartography of the Pretender." *South Asia Research* 35, no. 3 (2015): 298–317.

Slate, Nico. *Colored Cosmopolitanism: The Shared Struggle for Freedom in the United States and India.* Cambridge: Harvard University Press, 2012.

Smith, Anthony D. "The 'Golden Age' and National Renewal." In *Myths and Nationhood,* edited by Geoffrey Hosking and George Schopflin, 36–59. New York: Routledge, 1997.

Sreekumar, Sharmila. *Scripting Lives: Narratives of 'Dominant Women' in Kerala.* Hyderabad: Orient Blackswan, 2009.

Stoler, Ann Laura. *Race and the Education of Desire: Foucault's History of Sexuality and the Colonial Order of Things.* Durham: Duke University Press, 1995.

Subramanian, Ajantha. *Shorelines: Space and Rights in South India.* Stanford: Stanford University Press, 2009.

Sunny, Yemuna. "Communalisation of Education." *Economic and Political Weekly* 45, no. 23 (2010): 21–24.

Susuman, Sathiya A., Siaka Lougue, and Madusudana Battala. "Female Literacy, Fertility Decline, and Life Expectancy in Kerala, India: An Analysis from Census of India 2011." *Journal of Asian and African Studies* 51, no. 1, (2014): 32–42.

Swiderski, Richard Michael. "Northists and Southists: A Folklore of Kerala Christians." *Asian Folklore Studies* 47 (1988): 73–92.

T, Ajayan. "Dismissal of the First Communist Ministry in Kerala, and Extraneous Agencies." *The South Asianist* 5, no. 1. (2017): 282–303.

Tarlo, Emma. *Clothing Matters: Dress and Identity in India.* Chicago: University of Chicago Press, 1996.

Tartakov, Gary Michael. "Why Compare Dalits and African Americans? They Are Neither Unique nor Alone." In *Against Stigma: Studies in Caste, Race, and Justice since Durban,* edited by Balmurli Natrajan and Paul Greenough, 95–140. Hyderabad: Orient Blackswan, 2009.

Thapar, Romila. *The Aryan: Recasting Constructs.* Gurgaon: Three Essays Collective, 2008.

———. "The History Debate and School Textbooks in India: A Personal Memoir." *History Workshop Journal* 67 (2009): 87–98.

———. "National Curriculum Framework and the Social Sciences." In "Debating Education," special issue, *Social Scientist* 33, no. 9/10 (2005): 55–58.

———. "Secularism, History, and Contemporary Politics in India." In *The Crisis of Secularism in India,* edited by Anuradha Dingwaney Needham and Rajeswari Sunder Rajan, 191–207. Ranikhet: Permanent Black Press, 2007.

Tharakan, P. K. Michael. "Socio-economic Factors in Educational Development: The Case of Nineteenth-Century Travancore." *Economic and Political Weekly* 19, no. 45 (1984): 1913–28.

Tharu, Susie. "The Impossible Subject: Caste and the Gendered Body" In *Gender and Caste,* edited by Anupama Rao, 261–75. New Delhi: Kali for Women, 2003.

Thekkedam, Joseph Sebastian. "The Catholics and the New Education Policy of the Travancore Government." *Journal of Kerala Studies* 26, no. 9 (1999–2002): 125–36.

Thomas, Sonja. "Cowboys and Indians: Indian Catholic Priests in Rural Montana." Lecture presented at Colby College, 29 September 2016.

———. "Education as Empowerment? Gender and the Human Right to Education in Postcolonial India." In *Human Rights in Postcolonial India,* edited by V. G. Julie Rajan and Om Dwivedi, 66–92. New York: Routledge, 2016.

———. "Researching Minorities and Subalterns: South Asian Feminisms and the Problem of the Upper-Caste Hindu Referent." Paper presented at National Women's Studies Association conference, Montreal, Canada, November 2016.

———. "The Tying of the Ceremonial Wedding Thread: A Feminist Analysis of 'Ritual' and 'Tradition' Among Syro-Malabar Catholics in India." *Journal of Global Catholicism* 1, no. 1 (2016): 104–16.

Thomman, T. A. *Kerala Legislative Assembly Proceedings*, 30 June 1958. Trivandrum: Government Press, 1960.

Thorat, Sukhadeo. "Caste, Race, and United Nations' Perspective on Discrimination: Coping with Challenges from Asia and Africa." In *Against Stigma: Studies in Caste, Race, and Justice since Durban*, edited by Balmurli Natrajan and Paul Greenough, 141–67. Hyderabad: Orient Blackswan, 2009.

Thottathil, Swapna. *India's Organic Farming Revolution: What It Means for Our Global Food System*. Iowa City: University of Iowa Press, 2014.

Trautmann, Thomas R., ed. *The Aryan Debate*. New Delhi: Oxford University Press, 2005.

———. *Dravidian Kinship*. Cambridge: Cambridge University Press, 1981.

Upadhyaya, Prakash Chandra. "The Politics of Indian Secularism." *Modern Asian Studies* 26, no. 4 (1992): 815–53.

Vadakkan, Joseph. *A Priest's Encounter with Revolution*. Madras: Christian Literature Society, 1974.

Varshney, Ashutosh. *Ethnic Conflict and Civic Life: Hindus and Muslims in India*. New Haven: Yale University Press, 2002.

Vellapally, Susan, and Markos Vellapally. "Repeal of the Travancore Christian Succession Act: 1916 and Its Aftermath." *India International Centre Quarterly* 22, no. 2/3 (1995): 181–90.

Veluthat, Kesavan. *The Early Medieval in South India*. New Delhi: Oxford University Press, 2009.

———. "The Nambudiri Community: A History." In *St. Thomas Christians and Nambudiris: Jews and Sangam Literature—A Historical Appraisal*, edited by Bosco Puthur, 117–25. Kochi: LRC, 2003.

Venkitakrishnan, Usha, and Sunil George Kurien. "Rape Victims in Kerala." In *Confronting Violence against Women: Engendering Kerala's Development Experience*, edited by Vineetha Menon and K. N. Nair, 73–94. New Delhi: Daanish Books, 2008.

Vijayakumar, K. "The Influence of Caste in Kerala Politics: A Historical Perspective." *Journal of Kerala Studies* 8, pts. 1–4 (1981): 259–75.

Visvanathan, Susan. *The Christians of Kerala: History, Belief, and Ritual among the Yakoba*. New York: Oxford University Press, 1994.

———. "The Legends of St. Thomas in Kerala." *India International Centre Quarterly* 22, nos. 2/3 (1995): 27–44.

Viswanathan, Gauri. "Literacy and Conversion in the Discourse of Hindu Nationalism." In *The Crisis of Secularism in India*, edited by Anuradha Dingwaney Needham and Rajeswari Sunder Rajan, 333–55. Ranikhet: Permanent Black Press, 2007.

———. *Outside the Fold: Conversion, Modernity, and Belief*. Princeton: Princeton University Press, 1998.

Visweswaran, Kamala. *Un/common Cultures: Racism and the Rearticulation of Cultural Difference*. Durham: Duke University Press, 2010.

Visweswaran, Kamala, Michael Witzel, Nandini Manjrekar, Dipta Bhog, and Uma
    Chakravarti. "The Hindutva View of History: Rewriting Textbooks in India and the
    United States." *Culture & Society* 10, no. 1 (2009): 101–12.
Vithayathil, Varkey J. *The Origin and Progress of the Syro-Malabar Hierarchy.* Kottayam:
    Oriental Institute of Religious Studies, 1980.
Welter, Barbara. "The Cult of True Womanhood: 1820–1860." *American Quarterly* 18,
    no. 2, (1966): 151–74.
Yesudas, R. N. *A People's Revolt in Travancore: A Backward Class Movement for Social
    Freedom.* Trivandrum: Kerala Historical Society, 1975.
Zacharia, Scaria, ed. *The Acts and Decrees of the Synod of Diamper, 1599.* Edamattam:
    Indian Institute of Christian Studies, 1994.
———. "Introduction." In *The Acts and Decrees of the Synod of Diamper, 1599,* edited by
    Scaria Zacharia, 7–59. Edamattam: Indian Institute of Christian Studies, 1994.
Zachariah, K. C. "Religious Denominations of Kerala." Working Paper Series no. 468,
    Centre for Development Studies, Thiruvananthapuram, Kerala, 2016.
———. *The Syrian Christians of Kerala: Demographic and Socio-economic Transition
    in the Twentieth Century.* New Delhi: Orient Longman, 2006.

Index

brahmanical patriarchy and power
(*continued*)
  sustaining feature of, 104–5; use of
  term, 70, 158n20; from vedic culture,
  140–41. *See also* Aryan migration theory; Hinduism; upper-caste Hindus
Braidotti, Rosi, 150, 151, 152
breast cloth, 37
Breast Cloth Movement, 45*fig.*, 46–47,
  46–51, 47, 47*fig.*, 50, 122
Brogpa community, 75

California (USA) textbook revisions, 120,
  121
Cana, Thomas, 25, 81
capitation fees, 129, 132
caste differences: and breast cloth controversy, 49; phenotype differences, 79
caste system: among Christians, 5–6,
  22–28, 79, 87–88, 105–6, 112–13, 153, 155;
  British influence in, 20; critique of
  Hindu system, 9–10, 71, 77; discrimination in, 29, 56, 76, 88, 122–23, 167n72;
  divisions in Kerala, 21–22; as ethnicity
  or racial system, 168n2, 168n4; and
  gender equality, 8, 10; in Islam, 133–34;
  offenses and punishment, 47, 166n34;
  origination of, 78; reform of, 49–50
  (*See also* secularism in India). *See
  also* clothing and women's mobility;
  endogamous marriage; intercaste and
  interfaith marriages; lower castes; ritual customs; upper-caste identity
casteism: and California textbooks, 121;
  as socially constructed category, 70;
  studies of, 7–8
Catholic Church and protest over KEB, 97
Catholic schools, 29–30
Central Intelligence Agency, 91, 171n4
Chacko, P. T., 97, 172n34
Chakravarti, Uma, 9, 10, 23, 104–5, 109–10,
  140, 158n20
Chaldean Church, 25, 26
Charismatic movement, 147–56, 163n49
chatta and *thuni*: and change to sari,

50–51, 52–53; demise of, 55; description
  of, 37–38, 38*fig.*, 41*fig.*; domesticity
  symbolized by, 42–46; and dual nature
  of social standing, 41–42; and elderly
  women, 165n6; rejection of, 50; similarity to upper-caste Hindu clothing,
  37–41
Chatterjee, Partha, 118
Chavara, Kuriakos Elias (saint), 29
Chazhikadan, Joseph, 97, 100, 105
Chhachhi, Amrita, 12
children and families, 140, 144
Chowdhry, Prem, 9, 134, 135, 136, 137, 144
Christian Congress Party. *See* Kerala
  Pradesh Congress Committee
Christian women in liberation struggle,
  106–14
Christianity in India, 4, 5
Christophers, 111, 174n91
Chua, Jocelyn, 33
churidar (salwar kamize), 61–66, 62*fig.*,
  63*fig.*, 166n54
citizens, unmarked, 55, 57
Clark-Decès, Isabelle, 136
clothing and women's mobility, 35–66;
  Breast Cloth Movement, 46–51; communal dress and mobility in the early
  twentieth century, 37–46, 152; contemporary dress, 60–66; definition of
  clothing, 164n1; as embodiment of
  group identity and norms, 35–37, 48,
  50, 60, 65, 82, 155; evolution of, 60–61,
  61*fig.*; overview of, 35–37; seculariza-
  tion with sari, 52–57; sex segregation
  and sexual morality, 57–60; social
  policing of women's choices, 62–64.
  See also breast cloth; *chatta* and *thuni*;
  churidar (salwar kamize); *kaili*; *kavani*;
  kumpala; *kuppayam*; *mundu*; *mundum-
  neryathum*; *rouka*; sari, adoption of;
  set sari; *thorthu*
colleges, self-financing, 127–32, 178n66
colonialism and colonial histories, 48,
  68, 72, 74–75, 117–19, 175n7
communal garments of Syrian Christians,

GLOBAL
SOUTH
ASIA

Padma Kaimal
K. Sivaramakrishnan
Anand A. Yang
SERIES EDITORS

GLOBAL SOUTH ASIA takes an interdisciplinary approach to the humanities and social sciences in its exploration of how South Asia, through its global influence, is and has been shaping the world.

www.ingramcontent.com/pod-product-compliance
Lightning Source LLC
Chambersburg PA
CBHW031131270326
41929CB00011B/1576